NEW METHODS OF LITERACY RESEARCH

"...covers trends and methods that are evolving within the field of literacy research. Readers will gain knowledge, skills and advice from some of the most well-known and leading authorities on literacy and literacy research."

Stacie L. Tate, American University, USA

Literacy researchers at all stages of their careers are designing and developing innovative new methods for analyzing data in a range of spaces in and out of school. Directly connected with evolving themes in literacy research, theory, instruction, and practices—especially in the areas of digital technologies, gaming, and web-based research; discourse analysis; and arts-based research—this much-needed text is the first to capture these new directions in one volume. Written by internationally recognized authorities whose work is situated in these methods, each chapter describes the origin of the method and its distinct characteristics; offers a demonstration of how to analyze data using the method; presents an exemplary study in which this method is used; and discusses the potential of the method to advance and extend literacy research.

For literacy researchers asking how to match their work with current trends and for educators asking how to measure and document what is viewed as literacy within classrooms, this is THE text to help them learn about and use the rich range of new and emerging literacy research methods.

Peggy Albers is Professor of Language Education at Georgia State University, USA.

Teri Holbrook is Assistant Professor of Literacy and Language Arts at Georgia State University, USA.

Amy Seely Flint is Associate Professor of Language Education at Georgia State University, USA.

NEW METHODS OF LITERACY RESEARCH

Edited by Peggy Albers, Teri Holbrook, and Amy Seely Flint

Routledge
Taylor & Francis Group

NEW YORK AND LONDON

First published 2014
by Routledge
711 Third Avenue, New York 10017

Simultaneously published in the UK
by Routledge
2 Park Square, Milton Park, Abingdon, Oxon OX14 4RN

Routledge is an imprint of the Taylor & Francis Group, an informa business

Library of Congress Cataloging in Publication Data
A catalog record for this book has been requested.

ISBN: 978-0-415-62442-8 (hbk)
ISBN: 978-0-203-10468-2 (ebk)

Typeset in Bembo
by Wearset Ltd, Boldon, Tyne and Wear

CONTENTS

PREFACE

Teri Holbrook, Peggy Albers, and Amy Seely Flint

Shifting Times in Literacy Education

It is commonplace to note that terms using the phrase "new" contain the seeds of their own demise; as Gee (2008) opined of the term the New Literacy Studies, coined in the 1990s, it "is probably unfortunate, since anything that was once 'new' is soon 'old'" (p. 1). Thus the term "new literacies," with its emphasis on the Internet as the "defining technology for literacy and learning" (Coiro, 2008, p. xii), seems destined for a less temporal moniker. Even the heady thrill of calling today's students "21st century learners" and their communicative practices "21st century literacies" has the creaky feel of a soon-to-be-dated science fiction movie, where computers are big square boxes on a desk and cell phones cannot talk back.[1]

But while the terms themselves may be aging, the changes that literacy education are undergoing continue apace. The reason quite simply is that literacy technologies are in the midst of ongoing transformation, so profound that it can be hard for educators to keep up. While the Internet may now be a tool for everyday literacy practices, other information and communication technologies (ICTs) continue to come online that affect notions of what comprises a literate life. The affordances of these ICTs are renewing and solidifying definitions of literacy(ies) as multiple and multimodal and involving "forms of texts that can arrive via digital code as sound, text, images, video, animations, and any combination of these" (Lankshear & Knobel, 2011, p. 28).

A quick exercise in how swiftly literacy education is shifting from conventional, print-based concepts of literacy to digital and multimodal concepts can be found by looking at the programs for the Conference on College Composition and Communication (CCCC), held annually in the United States. A search of the online pdf of the 2004 conference program found the words "technology" on 50 out of 331 pages, "digital" on 17 pages, and "multimodal" on three pages—roughly 15%, 5%, and 1% respectively (see CCCC, 2004). In 2008, "technology" appeared on 36 pages out of 321, "digital" on 32 pages, and "multimodal" on 16 pages (11%, 10%, and 5%, respectively) (see CCCC, 2008). By 2012, those numbers had changed yet again: "digital" appeared on 91 out of 376 pages and "multimodal" on 33 pages (24% and 9% respectively) while "technology" stayed relatively static at 49 pages (13%) (see CCCC, 2012). Within an eight-year span, the word digital increased its real estate to nearly a quarter of program pages, while the word multimodal moved from barely mentioned to almost 1/10th of program pages. This fast calculation suggests that the papers presented by literacy and composition scholars at this leading conference mark a definite and ongoing shift in the field.

What this shift means for literacy classrooms, Pre-K through university, is profound. The texts that students read and create are no longer confined to alphabetic strings of symbols printed on paper and bound between fixed covers. The reader/writer relationship is not limited to the transaction that happens when the reader takes up the author's words on a page. Instead, texts are multimodal, multimedia, multi-platform, multi-authored, interactive, and dispersed (Jenkins, 2006). They are literally on the move, synching from desktop to laptop to e-book to smart phone. They are also more arts based as developing technology prompts calls for a renewed focus on the traditional arts—visual, music, drama, creative writing—reinvigorated within electronic and digital environments (Sanders & Albers, 2010). "Literacy" cannot possibly be singular anymore because words are no longer the only means by which students can express and represent their thoughts. From mash-ups to tweets to new media fictions and hypermedia architectures that combine images, sounds, and written and spoken words, the formats, modes, and distribution avenues of texts are expanding. Expanding with them are the qualities of "what it means to be literate in the 21st century" (Sanders & Albers, 2010, p. 1).

But it's not just texts and the reader/author relationship that are undergoing transformation. The affordances of technology that give humans the ability to collapse time and space are also having profound effects on literacy practices. An awareness of glocalization (Robertson, 1995)—"the simultaneity and the interpenetration of what are conventionally called the global and the local, or ... the universal and the particular" (p. 30) brings increased opportunities for English/Language Arts educators to engage students in explorations of cultural forces that impact the complex connections between the communities in which they are physically located and other communities around the world. "[C]hanges have occurred in the character and substance of literacies that are associated with larger changes in technology, institutions, media and the economy and with the rapid movement toward global scale in manufacture, finance, communications, and so on" (Lankshear & Knobel, 2011, p. 28). These forces, which are part of the social, economic, and political conditions in which students live, highlight the imperative for multiple discursive lenses through which students can analyze, question, articulate, represent, and change their worlds—lenses that literacy educators can make available to them.

These transformational changes in literacy education are not relegated to classrooms or even to conversations about (the recognized false binary of) in- and out-of-school literacies (see Hull & Schultz, 2002). They are changing literacy research as well. If research is made possible by the communicative and analytical technologies available to researchers, then developments in technology that disrupt long-standing notions of literacy can also disrupt long-standing practices of literacy research. Disruption, by its very definition an unsettling process, does the productive work of creating cracks, opening fissures, breaking up packed soil. In this kind of academic tilling, new research forms, concepts, and practices can emerge.

Two Texts: A Demonstration in Juxtaposition

The purpose of this book, then, is to look at how literacy researchers are using new and emerging inquiry methods in response to this transformative period— how, to use St. Pierre's words (1997), they engage in their work "to produce different knowledge and to produce knowledge differently" (p. 175). The researchers spotlighted in this book do not necessarily work with digital media or tools, nor do they necessarily focus on global influences; nevertheless, their work both affects and is affected by the currents described above. To demonstrate this assertion, we[2] juxtapose two texts, the first a 1976 research journal article that provided its readers with a historical view of literacy instruction and predictions for future trends in pedagogical inquiry and practices, and the second a 2009 cell phone video of a woman killed during an Iranian political protest.

In a *Theory into Practice* article entitled "Language arts and the curriculum," Burns (1976) gave a succinct and informative overview of U.S. language arts instruction to date, starting with the Massachusetts Education Act of 1647 that called for the creation of "schools for reading and writing" (p. 107) and briefly scanning the 17th, 18th, and 19th centuries as periods when handwriting, letter-sound relationships, elocution, grammar, and—late in the 19th century—comprehension were emphasized with the publishing of several well-used teaching texts, including the McGuffy readers (pp. 107–108). The bulk of the article focused on trends and innovations in 20th century language arts pedagogy, including instruction informed by applied linguistics, the recognized importance of preschool, a valuing of home cultures and dialects, awareness of gender issues in literacy development, and attention to composition and creative reading and writing (pp. 109–112). The inductive manner of much of the period's language arts instruction positioned language as "something that is alive and growing" (p. 111). Of particular note was the role of new media in the mid-20th century language arts classroom:

New media are being used by more and more teachers to add interest and effectiveness to the reading/language arts curriculum. From the small cassette tape recorder (used to listen to stories, to dictate stories, and to record original plays or dramatizations) to paperback books, there is a world of media at the teacher's disposal: records (of books, stories, and poetry to add to the enjoyment of literature); transparencies for overhead projectuals (to assist presentation of any topic); films (new loop films can be operated by the child and can be viewed individually or projected on a screen for group viewing); filmstrips and slides (animated and used to present concepts about language, poetry, literature); television (presenting information visually and orally to supplement text presentation); programmed instruction (booklet form or a machine); videotape machines (capture a classroom performance); computer (programming of learning).

(*p. 113*)

We include this quote not to evoke an easy response about the quaintness of a 35-year-old view of literacy that named paperbacks as new media but to demonstrate how conventional literacy was framed as firmly embedded in written and spoken language. Tape recorders were used to listen to and dictate stories. Records were an alternative conveyance for literature, and filmstrips presented language concepts. Films were designed to be operated or viewed by children—not created by them—although it's noteworthy that children could be seen as agents who recorded original plays and dramatizations. The remainder of the article spotlighted possible future developments for language arts curricula, including a lessened focus on grouping children by grade level; increased emphasis on diversity in instruction, the personal and relational aspects of language arts, and the integration of listening, speaking, reading, and writing; and more attention to "natural" or "non-school" learning (p. 114).

Shift now to Iran in 2009. On June 20 of that year, 26-year-old Neda Agha-Soltan was shot and killed during a demonstration protesting the outcome of the recently completed Iranian presidential election. Her death was recorded on a cell phone by a nearby witness, sent to a person in another country, and uploaded onto YouTube (Tait & Weaver, as cited in Mortensen, 2011). "Within minutes rather than hours" (Mortensen, 2011, p. 7) the video was picked up first by news organizations and then by various political groups and internationally circulated. Described as a "YouTube Martyr," Agha-Soltan's image became a dominant icon for the Iranian protest movement (p. 7) and more broadly for Iranian diasporic communities worldwide (Naghibi, 2011). Media-circulated still photos of her before the shooting were reproduced for t-shirts and posters, some using the same artistic techniques as the famous "Hope" poster of Barack Obama by Shepard Fairey. To indicate affinity and solidarity, people around the world uploaded photos of Agha-Soltan as their profile pictures on Facebook (Mortenson, 2011, p. 7). The video subsequently received journalistic recognition through the George Polk Award for Video-graphy, an annual distinction bestowed by Long Island University "to honor special achievement in journalism" with a premium placed on work that "brings results" (LIU, George Polk Awards). According to the LIU website, the 2009 award was given to "the anonymous individuals" who made the recording and uploaded it to the Internet, whereby it "became a rallying point for the reform-ist opposition in Iran" (LIU, Previous Award Winners).

We juxtapose these two texts because of what we perceive as the sea change in the conception and practice of literacies that they demonstrate. Imagine a researcher, scanning a classroom in 1976, well versed in the discourse of her field and anticipating the better integration of listening, speaking, reading, and writing in language arts instruction. Would she connect the dots that made the anonymously filmed video of Agha-Soltan's death such an impactful literacy artifact? Firmly grounded in a view of literacy and language arts as word based, would she conceptualize the video as a text that could be analyzed and the events, practices, and discourses circulating around it as instances of literacies? How would she think, write, inquire, investigate, frame questions that explored the rapid remixing, reproducing, deployment, and redeployment of a stranger's image by uncountable numbers of people for multiple purposes on a global scale? And how—or would she—make connections between such polit-ically charged texts and the English Language Arts classroom upon which she gazed?

These questions strike a chord with us—as did the texts that inspired them—because they point to the potency and fertility of the current moment in literacy research. Whatever the field of literacy research was in the last quarter of the 20th century, it is now something else. That is not to say that the concerns and questions expressed in the Burns (1976) article are obsolete—they are not. But they are complicated by and implicated in transformative cultural changes that affect the way literacies are conceptualized and literacy research is conceived and undertaken. Contemporary literacy researchers carry out their work within international and local discourses and movements that include but are not limited to immigration, global women's and minorities' rights, political springs and upheavals, and financial bubbles and collapses, all occurring amid and aided by developing communication technologies—YouTube, Facebook, Twitter, the quickly expanding seamless web. It is not possible to consider emerging forms of literacy research outside of the complex sociopolitical currents that both shape and are shaped by them.

Shifting Times in Literacy Research

Denzin and Lincoln (2000) famously categorized qualitative research as having moved through six "moments" during the 20th century, starting with the tradi-tional phase (roughly from 1900–1950), grounded in a positivist discourse and the myth of the Lone Ethnographer, and then moving apace through the modernist phase (a postpositivist paradigm); blurred genres (in which qualitative researchers drew from a variety of theories such as naturalistic inquiry, semiotics, phenomenology, and feminism, and in the process blurred writing genres of the social sciences and the humanities); the crisis of representation (in which epistemologies of color and feminist and critical theories challenged the notion that research could "capture lived experience" (p. 17) and problematized concepts of validity, generalizability, and reliability); the postmodern (which saw continued interrogation of written representation and called for activist-oriented research that pushes against grand narratives); and postexperimental inquiry (in which qualitative researchers produced a variety of genres, such as fiction, poetry, and multimedia) (pp. 12–17). This categorization has been critiqued as a progress narrative (Alasuutari, as cited in Denzin & Lincoln, 2011, p. xv), and Denzin and Lincoln have reiterated that these moments "overlap and coexist in the present" (p. xv). While we acknowledge the controvertible nature of any taxonomy, as qualitative researchers ourselves we find the language of Denzin and Lincoln's moments both evocative and provocative as we consider new and emerging methods of literacy research in the first two decades of the 21st century.

In their nomenclature, the 21st century thus far has involved two additional moments: the methodologically contested present (2000–2010), and the fractured future (2010–present) (Denzin & Lincoln, 2011, p. 3). In the seventh moment of the methodologically contested present, some qualitative researchers pushed back against the focus on evidence-based research promoted by No Child Left Behind while others took up multiple and mixed analytical methods (p. ix). The eighth moment of the fractured future—now—"confronts" the methodological response to evidence-based social science research and enacts renewed calls for critical inquiries:

> So at the beginning of the second decade of the 21st century, it is time to move forward. It is time to open up new spaces, time to explore new discourses. We need to find new ways of connecting persons and their personal troubles with social justice methodologies. We need to become better accomplished in linking these interventions to those institutional sites where troubles are turned into public issues and public issues transformed into social policy.
>
> *(p. ix)*

It is amid these historical movements of educational research—a past century of research shifts and paradigmatic proliferations (Lather, 2006), a new century of technological revolution, and a call for an opening up of spaces and discourses— that we consider new and emerging literacy research methods. In the chapters that follow, readers will see the tussle of contested methodologies, the appeal of a fractured future, the echoes and layers of blurred genres and postexperimental authorings. But to evoke Denzin and Lincoln (2011) again, we hope that readers will find in these chapters "a gentle, probing, neighborly, and critical conversation" (p. xii) in which they will want to engage.

New Forms of Literacy Research

This book, *New Methods of Literacy Research*, offers a look at emerging forms of literacy and qualitative research, either reinvigorated or freshly conceived in the midst of transformative times. The contributors to this volume bring to the forefront new and innovative research methods that employ discourse, arts-based, digital, and geographical analyses, among others, to examine various phenomena, including language, social contexts, identity, and multimodal texts. Their work suggests that research practices are diversifying to reflect how information is processed, internalized, and distributed; how social contexts in education are changing; and how understandings of literacies as multiple and glocal have influenced the very nature of learning and literacy.

Our goal is to acquaint a variety of audiences—doctoral students contemplating their dissertations, early career researchers developing their lines of inquiry, accomplished scholars seeking new perspectives and points of view—with exemplary samples of innovative methods used by researchers with a desire to take scholarly risks. Our charge to them was simple: write chapters that conveyed their methods in ways that readers might be able to take up and follow. As to be expected, the results were as individualistic as the authors who crafted them. In some cases, the chapters are well-crafted explanations of how the methods can be used, including an example study, while others are themselves instances of methodological innovation. We have no suggested order for reading the chapters; instead, each chapter is presented both to stand alone and in context with each other.

The work of these scholars pays testament to the fertility of this time, re-emphasizing that while the futuristic gleam may be off the term 21st century, the invigorating promise of new ideas, practices, and actions is embedded in this present period of literacy research. As the editors of this book, we invite you to join us in the discovery.

Notes

1. Lankshear and Knobel (2011) address this notion of "new" in relation to literacies by noting two ways in which the term is used—paradigmatically and ontologically. Gee's use of it in the New Literacy Studies is an example of paradigmatic use, in which his sociocultural framing of literacy was an alternative to existing literacy approaches. An ontology of "new," on the other hand, refers to the "'nature' or 'stuff' of new literacies" (p. 27) and maintains that technology and global currents have fostered changes "in the character and substance" (p. 28) of literacy that set new literacies as

fundamentally different from conventional literacies. These changes can be seen not only in the construction of texts as a result of technology but also in the "'ethos' of new literacies," which arise from "different *configuration of values* from conventional literatures ... [and] different kinds of social and cultural *relations*" [italics in original] (p. 28). As examples of the ethos of new literacies, Lankshear and Knobel offer the participatory, collaborative, and distributive characteristics of new literacies. In this sense, an ontological framing of "new" may diminish the impending aging of the term.

2. The use of "we" in the Preface refers specifically to the three editors of this book and not to a generic, universal "we."

References

Burns, P. C. (1976). Language arts and the curriculum. *Theory into Practice, 15*(2), 107–115.

Coiro, J. (2008). Preface. In J. Coiro, M. Knobel, C. Lankshear, & D. J. Leu (Eds.), *Handbook of research on new literacies* (pp. xi–xv). New York: Lawrence Erlbaum Associates.

Conference on College Composition and Communication. (2004). *Making composition matter: Students, citizens, institutions, advocacy.* Retrieved from www.ncte.org/cccc/review/2004program.

Conference on College Composition and Communication. (2008). *Writing realities, changing realities.* Retrieved from www.ncte.org/cccc/review/2008program.

Conference on College Composition and Communication. (2012). *Writing gateways.* Retrieved from www.ncte.org/cccc/review/2012program.

Denzin, N. & Lincoln, Y. (Eds.). (2000). *The SAGE handbook of qualitative research* (2nd ed.). Thousand Oaks, CA: Sage Publications.

Denzin, N. & Lincoln, Y. (Eds.). (2011). *The SAGE handbook of qualitative research.* Thousand Oaks, CA: Sage Publications.

Gee, J. (2008). *Social linguistics and literacies: Ideology in discourses* (3rd ed.). New York: Routledge.

Hull, G. & Schultz, K. (2002). *School's out: Bridging out-of-school literacies with classroom practice.* New York: Teachers College Press.

Jenkins, H. (2006). *Convergence culture: When old and new media collide.* New York: New York University Press.

Lankshear, C. & Knobel, M. (2011). *New literacies: Everyday practices and social learning* (3rd ed.). New York: Open University Press.

Lather, P. (2006). Paradigm proliferation as a good thing to think with: Teaching research in education as a wild profusion. *International Journal of Qualitative Studies in Education, 19*(1), 35–57.

Long Island University. (2012). George Polk Awards [Webpage]. Retrieved from www.liu.edu/polk.

Long Island University. (2012). George Polk Awards, Previous Award Winners [Webpage]. Retrieved from www.liu.edu/About/News/Polk/Previous#2009.

Mortensen, M. (2011). When citizen photojournalism sets the news agenda: Neda Agha Soltan as a web 2.0 icon of post-election unrest in Iran. *Global Media and Communication, 7*(1), 4–16.

Naghibi, N. (2011). Diasporic disclosures: Social networking, Neda, and the 2009 Iranian presidential elections. *Biography, 34*(1), 56–69.

Robertson, R. (1995). Glocalization: Time-space and homogeneity-heterogeneity. In S. Lash, R. Robertson, & M. Featherstone (Eds.), *Global modernities* (pp. 25–44). Thousand Oaks, CA: Sage Publications.

Sanders, J. & Albers, P. (2010). Multimodal literacies: An introduction. In P. Albers & J. Sanders (Eds.). *Literacies, the arts & multimodality* (pp. 1–25). Urbana, IL: National Council of Teachers of English.

St. Pierre, E. A. (1997). Methodology in the fold and the irruption of transgressive data. *Qualitative Studies in Education, 10*(2), 175–189.

ACKNOWLEDGMENTS

We would like to acknowledge the people who have been instrumental in helping us pull together this book. First, we would like to thank all of the chapter contributors; their insights and expertise certainly have shaped these methods of literacy research, and their immediate responses to our queries made our work that much easier. We also would like to thank Naomi Silverman who believed in this project from the start. We would like to thank Sally Quinn and Amy Ekins, copy editor and project manager, who helped us prepare this book. We would also like to acknowledge our doctoral students in the Middle and Secondary Education and Instructional Technologies at Georgia State: Eliza Allen, Ryan Boylan, David Brown, Nicole Dukes, Heather Lynch, Sarah Mantegna, Nicole Maxwell, Christi Pace, Kevin Powell, Sanjuana Rodriguez, Kelli Sowerbrower, Dru Tomlin, Alisha White, and Kamania Wynter-Hoyte. All of these young scholars worked directly with our authors and worked with us on editing and revising chapters. We especially want to acknowledge Nicole Dukes for acting as our student editor-in-charge.

PART I

Methods in Discourse Analysis

1

MICROETHNOGRAPHIC DISCOURSE ANALYSIS

David Bloome and Stephanie Power Carter

The What of Microethnographic Discourse Analysis

The study of discourse structures and processes has been conducted from a broad range of disciplinary perspectives (see Graesser, Gernsbacher, & Goldman, 2003; Schiffrin, Tannen, & Hamilton, 2001; van Dijk 1985, 1997, 2001) with a broad range of definitions of discourse (see Bloome, Carter et al., 2009; Potter, Wetherell, Gill, & Edwards, 1990). Applied to the study of literacy, these diverse perspectives and definitions of discourse have produced a body of educational studies across disciplines redefining literacy learning in and outside classrooms (see Gee & Green, 1998; Hicks, 1995; Rex et al., 2010). Microethnographic discourse analysis is a subset of perspectives within the broader field of discourse analysis studies.

Microethnographic discourse analysis is not a method but a perspective. This perspective is grounded in the insight that people act and react to each other; and they do so within a social context constructed by how they and others have been acting and reacting to each other over time. The primary, but not exclusive, means by which people act and react to each other is with language and related semiotic systems. Inherent to this perspective is the inseparability of people and their uses of language within the social events and social contexts of their interactions.

The foundations of a microethnographic discourse analysis perspective lie in the ethnography of communication (Erickson 2004; Gumperz & Hymes, 1972; Hymes, 1974) and interactional sociolinguistics (e.g., Gumperz, 1986). In brief, these foundations provide a systematic way to understand language and related semiotic systems as they are actually used in people's daily lives as part of their interactions with others within the local and broader social contexts of their lives (as opposed to views of language as an idealized, decontextualized linguistic system, cf., Chomsky, 1957). As applied to education, these foundations conceptualize teaching and learning as social linguistic processes (cf., Green, 1983b); that is, it is through their contextualized, interactional uses of language (and related semiotic systems) that educators and students constitute and define what counts as teaching, learning, curriculum, knowledge, achievement, gate keeping, and other educational processes (Hicks, 2003). Applied to the study of classrooms, researchers have employed this perspective to examine how cultural, racial, gender, and linguistic variation among school populations play out in educational processes and outcomes (e.g., Au, 1980; Camitta, 1993; Erickson & Mohatt, 1982; Phillips, 1983) as well as how classroom conversations are related to and define academic learning (e.g., Cazden, 1988, 2001; Michaels, Sohmer, & O'Connor, 2004).

Building on foundations in the ethnography of communication and interactional sociolinguistics, educational researchers (e.g., Bloome, Carter, Christian, Otto, & Shuart-Faris, 2005; Hicks, 2003) sought to incorporate additional theoretical perspectives that would address the complexities of dialogue (e.g., Bakhtin, 1935/1981; Volosinov, 1929/1973), power relations (e.g., Apple, 1995; Bourdieu & Thompson, 1991; Foucault, 1980), the relationship of language and culture (e.g., Agar, 1996; Duranti & Goodwin, 1992; Sherzer, 1987; Street, 1993); critical discourse analysis (e.g., Blommaert & Bulcasen, 2000; Fairclough, 1992, 1995; Rogers, Malancharuvil-Berkes, Mosley, Hui, & Joseph, 2005), cultural studies (e.g., Walkerdine, 1984; Wohlwend, 2009), gender and language studies (e.g., Cameron, 1998; Coates, 1993; Holmes & Meyerhoff, 2008), critical race studies (e.g., Crenshaw, Gotanda, Peller, & Thomas, 1995), among others. In so doing, educational researchers addressed: (a) the relationship of local, interactional events with events and processes in other locales and at broader levels of social, cultural, economic, political, and educational contexts; (b) the ways in which social structures structure daily life and institutional life including schooling; and (c) the ways in which people, including teachers and students, together adapt and resist given structures and social, cultural, economic, political, and semiotic practices as well as the ways in which new structures and practices are created. This laminating of multiple theoretical perspectives seeks to capture and theorize the inherent inseparability of local interactions and the contexts in which they occur. At the same time, it seeks to maintain the insight that social events, practices, institutions, ideologies, are constructed, maintained, and changed by people in interaction with others; the histories and material nature of those practices, institutions, and ideologies not withstanding. As such, from a microethnographic discourse analysis perspective one must simultaneously view local, interactional events as reflections and refractions of broader social and historical contexts while viewing broader, social contexts as reflected in and refracted by local, interactional events.

Microethnographic Discourse Analysis Perspectives of Literacy

The study of literacy from a microethnographic discourse analysis perspective incorporates theoretical frames and constructs from scholarship on literacy as a social and cultural process (e.g., Barton & Hamilton, 1998; Cook-Gumperz, 1986; Gee, 1996; Heath, 2012; Street, 1995). With roots in social and cultural anthropology and sociology, literacy is defined as a set of social and cultural events and practices in which the involvement of written language is more than trivial (cf., Heath, 1980). From this perspective, literacy is always *literacies* (referring to multiple and diverse social and cultural events and practices involving written language; hereafter referred to as literacy events and practices) and literacies are always a part of reflecting and refracting the cultural ideology of institutional and broader contexts.

A microethnographic discourse analysis perspective views literacy events and practices as constructed by people acting and reacting to each other with, through (and possibly about) written language. Literacy events and practices may involve spoken language and other modes of communication, and the relationships of written and spoken language and other modes of communication to each other vary depending upon the nature of the social events and practices themselves (and as people adapt and change those events and practices). Thus, there is no a priori characterization of the nature or functions of written language or an a priori framework for the interpretation or meaningfulness of written language. Rather, what written language is used for, its nature, and how it is interpreted depend on what people in interaction with each other do with it and what frames of interpretation they construct (Santa Barbara Classroom Discourse Group, 1992). And, while these constructions are not predetermined, neither are they indifferent to the history of the use of written language within local and broader contexts. Indeed, people may hold each other accountable for using written language in ways consistent with its history of use in particular types of social situations.

Questions Asked About Literacy(ies) from a Microethnographic Discourse Analysis Perspective

A key research question from a microethnographic discourse analysis perspective is on how the ways people act and react to each other constitute literacy events and practices and the relationship of such social interactions to other social events and practices and to broader social contexts. Simply put, questions are asked about who is doing what, with whom, when, where, and how in a literacy event and across a series of literacy events. Related questions include how, *in situ*, the ways people act and react to each other define literacy and literacy learning, construct social identities in relationship to literacy, constitute inclusion and exclusion from a broad range of social groups and social institutions, enact and challenge the relationship of literacy and social structures and power relations, define and naturalize rationality, as well as provide opportunities for people to use written language and related semiotic systems to construct their daily lives in and out of classrooms, make their lives meaningful, and develop caring and loving relationships.

Some Theoretical Tools for Conducting Microethnographic Discourse Analysis Studies of Literacy Events and Practices

As part of a broader approach to describing and theorizing how the diverse and evolving ways people act and react to each other with, through, and about written language, we note six key theoretical tools: attention to indexicality, contextualization cues, boundary making, thematic coherence, intertextuality, and intercontextuality.

Indexicality refers to the signaling of a context (cultural, social, historical, geographic, economic, etc.) and social relationships through the use of varied communicative means. As people act and react to each other they are continuously signaling, validating, and negotiating the contexts that are framing what they are doing, what and how their actions and reactions have meaning, and how what they are doing is connected to social and cultural phenomena outside the event. From a microethnographic discourse analysis perspective, indexicality is not established with an isolated word or singular sign, but rather in the ways people build their actions and reactions on each other.

Gumperz (1986) noted that as people act and react to each other they use *contextualization cues*, any linguistic feature or form – verbal, prosodic, non-verbal – to index an interpretive frame and context. Because people must signal to each other their intentions, contextualization cues are visible, usually multiple, and redundant. Contextualization cues provide a material basis for producing a description of what is happening in a social event. It is important to note that simply identifying a contextualization cue does not necessarily indicate what the cue means as the meaning depends on many factors; rather, contextualization cues need to be described as part of people's evolving actions and reactions.

The boundaries between social events cannot be determined a priori, and similarly so the boundaries among texts, social groups, institutional contexts, and other social contexts. Rather, *boundary making* is accomplished by people concertedly as they interact with each other. Boundaries have to be proposed and ratified, actively maintained, and are highly contestable by participants during a literacy event. Boundary making is a communicative tool that people use to help mutually construct meaning by identifying units of analysis at multiple levels including social events, institutions, and contexts.

Thematic coherence within a microethnographic discourse analysis perspective refers to the construction of meaning at multiple levels across an event and across events through people acting and reacting to each other. Thematic coherence answers the question for interlocutors: what is this interaction and event about? It also answers the question, what is the meaning of a series of structurally related events? Thematic coherence is not static but may evolve over the course of an event and across related events. The mapping of thematic coherence is similar for interlocutors and researchers. That is, interlocutors must continuously signal to each other the thematic coherence of an event; and the contextualization cues and other communicative means they use to do so need to be visible and material. A researcher observing the event (either as the event occurs or with the assistance of video technology) can track the construction of thematic coherence by noting those visible signals and mapping them on a moment-by-moment, utterance-by-utterance basis (cf., Green & Wallat, 1981).

Intertextuality refers to the juxtaposition of texts. From a microethnographic discourse analysis perspective, the juxtaposition of texts – what texts are juxtaposed, when, where, how, and by whom – is viewed as part of the process of people acting and reacting to each other (cf., Bloome & Egan-Robertson, 1993). By juxtaposing texts – spoken, written, signed, etc. – people concertedly construct shared meanings both for the event and for the texts themselves. That is, the meaningfulness of a text depends both on how it is used within a social event and on how it is positioned in relationship to other texts within and across events.

Intercontextuality is a complimentary construct to intertextuality. It refers to the juxtaposition of contexts as part of the process of people acting and reacting to each other. By juxtaposing contexts, people construct shared meanings, interpretive frames, and histories. Interpellation, the process whereby one context redefines another, from a microethnographic discourse analysis perspective, is a function of how people construct intercontextuality. For example, the redefining of classroom education as a business enterprise depends on people, as they interact with each other, juxtaposing business contexts with classroom contexts and redefining the latter in terms of the former. Intercontextuality is also a component of how people narrativize their experiences and create collective memories. That is, as people act and react to each other, they construct shared narratives employing select events and contexts to constitute those narratives and give them meaning.

Telling Cases, Type-Case Analysis, Over Time, and Grounded Theoretical Constructs in the Microethnographic Discourse Analysis Study of Literacies

The descriptions generated through the moment-by-moment descriptions and analyses of specific literacy events yield theoretical insights in at least four ways. First, the descriptions and analyses may be located in what Mitchell (1984) calls a "telling case." A telling case is not necessarily representative or typical but its nature is such that it reveals taken-for-granted cultural processes and ideologies operant in a set of situations or in an institution or society. For example, in a classroom literature discussion a student expresses an interpretation of a character that differs from the way that is consistent with the shared expectations held by the teacher and other students. The teacher or another student may react by "repairing" (i.e., correcting) the interpretation and making public both the errant interpretation and the appropriate interpretive framework. Such an errant interpretation and its repair may not be frequent or typical, nonetheless in combination they are revealing about the cultural models of reading to which the participants hold each other accountable. A microethnographic analysis of what happens in such an event not only yields insights into how repairs are made in instructional conversations but also what constitutes the appropriate cultural model and interpretative framework for reading literature in this classroom. That is, the detailed, moment-by-moment description of how the teachers and students use spoken and written language to hold each other accountable for a particular model of reading comprehension in this literature class is made visible both to the people in the event and to researchers studying the event.

A microethnographic discourse analysis perspective may also yield theoretical insights through *type-case analysis*. Through detailed, moment-by-moment description of how people are acting and reacting to each other in a literacy event, patterns may be identified. A type-case analysis provides a systematic means for examining the recurrence of a particular pattern in analogous and non-analogous events. Engaging in a type-case analysis requires identifying through an ethnographic methodology what events are analogous and non-analogous, and doing so based on an emic understanding of the organization of events in the classroom (or other social setting). As a pattern is checked for its recurrence in analogous events attention is paid to how the pattern varies across those analogous events and is refined. By checking for the recurrence of the pattern in analogous events, a researcher can check how the pattern is connected to a particular set of situations. If the pattern is present in non-analogous events then questions can be raised about its function and significance in these non-analogous events (and thus provide insights into the relationship of events to each other and to how people adapt a particular literacy practice to different types of events). For example, consider a literature classroom in which the teacher presents a model of reading that involves a particular way of juxtaposing literary texts. The teacher and students may be reading a core novel, such as *The House on Mango Street* (Cisneros, 1984) and as the students read various chapters the teacher introduces additional short stories, excerpts from novels, poems, and essays for the students to read with the chapter. They discuss similarities and differences between the chapter from the core novel and the supplemental readings. Through a microethnographic discourse analysis perspective, researchers identify interactional patterns in how the teacher and students construct an interpretative framework for what counts as a similarity or difference and what those mean for the interpretation of the core novel. Using type-case analysis, researchers would then look for the recurrence of the interactional pattern across analogous events in that classroom. The result is a detailed description of the literacy practice in this classroom for reading novels. An agenda for such a program of research might be identifying how cultural models for reading literature vary across classrooms (even if they are reading the same novels) and what the implications of that variation might be for what reading practices students differentially acquire.

Similar to the use of type-case analysis with a microethnographic discourse analysis perspective is the use of the *over time* case. The underlying assumption of the over time case is that particular social settings are emically structured (either explicitly or implicitly) for change over time; that is, the people in those social settings have an agenda oriented to change over time. Classrooms would be one example as teachers and students work together to change the situated literacy practices in which they engage. Through a microethnographic discourse analysis perspective, the interactional construction of a situated literacy practice is identified within a particular key event or set of key events. Then, subsequent related events are examined to identify how the literacy practice is modified. Rather than refine the description of the identified practice (pattern) from the analogous events, what is foregrounded are the changes in the practice over time and the ways in which those changes were constructed, reconstructed, and validated.

Implied in the discussion of cases and microethnographic discourse analysis above is an agenda oriented to making visible how people acting and reacting to each other together constitute enacted definitions of key literacy and education concepts such as reading, writing, text, curriculum, learning, teaching, lesson, task, achievement, and thinking. Although educators and students often hold formal or folk definitions of such concepts, perhaps from the educational field or teacher education or popular culture, how these concepts are realized in the dynamics of the social interactions of teachers and students in classrooms may differ significantly from those formal or folk definitions. The result is a series of grounded theoretical constructs that supplant the decontextualized and abstractly held definitions and reveal what counts as such concepts *in situ*. These grounded theoretical constructs constitute a set of findings that can reframe and reconceptualize what educators and researchers assume to be occurring in classrooms. For example, consider a classroom lesson in which the teacher provides a list of questions for students to answer from their textbook; the teacher asks questions, the students respond, and the teacher evaluates their answers. The teacher and students define the event as a classroom lesson in which they are attempting to teach and learn information from the textbook by being engaged in reading comprehension. However, a description of what is happening during this lesson using a microethnographic discourse analysis perspective might show what the teacher and students were doing was enacting an interactional pattern for what counts as a lesson (a particular performative literacy practice) and that what counted as reading comprehension was reproducing printed text in spoken response to teacher questions (text reproduction). In brief, rather than view the students' inability to "learn" the information they read as a failure indicative of poor reading skills or poor teaching, from a microethnographic discourse analysis perspective the teacher and students successfully produced a social event that counts as *doing lesson* and as doing *reading comprehension*. In brief, a microethnographic perspective provides a way to describe what is happening distinct from the etic descriptors of prescriptive educational lexicons.

An Exemplar – Learning Over Time in a Language Arts Classroom

Bloome, Beierle, Grigorenko, and Goldman (2009) conducted a microethnographic discourse analysis of the classroom events in a ninth grade language arts classroom. In collaboration with the teacher, video recordings were made every day during the first eight weeks of the school year in one of her classes. As an aside, we note that video recordings are not themselves data but rather a level of data analysis. That is, during video recordings decisions have to be made about what to video and what not to record, what angle to use, how broad or narrow a visual frame, where to place microphones to collect accompanying audio, how many cameras to use, among myriad other decisions. The collection of video recording decisions reflects a particular perspective of classroom events (see Baker, Green, & Skukauskaite, 2008; Erickson, 2006).

Of particular interest in this classroom were the uses of intertextuality since the teacher had spent the previous summer working with Bloome and Goldman studying theories and research on intertextuality and had designed the instructional unit for the first eight weeks to emphasize and foreground intertextuality. Specifically, she selected one novel for study (*The House on Mango Street*) and as she and her students moved through the chapters of the book they read related stories, poems, and chapters from other novels. In addition, the writing assignments and the classroom discussions were all related to *The House on Mango Street* including the final assignment which was to write a short story about their family history (the family history could be fictional) using *The House on Mango Street* as a mentor text. In addition to the video recordings, data collection also included interviews with the teacher and students and collection of all student written work.

It should be noted that Bloome and Goldman were also collecting data on a second classroom, a seventh grade language arts class in another school, for a comparative perspective. The teacher of this second classroom had also spent the previous summer studying intertextuality but her approach in her first instructional unit differed in that she had her students read two novels at the same time.

As a first step, the research team reviewed the various daily instructional activities across the eight weeks seeking to identify activities that were core to classroom instruction over time (e.g., writing, read alouds, discussion, analysis of a literary text) and to identify the written texts used. Then, a target lesson was identified that appeared to contain key literacy events and practices that were key to literacy learning as defined by the teacher, that were consistent with an ethnographic (anthropological) perspective of literacy events, and that had have emic validity (based on preliminary analysis). In this classroom, two such literacy events and practices were identified: the analysis of a literary text and writing – and both of these activities were found in the target lesson. (Please note that each of these events involved spoken, written, and nonverbal language). One quality of both of these events is that they were about written language; that is, students were not just using multiple modalities of language to share their views, knowledge, and experiences, but a primary purpose was to talk and write about written language (i.e., the literary texts, their own writing – one of the hallmarks that Street and Street, 1991, identify as indexing the schooling of literacy). In brief, the identification of these key events was driven by theoretical perspective associated with microethnographic discourse analysis and was systematic and transparent.

After identifying the target lesson, the two previous lessons and the two subsequent lessons were also identified; the purpose was to examine how the key events of the target lesson evolved from what came before and what came later. In some cases, what precedes the key events in a target lesson does not appear in the immediately preceding lessons. Therefore, a researcher has to examine the key events in the target lesson to identify what intercontextual links the interlocutors make. In the Bloome et al. (2009) study, the two previous and two subsequent lessons were explicitly linked by the references of teacher and students.

Transcripts were made of the key events in all five lessons. As Ochs (1979) and Green, Franquiz, and Dixon (1997) note, making a transcript is a theorizing task. That is, decisions are made about what to transcribe and what not to transcribe and how to represent the instructional conversation. Each of these decisions reflects a particular set of theoretical assumptions about how talk in classrooms matters. One of the assumptions that Bloome et al. (2009) made is that interlocutors signal to each other units of conversational analysis and they signal to each other the shared interpretative frameworks to be employed; both are signaled through the use of contextualization cues. Thus, in making a transcript it is important to transcribe both the boundaries of conversational units *as they are signaled by the interlocutors* and to record the contextualization cues that provide evidence of the unit boundaries and of the register, key, tone, and substance of the interpretive framework. As an aside, given the discussion of transcription above, a transcript is not data but rather it is a level of analysis.

After transcribing key events in the target lesson, a description is made of each message unit (cf., Green & Wallat, 1981; similar to an utterance) based on the foundations theories discussed earlier and on other theories of the social uses of language (e.g., Austin, 2005; Goffman, 1981; Hanks, 1995; Searle, 1969). The theoretical frameworks one brings to the descriptive analysis depend in part on the goals of the research study and in part of what the preliminary ethnographic analysis suggests may be occurring with, through, and about written language in the event. Description is similar to coding but not the same. Coding involves using a set of distinct and mutually exclusive descriptors based on the message unit (utterance) itself. Description, as we are using it, is oriented to describing the multiple, overlapping, and often ambiguous functions and meanings of a message unit. Further, and key to the distinction between description and coding, description is based on *post hoc* analysis rather than simply on the message unit itself. Thus, the function and meaning of a message unit depends on what comes before and what comes after and how that refracts what the shared, public, and visible meaning of a message unit is. That is, the meaning and function of a message unit depends on how interlocutors take it up.

Once a message unit by message unit description is made, the transcription and description are analyzed for thematic coherence. The identification of thematic coherence depends on the *post hoc* reactions of the interlocutors. That is, thematic coherence does not lie in the decontextualized meanings of the words, utterances, and texts employed in the event. Rather, thematic coherence is a social construction that interlocutors make public to each other. On occasion the thematic coherence of an event can be identified by a jointly constructed repair. For example, imagine that a teacher is discussing a classroom writing task with her students. One student asks, "When are they taking yearbook photographs?" to which the teacher replies, "We are not talking about that now. We are talking about the writing task to write about a holiday memory." The students in the classroom look at the student who asked the question with disapproving facial expressions and make eye contact with each other in a manner indicating the student's inappropriate behavior. The teacher's repair makes visible what they are and have been talking about; one theme that gives coherence to that instructional conversation.

Thematic coherence is not limited to identifying the formal or academic themes of the lessons. Thematic coherence can refer to aspects of the hidden curriculum such as appropriate social behavior, social identities, the valuing of particular cultural practices, gender roles, power relations, what counts as knowledge and knowing, etc.

The analysis of the target lesson is examined for how the instructional themes evolve and change over time. Of particular importance, is the ways in which those themes and their evolution are constructed. We take it as a given that a goal of an instructional conversation is to construct a change; and that change is a visible and public definition of learning. However, although it may be a goal of instructional conversations, evolution and change might not occur. This is also noteworthy and from the perspective of microethnographic discourse analysis is also considered an accomplishment. That is, both change and stability are social constructed productions.

After the target event is analyzed, a similar analysis is conducted on analogous events in the previous and subsequent lessons (as described earlier in the "over time" case study). By looking across days and lessons, a description and interpretation can be made of change and stability in the literacy practices that are central to these classroom events. This description and interpretation brings together an emic perspective and an etic perspective, both of which are grounded in the ways people (the teacher and the students) acted and reacted to each other over time.

The study by Bloome et al. (2009) detailed, on a message unit by message unit basis, how the teacher and students connected their lessons to other contexts, constructed collective memories, and shared chronotopes (ideologies of movement through time and space), and how these interactionally accomplished constructions provided an interpretive framework for understanding both literary texts and their own narrativized present and future lives.

A Microethnographic Perspective and the Hidden Curriculum of Classroom Literacy Events

Because a microethnographic discourse analysis perspective emphasizes the inseparability of people and the events and contexts of which they are apart, the perspective lends itself to understanding how the hidden curriculum of reading and literacy instruction is constructed by teachers and students, how such a curriculum "naturalizes" the use of literacy to privilege some cultural, racial, ethnic, socio-economic, and linguistic groups over others, and how a literacy curriculum defines what it means to be human (cf., Williams, 1977).

An exemplar is Stephanie Power Carter's (Carter, 2007) study of race and gender in a twelfth grade English classroom. Carter incorporated a Black feminist perspective (cf., Collins, 2000; Guy-Sheftall, 1985; Smith, 1983) with a microethnographic discourse analysis perspective in the study of African-American female students in a predominately White twelfth grade English language arts classroom focused on British literature. Using a telling case research design she used participant observation, ethnographic interviewing, and audio recording of classroom lessons. She focused primarily on two African-American female students who were mostly silent during classroom lessons. Despite their verbal silence there was a great deal of nonverbal interaction between the two young women during classroom lessons; mostly the nonverbal behavior involved eye contact.

Figure 1.1 shows how Carter displayed the nonverbal eye gaze behavior between the two young women. Carter used interviews with the two young

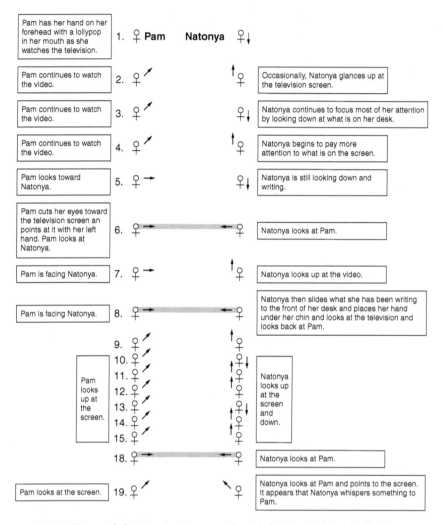

Transcript segment of Pam and Natonya's eye contact
During Huck Finn *Event*
15 seconds

Pam has her hand on her forehead with a lollypop in her mouth as she watches the television.	1. ♀ **Pam**	**Natonya** ♀↓	
Pam continues to watch the video.	2. ♀⬈	↑♀	Occasionally, Natonya glances up at the television screen.
Pam continues to watch the video.	3. ♀⬈	♀↓	Natonya continues to focus most of her attention by looking down at what is on her desk.
Pam continues to watch the video.	4. ♀⬈	↑♀	Natonya begins to pay more attention to what is on the screen.
Pam looks toward Natonya.	5. ♀→	♀↓	Natonya is still looking down and writing.
Pam cuts her eyes toward the television screen an points at it with her left hand. Pam looks at Natonya.	6. ♀→←♀		Natonya looks at Pam.
Pam is facing Natonya.	7. ♀→	↑♀	Natonya looks up at the video.
Pam is facing Natonya.	8. ♀→←♀		Natonya then slides what she has been writing to the front of her desk and places her hand under her chin and looks at the television and looks back at Pam.

	9. ♀⬈	↑♀	
	10. ♀⬈	↑♀↓	
Pam looks up at the screen.	11. ♀⬈	↑♀	Natonya looks up at the screen and down.
	12. ♀⬈	↑♀	
	13. ♀⬈	↑♀↓	
	14. ♀⬈	↑♀	
	15. ♀⬈	↑♀	
	18. ♀→←♀		Natonya looks at Pam.
Pam looks at the screen.	19. ♀⬈	↘♀	Natonya looks at Pam and points to the screen. It appears that Natonya whispers something to Pam.

FIGURE 1.1 Non-verbal transcript (source: adapted from "Inside Thing": Negotiating race and gender in a high school British literature classroom (p. 105) by S. P. Carter in M. Blackburn & C. Clark (Eds.) *Literacy Research for Political Action and Social Change* (2007), New York: Peter Lang. Adapted with permission.)

women to gain insight into how to interpret those nonverbal behaviors. The diagram of nonverbal behavior shows that the two young women made eye contact when a confederate flag was displayed in a student video being shown to the class. In interviews with the young women focusing on their use of eye gaze, Carter shows how such nonverbal behavior indexes solidarity between the young women and their identity as young African-American women who are supporting each other as they negotiate a Eurocentric curriculum that marginalizes their cultural heritage (e.g., the display of the confederate flag, the absence of literature by people of African descent) and gender as Black women (e.g., poems praising whiteness as beauty). Theoretically, Carter showed how "silence" was not necessarily void of communication or necessarily a passive response to marginalization. Rather, silence could be constructed as a proactive response to a hostile social context that allows people to pursue their educational agendas maintaining positive social and cultural identities.

Summary

Microethnographic discourse analysis is a perspective for researching language and literacy events grounded in the theoretical insight that people act and react to each other and that they do so primarily with and through language, over time. Such a perspective calls into question taken-for-granted definitions of literacy, reading, writing, learning, achievement, teaching, as well as the dichotomies implied by their definitions (literate v. illiterate, reader v. nonreader, success v. failure, etc.). It focuses attention on how literacy events and practices are constructed and refuses to allow a separation between events and the people in them. It places emphasis on detailing and describing how local, interactional literacy events are connected to other social events and how they are connected to broader social and cultural contexts. It is the nature of microethnographic discourse analysis to create a dialectic between the theoretical perspective it brings to the research effort and what people do and construct together in literacy events. These dialectics guide the process of data collection and analysis as well as refine the principles that guide microethnographic discourse analysis.

Researchers employing a microethnographic discourse analysis perspective may incorporate other social science, humanistic, and critical perspectives. But, such incorporation is done in a systematic manner that maintains the core principles of microethnographic discourse analysis. When incorporating other perspectives, a series of dialectic relationships is created: (a) between the theoretical principles and the material basis of how people act and react to each other, and (b) between microethnographic discourse analysis and the other perspectives such that new heuristics evolve.

References

Agar, M. (1996). *Language shock: Understanding the culture of conversation.* New York: HarperCollins.

Apple, M. (1995). *Education and power* (2nd ed.). New York: Routledge.

Au, K. (1980). Participation structures in a reading lesson with Hawaiian children. *Anthropology and Education Quarterly, 11*(2), 91–115.

Austin, J. L. (2005). *How to do things with words* (2nd ed.). Cambridge, MA: Harvard University Press.

Baker, W. D., Green, J., & Skukauskaite, A. (2008). Video-enabled ethnographic research: A microethnographic perspective. In G. Walford (Ed.), *How to do educational ethnography.* London: Tufnell Press.

Bakhtin, M. M. (1935/1981). *The dialogic imagination: Four essays.* Austin, TX: University of Texas Press.

Barton, D., & Hamilton, M. (1998). *Local literacies.* London: Routledge.

Blommaert, J., & Bulcasen, C. (2000). Critical discourse analysis. *Annual Review of Anthropology, 29*, 447–466.

Bloome, D., Beierle, M., Grigorenko, M., & Goldman, S. (2009). Learning over time: Uses of intertextuality, collective memories and classroom chronotopes in the construction of learning opportunities in a ninth-grade language arts classroom. *Language and Education, 23*(4), 313–334.

Bloome, D., Carter, S., Christian, B., Otto, S., & Shuart-Faris, N. (2005). *Discourse analysis and the study of classroom language and literacy events A Microethnographic approach.* Mahwah, NJ: Erlbaum.

Bloome, D., Carter, S., Christian, B., Otto, S., Shuart-Faris, N., Madrid, S., & Smith, M. with Goldman, S., & Macbeth, D. (2009). *On discourse analysis: Studies in language and literacy.* New York: Teachers College Press.

Bloome, D., & Egan-Robertson, A. (1993). The social construction of intertextuality and classroom reading and writing. *Reading Research Quarterly, 28*(4), 303–333.

Bourdieu, P., & Thompson, J. B. (1991). *Language and symbolic power.* Cambridge, MA: Harvard University Press.

Cameron, D. (1998). *The feminist critique of language.* New York: Psychology Press.

Camitta, M. (1993). Vernacular writing: Varieties of writing among Philadelphia high school students. In B. Street (Ed.), *Cross-cultural approaches to literacy.* Cambridge, UK: Cambridge University Press.

Carter, S. P. (2007). "Inside thing": Negotiating race and gender in a high school British literature classroom. In M. Blackburn & C. Clark (Eds.), *Literacy research for political action and social change* (pp. 97–111). New York: Peter Lang.

Cazden, C. (1988). *Classroom discourse: The language of teaching and learning.* Portsmouth, NH: Heinemann.

Cazden, C. B. (2001). *Classroom discourse: The language of teaching and learning* (2nd ed.). Portsmouth, NH: Heinemann.

Chomsky, N. (1957). *Syntactic structures.* The Hague, Netherlands: Mouton de Gruyter.

Cisneros, S. (1984). *The house on Mango Street.* Houston, TX: Arte Publico Press.

Coates, J. (1993). *Women, men, and language: A sociolinguistic account of gender differences in language* (2nd ed.). New York: Longman.

Collins, P. H. (2000). *Black feminist thought: Knowledge, consciousness, and the politics of empowerment.* New York: Routledge.

Crenshaw, K., Gotanda, N., Peller, G., & Thomas, K. (Eds.). (1995). *Critical race theory: The key writings that formed the movement.* New York: The New Press.

Duranti, A., & Goodwin, C. (Eds.). (1992). *Rethinking context: Language as an interactive phenomenon.* Cambridge, UK: Cambridge University Press.

Erickson, F. (2004). *Talk and social theory: Ecologies of speaking and listening in everyday life.* Malden, MA: Polity.

Erickson, F. (2006). Definition and analysis of data from videotape: Some research procedures and their rationales. In J. Green, G. Camilli, & P. Ellmore (Eds.), *Handbook of complementary methods in education research* (pp. 177–191). Mahwah, NJ: Erlbaum.

Erickson, F., & Mohatt, G. (1982). Cultural organization of participation structures in two classrooms of Indian students. In G. Spindler (Ed.), *Doing the ethnography of schooling: Educational anthropology in action* (pp. 132–175). Prospect Heights, IL: Waveland Press, Inc.

Fairclough, N. (1992). *Discourse and social change.* Cambridge, UK: Polity Press.

Fairclough, N. (1995). *Critical discourse analysis.* London: Longman.

Foucault, M. (1980). *Power/knowledge: Selected interviews and other writings, 1972–1977.* C. Gordon (Ed.). New York: Pantheon Books.

Gee, J. P. (1996). *Social linguistics and literacies: Ideology in discourses* (2nd ed.). London: Taylor & Francis.

Gee, J. P., & Green, J. L. (1998). Discourse analysis, learning, and social practice: A methodological study. *Review of Research in Education, 23,* 119–169.

Goffman, E. (1981). *Forms of talk.* Philadelphia: University of Pennsylvania Press.

Graesser, A., Gernsbacher, M., & Goldman, S. (Eds.). (2003). *Handbook of discourse processes.* Mahwah, NJ: Erlbaum.

Green, J., & Wallat, C. (Eds.). (1981). *Ethnography and language in educational settings.* Norwood, NJ: Ablex.

Green, J. L. (1983a). Exploring classroom discourse: Linguistic perspectives on teaching-learning processes. *Educational Psychologist, 18*(3), 180–199.

Green, J. L. (1983b). Teaching as a linguistic process: A state of the art. *Review of Research in Education, 10,* 151–252.

Green, J. L., Franquiz, M., & Dixon, C. (1997). The myth of an objective transcript: Transcribing as a situated act. *TESOL Quarterly, 31*(1), 172–176.

Gumperz, J. (1986). *Discourse strategies.* New York: Cambridge University Press.

Gumperz, J., & Hymes, D. (Eds.). (1972). *Directions in sociolinguistics: The ethnography of communication.* New York: Holt, Rinehart & Winston.

Guy-Sheftall, B. (Ed.). (1985). *Words on fire: An anthology of African-American feminist thought.* New York: The New Press.

Hanks, W. (1995). *Language and communicative practices.* New York: Westview Press.

Heath, S. (1980). The functions and uses of literacy. *Journal of Communication, 30*(1), 123–133.

Heath, S. B. (2012). *Words at work and play: Three decades in family and community life.* New York: Cambridge University Press.

Hicks, D. (1995). Discourse, learning and teaching. *Review of Research in Education, 21,* 49–95.

Holmes, J., & Meyerhoff, M. (Eds.). (2008). *Handbook of language and gender.* Malden, MA: Blackwell.

Hymes, D. (1974). *The foundations of sociolinguistics: Sociolinguistic ethnography.* Philadelphia: University of Pennsylvania Press.

Michaels, S., Sohmer, R. E., & O'Connor, M. C. (2004). Classroom discourse. In H. Ammon, N. Dittmar, K. Mattheier, & P. Trudgill (Eds.), *Sociolinguistics: An international handbook of the science of language and society* (2nd ed., pp. 2351–2366). New York: Walter de Gruyter.

Mitchell, J. C. (1984). Typicality and the case study. In R. Ellen (Ed.), *Ethnographic research: A guide to general conduct* (pp. 238–241). New York: Academic Press.

Ochs, E. (1979). Transcription as theory. In E. Ochs & B. B. Schieffelin (Eds.), *Developmental pragmatics* (pp. 43–72). New York: Academic Press.

Philips, S. (1983). *Invisible culture: Communication in classroom and community on the Warm Springs Indian reservation.* New York: Longman.

Potter, J., Wetherell, M., Gill, R., & Edwards, D. (1990). Discourse: Noun, verb or social practice? *Philosophical Psychology, 3*(2), 205–217.

Rex, L., Bun, M., Davila, B. A., Dickinson, H. A., Ford, A., Gerben, C., Orzulak, M. J. M., & Thomson, H. (2010). A review of discourse analysis in literacy research: Equitable access. *Reading Research Quarterly, 45*(1), 94–115.

Rogers, R., Malancharuvil-Berkes, E., Mosley, M., Hui, D., & Joseph, G. O. (2005). Critical discourse analysis in education: A review of the literature. *Review of Educational Research, 75*(3), 365–416.

Santa Barbara Classroom Discourse Group. (1992). Constructing literacy in classrooms: Literate action as social accomplishment. In H. Marshall (Ed.), *Redefining student learning: Roots of educational change* (pp. 119–150). Norwood, NJ: Ablex.

Schiffrin, D., Tannen, D., & Hamilton, H. E. (2001). *The handbook of discourse analysis.* Malden, MA: Blackwell Publishers.

Searle, J. (1969). *Speech acts.* Cambridge, UK: Cambridge University Press.

Sherzer, J. (1987). Discourse-centered approach to language and culture. *American Anthropologist, 89*(2), 295–309.

Smith, B. (Ed.). (1983). *Home girls.* New York: Women of Color Press.

Street, B. (1993). Culture is a verb: Anthropological aspects of language and cultural process. *Language and culture* (pp. 23–43). Clevedon, UK: British Association for Applied Linguistics.

Street, B. (1995). *Social literacies: Critical approaches to literacy in development, ethnography and education.* London: Longman.

Street, B., & Street, J. (1991). The schooling of literacy. In D. Barton & R. Ivanic (Eds.), *Writing in the community* (pp. 143–166). London: Sage.

Van Dijk, T. A. (Ed.). (1985). *Handbook of discourse analysis* (Volumes 1–4). London: Academic Press.

Van Dijk, T. A. (Ed.). (2001). *Discourse as social interaction.* Thousand Oaks, CA: Sage.

Volosinov, V. (1929/1973 trans.). *Marxism and the philosophy of language* (trans. L. Matejka & I. Titunik). Cambridge, MA: Harvard University Press.

Walkerdine, V. (1984). Someday my prince will come. In A. McRobbie & M. Nava (Eds.), *Gender and generation* (pp. 162–184). London: Macmillan.

Williams, R. (1977). *Marxism and literature.* Oxford, UK: Oxford University Press.

Wohlwend, K. (2009). Damsels in discourse: Girls consuming and producing identity texts through Disney princess play. *Reading Research Quarterly, 44*(1), 57–83.

2

CRITICAL DISCOURSE ANALYSIS IN LITERACY RESEARCH

Rebecca Rogers

Critical Discourse Analysis: Origins and Traditions

Critical discourse analysis (CDA) is a set of theories and methods that have been widely used in literacy research to study the relationships between discourse processes and social structures. The critical study of discourse has a long history and can be traced to philosophers and theorists such as Bakhtin (1981), DuBois (1903/1990) and Pecheux (1975). Bringing together decades of scholarship in critical discourse traditions, a group of scholars (Fairclough, Kress, van Dijk, van Leeuwen, Wodak) gathered in the early 1990s for a symposium in Amsterdam to discuss theories and methods specific to CDA. What resulted was a more formalized tradition of CDA, still diverse and interdisciplinary, but having enough commonalities to be taken up in a variety of disciplines, including literacy studies. CDA in literacy research grew out of the work of sociolinguistics, linguistic anthropology and cultural and media studies. Schools, classrooms and literacy practices have been looked to as sites for studying not only the micro-dimensions of classroom talk but also how social structures are reproduced at macro-levels. Indeed, it has been this orientation toward critique and resistance of injustice that has fueled much of the work in critical discourse studies. In 1994, a group of scholars that became known as the New London Group met in New London, New Hampshire to work out a vision for critical discourse studies. Fairclough, Gee and Kress were among this group and their approaches to discourse analysis have been widely used in literacy research (New London Group, 1996; Rogers, 2011/2004). Some of the early examples of literacy research that used critical discourse analysis include Orellana (1996), Comber (1997), Egan-Robertson (1998) and Young (2000).

Over the past decade, there has been a surge of studies in literacy research using CDA on many different fronts and across the age span with a full range of research questions and approaches (Rex et al., 2010; Rogers & Schaenen, under review). The increased prominence of CDA in literacy research can be attributed to the commensurability that exists between the areas. Both are traditions that address language as a social semiotic practice that constructs and represents the social world. Further, both address problems through a range of theoretical perspectives. Many of the problems that are addressed, particularly in a globalized world system, have to do with power and inequality. Much less scholarship has focused on the productive uses of power, or moments of equity and transformation. CDA is amply prepared to address both domination and liberation in our increasingly global and digital world.

Guiding Tenets of Critical Discourse Analysis

CDA has been used within many areas in literacy studies – from the preparation of literacy teachers and professional development (Assaf & Dooley, 2010; Haddix, 2010; Mosley & Rogers, 2011), to literacy policies and politics (Dworin & Bomer, 2008; Woodside-Jiron, 2003), to early literacy (Dutro, 2010; Wohlwend, 2007), to bilingual education (Martínez-Roldán, 2005). The approaches to CDA drawn on most readily are those associated with Gee, Fairclough and Kress whose scholarship offers guiding tenets around key concepts (see also Rogers, 2011/2004, for an overview of these approaches).

Considering Critical in CDA

Critical social theory (CST) provides a foundation for CDA (e.g., Bowles & Gintis, 1976; Callinicos, 1995; Giddens, 1984; Giroux, 1983). Critical social theory leans on the rejection of naturalism, rationality, neutrality and individualism. CST's intellectual heritage is diverse and has been influenced by the Frankfurt School and British Cultural Studies. Enduring tensions in CST are oppression and liberation, as well as structure and agency. The project of critique helps penetrate domination, whether it is based in racism, classism, sexism, heterosexism or neo-colonialism. Rather than only critiquing domination, those inspired by critical social theory seek to create a society free of domination. This part of CDA has been neglected, an idea to which I return.

Considering Discourse in CDA

Located between the linguistic and the social, discourses are social practices, processes and products. Given the broadness in parameters of what constitutes discourse, it is useful to turn to Gee, Fairclough and Kress for their conceptualizations of discourse.

Gee (1996) defines discourse in this way, "[a] discourse is an association of socially accepted ways of using language, other symbolic expressions and artifacts of thinking, feeling, believing, valuing, and acting that can be used to identify yourself as a member of a socially meaningful group" (p. 144). Discourses are always intertextual, linked across time, place and speakers. Fairclough (1992), blending Hallidayian linguistics with Marxist inspired theories of discourse, writes,

> In using the term discourse, I am proposing to regard language use as a form of social practice, rather than a purely individual activity or a reflex of situational variable.... Discourse is a practice not just of representing the world, but of signifying the world, constituting and constructing the world in meaning.

Gee and Fairclough recognize how discourses navigate between structure and agency.

Kress (2009), from a social semiotic tradition, views meaning making as a social process where people use the modes, or resources, at their disposal to design meanings. Modes are the material-semiotic resources that people have available for achieving representational work. Hodge and Kress (1988) define discourse as: "The site where social forms of organization engage with systems of signs in the production of texts, thus reproducing or changing the sets of meanings and values which make up a culture" (p. 6).

Considering Analysis in CDA

There are many different approaches to analysis within CDA. For instance, nexus analysis, systemic functional approaches and positive discourse analysis are just a few of the approaches used by literacy researchers. The view of methods is that one finds a research topic, consults a set of theoretical frames and then selects methods, depending on the questions. While there is no one approach, it is instructive to look at key concepts embedded within Gee, Fairclough and Kress's approaches (see also Rogers, 2011/2004).

Gee's Approach. Gee's approach draws on American anthropological linguistics, social discourse theories and cognitive psychology. Starting from his distinction "d"iscourse and "D"iscourse, Gee's work (2011) brings together his theory of language with devices for inquiry. Situated meanings, social languages, figured worlds and Discourses are "tools of inquiry." These are frameworks for understanding how people use language to accomplish social goals. The "building tasks" are the things that are being built as people interpret meanings and include questions that guide the analyst.

Fairclough's Approach. Fairclough draws from Marxist inspired linguistics, sociolinguistics and social theories of discourse. Fairclough (2011) explores the kinds of semiotic resources people draw on as they design and interpret social practices through *ways of interacting* (genres), *ways of representing* (discourse) and *ways of being* (style). This heuristic – or order of discourse – provides a means for understanding the relationships between the textual and the social. A key element of Fairclough's framework is the interdiscursive relationship between and amongst genres, discourses and styles. The analyst describes, interprets and explains the relationships between texts and social practices at local, national and global scales.

Kress's Approach. Kress is one of the people credited with developing critical linguistics. He, alongside Fowler, Hodge and Trew developed an approach for understanding the relationships between material relations of the socioeconomic base and superstructures as mediated through ideology (Fowler, Hodge, Kress & Trew, 1979). This interest in ideology and sign systems was transferred to how images are ideologically constructed, how subjectivities are constituted and through what modes, or social semiotics (Kress, 2009). A social semiotic approach is concerned with how meanings are made, in the outward representation of signs and also the inner interpretation of signs. Upon looking at a social practice the analyst identifies how meanings are made through multiple modes.

A Shift in Analytic Focus, Positive Discourse Analysis

It has been argued that CDA has, for too long, studied how oppression is discursively constructed (e.g., Baxter, 2002; Luke, 2004; Martin, 2004). Indeed, a substantial number of critical discourse analyses focused on injustice and inequity have been carried out in literacy studies. This work has drawn our attention to how domination (say, racism, sexism or classism) is reinforced, through literacy practices. However, fewer studies have investigated the discursive contours of inclusive and democratic literacy practices. Recognizing this gap, a number of scholars are calling for a focus on productive uses of power, what has been referred to as Positive Discourse Analysis (Bartlett, 2012; Janks, 2005; Luke, 2004; Martin, 2004; Scollon & Scollon, 2004; Mosley & Rogers, 2011). Macgilchrist (2007) writes, "[PDA] analyzes the discourse we like rather than the discourse we wish to criticize" (p. 74). This is not a new approach to CDA but, rather, a shift in analytic focus.

Positive Discourse Analysis: A Demonstration

My own approach is a synthesis of different kinds of CDA, with an orientation toward transformation and agency. I illustrate this approach by attending to a moment of agency and leadership in the life of Leslie Barton, a pre-service teacher. This example comes from a year-long teacher-research study in a teacher education program (Rogers & Mosley, 2010; Rogers & Mosley Wetzel, 2013). I focus on an excerpt from Leslie's presentation of a workshop at the

Educating for Change Curriculum Fair where she used a narrative of her own awakening to the importance of culturally relevant teaching (Ladson-Billings, 1994) as a vehicle to teach others the value of this approach. I asked: What might we say about the discursive composition of agency as it is signaled through this presentation? What storylines does Leslie construct about herself, her student and the field of literacy education?

Leslie Barton is a white middle class female who identified as both Jewish and Christian. She lived in the same Midwestern City for her whole life and attended public schools. Leslie majored in Elementary Education and Anthropology. In college, Leslie identified as a social justice activist and participated in a living wage campaign and a teachers for social justice group. She worked with Martin, a second grader who was African-American and reading below grade level, throughout the year-long study. The Educating for Change Curriculum Fair is a yearly event sponsored by a teachers for social justice group in St. Louis. Leslie's 30-minute presentation at the Fair occurred during a peak in her teaching when she recognized her student's literacy growth was a result of culturally relevant teaching. Ladson-Billings (1994) defined the goal of culturally relevant teaching as empowering "students intellectually, socially, emotionally, and politically by using cultural referents to impart knowledge, skills, and attitudes" (p. 382). Leslie's workshop was video-recorded. For the purposes of this demonstration, I focus only on stanza 4 to provide a closer look at the details of the analysis. The complete analysis of this event can be found in Rogers & Mosley Wetzel (2013).

Analytic Procedures

There are a number of steps involved in conducting CDA. I chose this event for analysis because it was a significant event, according to Leslie, where she represented the empowering potential of culturally responsive pedagogy. And, in the spirit of positive discourse analysis, I was drawn to this example because I found Leslie's agency impressive and wanted to look more closely at its discursive composition. The first step in analysis was creating a multimodal transcript, including the verbal and nonverbal discourse (Norris, 2004). The nonverbal action (represented in italicized font) is inserted as closely to the verbal discourse (represented in regular font) that overlaps it. See Appendix Table 2.A.1.

The next step was to segment the transcript into idealized lines, stanzas and narrative structure, to learn about *what* was said and *how* it was said (Gee, 1985; Labov & Waletsky, 1997). Appendix Table 2.A.2 displays all of the stanzas in the workshop. Next, the multimodal transcript was converted into a table and the corresponding image and time stamp were added. Notice in Table 2.1 how the image is privileged because of its position on the left side of the table.

TABLE 2.1 Multimodal Transcript – Example from Stanza 4

Time stamp	Images from Quicktime	Verbal transcription	Nonverbal transcription
3:05		We will kinda talk about what that means to be a culturally relevant text	*Sitting comfortably in a student's chair, slightly lower than other workshop attendees. Handout is in her lap. "Dreamkeepers" is represented behind her and is pivotal in her narrative. Brushes her hair behind her ear with her hand as she begins talking.*
3:14		and then how did it change specifically from writing samples that came out of our lessons together.	*Turns her body to face the display of books and uses a hand gesture to draw attention to them. Uses a metaphoric gesture to reference the literacy artifacts.*

From here, I surveyed the linguistic features of the text to get a sense of the organization of the text (e.g., Fairclough, 1992; Gee, 2006; Janks, 2005). Informed by systemic functional linguistics, my analysis operated on the basis that each utterance has both a form and function. Halliday (1994) discusses three functions of language – textual (mode), interpersonal (tenor) and ideational (field). Fairclough (2011) translated these functions into "orders of discourse" and while the language is different, the concepts are the same: genre or "ways of interacting" refers to the mode of language. "Ways of representing" refers to the ideational component of language or the discourse. And "ways of being," or style, refers to the interpersonal, the tenor. I marked each utterance with its meanings at the level of genre, discourse and style.

As an example, I will unpack one statement. Leslie states, "What I kind of did is thought about 'what is a culturally relevant text?'" (line 87). To analyze this utterance, I consulted my chart of linguistic features (see Appendix Table 2.A.3). At the level of genre, I looked for features such as cohesion, parallel structure, repetition and intertextuality. These are the textual features that define this workshop as a particular kind of social practice.

I circled and underlined parts of speech. I underlined the verbal phrase "kind of did" which is repeated and creates coherence (genre, see lines 33, 70, 85, 86). At the level of style, I noted that the phrase tempers the action. But at the level of discourse, it is in the position of the theme, the place where given information is noted. The rheme, or the new information, is structured through a rhetorical question "what is a culturally relevant text?" This is an example of how Leslie leveraged new thinking about culturally relevant pedagogy (discourse) and it functions as a teaching tool in this context (style). I noted that she consistently used this modifier "kind of did" when she steps into the role of "educator of educators." It allows her to soften her stance and also assert authority with the information in the rheme.

My goal was to find connections amongst genre, discourse and style, keeping in mind that each level may include multiple modes of semiosis. What became clear during this stage in the analysis was that Leslie was creating different roles for herself even within one stanza – as an educator, an educator of educators and as a change agent. I brought theoretical frames to the foreground and was reminded of how people discursively construct the worlds they inhabit, bringing them to life (Davies, 1990; Giddens, 1984). Appendix Table 2.A.4 is a visual display of a portion of my analysis of Stanza 4. At this point, I recontextualized the analysis in the ethnographic context and developed a plan for representing my findings.

Representing the Findings: Designing Possible Teaching Selves

I structured the findings through the different stances Leslie enacted in the workshop: educator, teacher educator and change agent. In each section, I weave in the analysis of the genre, discourses and associated multimodality.

Positioning herself as an educator. Leslie casts herself as a culturally relevant educator both in the content and structure of the workshop. She deconstructs power relationships in the workshop with her verbal discourse and in her use of gesture, her arrangement of space and her gaze. She arranges the chairs in a semi-circle and chooses a student's chair so that she sits lower than others in the room. She creates a chronological display of children's books, teacher resources and her student's writing samples. Stanza 4 begins with her verbal and gestural reference to "an assortment of books" (line 37) and "writing samples" (line 40) generated in her teaching sessions. The book *Dreamkeepers* (Ladson-Billings, 1994) is the first book in the display.

Early on, she states she is a student but quickly steps into the role of an educator. She consistently uses third person, collective pronouns to build solidarity. She states, "we will kind of talk about what that means to be a culturally relevant text" (lines 33–34). In lines 43–44, she positions herself as an educator, "the idea is to empower the students who are in our classes." This inclusive talk about students and teaching creates cohesiveness throughout the presentation. Coupled with her choice of pronouns is the kinds of statements she makes — they are declarative, framed through an active voice and assertive. Leslie explains the goal of culturally relevant teaching,

42. But, um, at the top with culturally relevant teaching,
43. the idea is to empower the students
44. who are in our classes
45. by bringing,
46. instead of asking the students
47. to come to the school culture,
48. the white middle class culture,
49. to actually bring the school to our students.
50. To bring our students' communities and the students' cultures into the schools
51. through books that we use

She creates a narrative about herself as a teacher who has a philosophy about texts, instruction and the culture of schools.

60. So instead of asking our students
61. to come to this new culture and these new texts.
62. Um, this whole new meaning.
63. So instead of,
64. in a reading program to use culturally relevant texts
65. so that when we are working on reading
66. we are not,
67. we are focusing more

68. on where the students are
69. instead of trying to bring them into this white middle class culture.

Her statement, "we are focusing more on where the students are" (lines 67–68) indicates she is an asset-based teacher. She understands that texts contain values that make up the culture of the school and names the racialized space of schools "this white middle class culture" (line 69). She evokes the work of Ladson-Billings and Delpit to build credibility and position herself as part of a larger community of educators. In lines 73–74 she talks about "silenced voices," reminiscent of Delpit's (1988) work. She sees herself in dialogue with her student expressed through her use of collective pronouns when she talks about Martin ("I have an assortment of books that we read throughout the semester"; line 37). Her literal and verbal movement from the books to the writing samples emphasizes her belief in the interconnectedness of literacy processes.

Positioning herself as an educator of educators. Leslie also positions herself as an educator of other teachers. She designs an interactive workshop, filled with visual displays, enhanced by the presence of the student she taught, has additional resources for educators and has time for dialogue. Rather than take on an authoritative tone of a lecture as some novice teacher educators might feel compelled to do, Leslie designs an interactive workshop. This invites people to co-construct but also opens the potential for critiques and challenges to her approach. She traverses this delicate balance of authority and openness in several places in the workshop. For example, she states,

33. We will kinda talk about what that means
34. to be a culturally relevant text

The verbal phrase "kinda talk" softens her authority and demonstrates her belief in co-constructing knowledge with other educators. "What that means," suggests the concept of culturally relevant texts is open to interpretation. In other places, her statements are authoritative and indicate the complexity of balancing personal and cultural relevance when choosing texts:

78. So, a lot of it really has to do with
79. really bringing in a multicultural aspect,
80. because we are bringing in the cultures of our students.
81. But we are also honing in on each individual student.
82. You really have to know the student
83. to know what is a culturally relevant text.

Stanza 4 focuses centrally on explaining the theory of culturally relevant pedagogy and she translates theory into everyday language that is likely to resonate with her audience. After she has explained the philosophy, she states, "so that is kind of the idea that comes behind it" (lines 70–71). Leslie also uses think alouds to provide people with a view of her thought processes:

86. What I kind of did is thought about
87. "what is a culturally relevant text?"
88. I thought,
89. "these are texts that reflect the students in their culture, gender and class experience"

(Stanza 4)

This was a pivotal moment in her teaching when she chose a text with an African-American character set on a farm whereas Martin lived in the city. She had mistakenly assumed that because the black characters made the text culturally relevant. She does not discuss this here, perhaps leaving space for others to notice it in the discussion. She foreshadows a time when the participants will share their ideas "We can kind of talk about that later" (line 84).

Positioning herself as a change agent. Leslie also projects herself as a change agent through her use of counter-narratives that are organized in opposition to dominant worldviews (Solórzano & Yosso, 2002). In Leslie's narrative, the traditional goal of education is to maintain the status quo. Schools are structured through white norms and, as such, are discriminatory to those not part of the "white middle class culture" (line 48). Also embedded in this narrative is an alternate vision for schools. Culturally relevant texts are the vehicle for navigating the gap between what is and what might be, most readily articulated in lines 42–51 (see above). The adverbial phrase "instead of" (line 46) is used repetitively (four times in stanza 4) and serves to build a contrastive structure between the traditional goals of school and the goal to "empower the students in our classes" (line 43). The route to empowerment lies in bridging the distance between home and school,

73. to bring up some of the silenced voices
74. and some of the silenced cultures
75. that are not in the schools right now.

While many new educators may be tempted to align themselves with the values of the school, Leslie sides with students who are marginalized. She positions herself as an agent of transformation through the design of culturally relevant pedagogy.

Important Contributions and Exemplar Studies

This turn toward the positive in literacy studies holds potential to deepen our understanding of the complexities of literacy practices and also contribute to the field of critical discourse studies. There are examples of recent scholarship making this turn toward the positive. I will share two examples.

First, Dutro (2010) presents a CDA of third graders' experiences reading and responding to a story about a Depression-era farm family's economic hardships from the district-mandated reading curriculum. Her CDA demonstrates how middle class privilege is reproduced through the curriculum. Many analysts would have stopped by describing the reproduction of ideologies. Dutro does not. She recognizes the difficulty in disentangling structure and agency; the epistemic and ontological stronghold of commercially produced and mandated reading materials and the lived experiences of children living in urban poverty. She turns toward the "positive," which means shining light on the *struggle* toward liberation. Just as the story set in the 1930s obscures poverty, her students bring their present day experiences with poverty into the dialogue. And, while the teacher's guide urges teachers to focus on overcoming poverty, the third graders' writing reveals the enduring dimensions of living in poverty. In this way, Dutro's analysis does not deny the structural constraints of poverty reinforced through mass-produced curricular materials but neither does it underestimate the power of children and teachers to make room for themselves in the world by naming their own class-based realities (Martin, 2004). Dutro takes the reader with her as she imagines different scenarios with the curriculum; what she refers to as "imagined revisions" (p. 285). This act of imagining different futures is a key piece of CDA, one that is often neglected.

The second example is Haddix (2010) who presents two, in-depth case studies of pre-service teachers to understand the enactment of linguistic identities. As she writes,

> the discursive ways that Black and Latina preservice teachers reconcile tensions between their racial and linguistic identities and the construction of teacher identities in the current context of preservice teacher education in the US.... This examination of their literacy and language practices elucidates a move beyond marginalization and inferiority toward agency and linguistic hybridity.
>
> *(p. 97)*

Rather than focus on the tensions that these teachers faced navigating between their primary discourse (home culture) and secondary discourse (university/school culture) communities, she shifts the analytic focus to how they *reconciled* these tensions. She chose teachers who demonstrated a metacognitive awareness of their language use. She found that both teachers were able to create spaces where they took on the identities of being a new teacher and also asserted their affiliation to African-American language. As she writes, "neither fully accepting nor completely rejecting the dominant discourses in teacher education" (p. 102). Haddix admits that this move toward agency was context dependent. Both teachers were able to create a hybrid discourse in classrooms where they shared cultural and linguistic experiences with their students.

Looking across the examples, we can see common dimensions of this type of analysis. First, while Haddix and Dutro do not refer to their orientation as positive discourse analysis, their analysis demonstrates that it is hard to disentangle structure and agency. Focusing on one without the other will not do. So, while both name the structures — social class privilege and dominant language ideologies, respectively — they do not stop there. They demonstrate how their participants struggle against the stronghold of dominant ideology and forge counter-representations and new realities.

Second, Dutro and Haddix were both participants in the social practices they sought to understand. Because literacy researchers are often studying their own practices and doing so within long-term, ethnographically grounded projects, there is a greater likelihood of honoring the complexity of the human experience. Indeed, it is easier to wage only critique against those with whom we do not have a relationship. However, focusing only on unrealized moments (through critique) denies the complexity of human experience and the process of learning and becoming. We see this in both studies. Further, the closeness with the participants leads them to privilege the epistemic perspective of the marginalized or those working against marginalization. As Haddix (2010) wrote, "I sought to amplify the muted voices of Black and Latina preservice teachers within the larger context of preservice teacher education and research" (p. 98). This is the kind of movement toward action that we might expect to see within studies oriented toward the positive.

This kind of scholarship is on the rise in literacy studies but there is a continued need to move beyond describing marginalization to describing agency. This turn is not meant to deny domination but, rather, acknowledge the struggle toward liberation. And, while I am not a proponent of an endless proliferation of new terms that describe old theories and methods, I do think that recognizing such approaches as "positive discourse analysis" may help to draw attention to some of the issues associated with this shift which, in turn, might sensitize our own and others' attention to what is going well, instead of what is not. This shift holds tremendous potential for the design of more just learning spaces and to contribute to the field of critical discourse studies, more generally.

Appendix

TABLE 2.A.1 Transcript of Stanza 4

3:05	*Sitting comfortably in student's chair, slightly lower than workshop attendees. Handout is in her lap. The book "Dreamkeepers" is represented behind her and is pivotal to her narrative. Uses hand gestures in front of her face as she speaks.*
	We will kinda talk about what that means to be a culturally relevant text
	Brushes her hair behind her ear with her hand.
3:14	and then how did it change specifically from writing samples that came out of our lessons together.
	Turns her body to face the display of books and uses a hand gesture to draw attention to them.
3:15	I have an assortment of books that we read throughout the semester, actually throughout the year.
	Rotates her body and, with her hand, gestures to show the books on display.
3:16	And then some of his writings samples that we have and we will look at some more closely.
	Gestures with her hand and motions across the display of texts.
3:28	But, um, at the top with culturally relevant teaching, the idea is to empower the students
	Camera scans across the room at the texts as Leslie continues speaking.
3:34	who are in our classes by bringing, instead of asking the students to come to the school culture, the white middle class culture, to actually bring the school to our students.
	Touches her glasses and presses them against her face as she speaks.
3:53	To bring our students' communities and the students' cultures into the schools through books that we use.
	Hand gestures.
3:59	So that, um, so that they will have a better experience. *Continues to use hand gestures for emphasis.*
	Looks to her side as if talking to a specific person. Continues to use hand gestures for emphasis.
4:10	I think that what a lot of that comes out of is, um, there is less
	Touches her face, then her hair, then adjusts glasses.
	I can't think if what
	Hands raised in emphatic gesture.

continued

TABLE 2.A.1 continued

4:19	Less of a *pause* discomfort from the students trying to figure out, how do we talk this language of the school. How do we learn these new customs
	Pauses and gazes up as if concentrating on a thought.
4:30	So instead of asking our students to come to this new culture and these new texts.
	Continues to use hand gestures for emphasis in her speech.
4:40	Um, this whole new meaning. So instead of, in a reading program to use culturally relevant texts so that when we are working on reading we are not, we are focusing more on where the students are instead of trying to bring them into this white middle class culture.
	Repositions her chair and moves it slightly to make room for a student to come sit in front of the book display while holding paper. Student rolls his chair a little and comes into the frame.
4:54	So that is kind of the idea that comes behind it
	Looks down to see notes that are in her lap; brushes hair behind her ear as she begins talking. Turns her body to face the display of books and uses a metaphoric gesture to draw attention to them.
5:01	Also, it is to bring up some of the silenced voices and some of the silenced cultures that are not in the schools right now
	Raises her right hand in an emphatic hand gesture
5:05	To really try to incorporate them into the classroom as much as possible.
	Camera zooms out.
5:09	So, a lot of it really has to do with really bringing in a multicultural aspect, because we are bringing in the cultures of our students.
	Young boy looks at Leslie as she speaks.
	But we are also, honing in on each individual student.
5:23	You really have to know the student to know what is a culturally relevant text.
	We can kind of talk about that later.
	Leslie looks down at her notes.

TABLE 2.A.2 Overview of presentation

Time	Stanza	Content
00:00	Stanza 1	Leslie presents the goal of the workshop.
01:54	Stanza 2	Leslie aligns herself with Ladson-Billings (1994).
02:50	Stanza 3	Leslie talks about how using culturally relevant texts with Martin made a difference in his writing.
03:05	Stanza 4	Leslie describes culturally relevant teaching.
06:07	Stanza 5	Leslie explains how to accelerate students' reading and writing through culturally relevant texts.
06:53	Stanza 6	Leslie addresses the importance of book choice.
09:23	Stanza 7	Leslie connects conventional spelling to culturally relevant teaching.
10:06	Stanza 8	Leslie describes how Martin's writing improved when she used culturally relevant texts.
14:38	Stanza 9	Martin reads the songs he wrote.
16:39	Stanza 10	Leslie raises questions about the value of this approach.
20:40	Stanza 11	Leslie facilitates a discussion about culturally responsive pedagogy.

TABLE 2.A.3 Survey of linguistic features and functions

Discursive feature	Description	Questions to ask of the text
GENRE "WAYS OF INTERACTING"		
Turn taking	Description of the structure and sequence of an interaction.	• What is the sequence of turns? • How many turns are taken? • How long are the turns?
Cohesion	Lexical or grammatical features that help a text to hang together across sentence boundaries and form larger units.	• What relations exist between the clause and the sentence?
Parallel structure	Similar textual features within the text; at the level of semantics or syntax, across semiotic modes.	• What features of this text function to create flow and rhythm?
Intertextuality	*Manifest intertextuality*: intertextual features such as: quoted speech, irony, parody, negation, presupposition, scare quotes. *Constitutive intertextuality*: interdiscursive features between texts such as: structure, form, genre.	• How does this text draw on other voices, texts and genres?
DISCOURSE "WAYS OF REPRESENTING"		
Information focus	Themes are represented in the first part of the clause and are generally the known information. Rhemes include the new information and are generally included in the last part of the clause.	• What ideas are represented? • What information is foregrounded by being in the theme position?
Lexical relations	The relation and classification of experiences through an unfolding series of activities.	• What social categories underlie the lexical strings in the text? • What taxonomies are represented?
Lexicalization	The selection of wordings.	• How are ideas represented through word choice? • What is the level of formality?
Relexicalization	Renaming/re-voicing.	• What words or phrases show up again and again in the transcript?

Term	Description	Questions
Pronouns	First/second/third person. Inclusive/exclusive pronouns. Sexist/non-sexist pronouns.	• Which pronouns are used and where?
Verbal processes	Verbs of doing (material, behavioral) Verbs of sensing/saying (mental) Verbs of being (relational) Existential verbs ("There is...")	• What verbs are drawn upon in the interaction?
Exclusion	Suppression of information: Topical silence; lexical silence; presuppositional silence.	• What information is being excluded?
STYLE "WAYS OF INTERACTING"		
Transitivity	Processes in verbs	• To what degree does an action affect its object? • When is this process occurring? • Is the agent represented? Are participants agents or recipients of actions?
Tense	Tense sets up when an event occurs in time.	
Voice	Active and passive voice.	
Modality	Aspects of grammar that express obligation, permission and probability (e.g., may, might, can, could, will, should, must need).	• How is obligation expressed in this text?
Mood	Grammatical aspects that allow the speaker to express their attitude toward what is being said/written. Indicative (I am here) Imperative (Be here) Subjunctive (If I were here) Interrogative (Is he here?) Rhetorical (Am I here?)	• Through what forms does the speaker express their stance toward what is being said?
Nominalization	Turning the verb or adjective into a noun.	• Are verb processes turned into nouns in this text? • (e.g. Administrators closed 10 schools. There were 10 school closings.)
Appraisal	Systems of evaluation that are used to negotiate social relationships by communicating attitudes (affect, judgment, appreciation).	• What kinds of attitudes are negotiated in the text? What is the strength of the feelings involved? How are values sourced and positions aligned?

TABLE 2.A.4 Conducting critical discourse analysis: an example

Stanza 4	Description of linguistic features	Interpretations	Connections/patterns across the stanza
Orientation Lines 33–41	*Verbal phrases (style)/pronouns (discourse)* "We will kinda talk about what that means to be a culturally relevant text" (lines 33–34) "we will look at some more closely" (line 41) "we read throughout the semester" (line 38)	Collective pronoun "we" references the participants and positions her as an educator of educators and as a teacher who collaborates with her students.	See lines 72–84 for examples where she positions herself dually as a teacher and as a teacher educator.
	Intertextuality (genre) "what that means to be a culturally relevant text"	Evokes Ladson-Billings' culturally relevant teaching and suggests that there are multiple interpretations of this concept.	See also lines 73–74; 79.
	Declarative statements/lexicalization (discourse) "I have an assortment of books…" "And then some of his writing samples…"	She is part of a community of educators who use a variety of books and genres for writing.	See also lines 63–69 where she positions herself as a teacher.
Free clauses Lines 42–62	*Verbal phrases (style)* "to empower" (line 43) "bringing" (line 45) "bring the school culture" (line 49) "bring our students' communities" (line 50)	Repetitive use of mental and material verbs signals her active stance as a change agent.	See also lines 33, 53, 69.
	Adverbial phrases (discourse/style) "instead of asking" (line 46) "to actually bring the school" (line 49) "so instead of asking our students" (line 60)	Repetition of the adverbial phrase "instead of" creates cohesion and emphasis. Sets up contrastive structure needed for a counter-narrative. Signals she is knowledge about traditional pedagogy and culturally relevant pedagogy. Steps into the role of a change agent.	See also lines 63, 69.

Lexialization (discourse) "to come to the school culture, the white middle class culture …" (lines 47–48) "to bring our students' communities and the students' cultures into the schools" (line 50) "this new culture and these new texts" (line 61)	Recognizes that schools privileged white middle class students. Represents herself as a teacher who understands that schools are constituted by social practices and identities.	See also lines 46–49 and 60 where she steps into the role of a teacher.
Intextextuality/revoicing students (genre) "How do we talk this language of the school?" (line 58) "How do we learn these new customs?" (line 59)	She is a teacher who understands the power of language. Empathizes with future students and the questions they might ask.	See also lines 86–87 where she revoices herself.
Pronouns (discourse) "empower the students who are in our classes" (lines 43–44) "bring the school to our students" (line 49) "asking our students" (line 60)	Use of the collective pronoun "our" signals her membership in a community of educators. Creates solidarity around the ideas she is presenting.	See also lines 33–34, 60, 80.

References

Assaf, L., & Dooley, C. (2010). Investigating ideological clarity in teacher education. *The Teacher Educator, 45*(3), 153–178.

Bakhtin, M. (1981). *The dialogic imagination: Four essays by M. M. Bakhtin* (C. Emerson & M. Holoquist, Trans.). Austin, TX: Texas University Press.

Bartlett, T. (2012). *Hybrid voices and collaborative change: Contextualizing positive discourse analysis.* New York: Routledge.

Baxter, J. (2002). Competing discourses in the classroom: A post-structuralist discourse analysis of girls and boys' speech in public contexts. *Discourse and Society, 13*(6), 827–842.

Bowles, S., & Gintis, H. (1976). *Schooling in capitalist America.* New York: Basic Books.

Callinicos, A. (1995). *Race and class.* London: Bookmark Publications.

Comber, B. (1997). Managerial discourses: Tracking the local effects on teachers' and students' work in literacy lessons. *Discourse: Studies in the Cultural Politics of Education, 18*(3), 389–407.

Davies, B. (1990). Agency as a form of discursive practice. *British Journal of Sociology of Education, 11*(3), 341–361.

Delpit, L. (1988). The silenced dialogue: Power and pedagogy in educating other people's children. *Harvard Educational Review, 58*(3), 289–298.

DuBois, W. E. B. (1903/1990). *The souls of black folks.* New York: Vintage Books.

Dutro, E. (2010). What "hard times" mean: Mandated curricula, class-privileged assumptions, and the lives of poor children. *Research in the Teaching of English, 44*(3), 255–291.

Dworin, J., & Bomer, R. (2008). What we all (supposedly) know about the poor: A critical discourse analysis of Ruby Payne's "framework." *English Education, 40*(2), 101–121.

Egan-Robertson, A. (1998). Learning about culture, language and power: Understanding relationships among personhood, literacy practices and intertextuality. *Journal of Literacy Research, 30*(4), 449–487.

Fairclough, N. (1992). *Discourse and social change.* Oxford, UK: Polity Press.

Fairclough, N. (2011). Semiotic aspects of social transformation and learning. In R. Rogers (Ed.), *An introduction to critical discourse analysis in education* (2nd ed., pp. 119–126). New York: Routledge.

Fowler, R., Hodge, R., Kress, G. & Trew, T. (1979). *Language and control.* London: Routledge & Kegan Paul.

Gee, J. (2006). *An introduction to discourse analysis: Theory and method.* New York: Routledge.

Gee, J. P. (1985). The narrativization of experience in the oral style. *Journal of Education, 167*(1), 9–35.

Gee, J. P. (1996). *Social linguistics and literacies: Ideology in discourses.* London: Falmer Press.

Gee, J. P. (2011). *How to do discourse analysis: A toolkit.* New York: Routledge.

Giddens, A. (1984). *The constitution of society: Outline of the theory of structuration.* Berkeley, CA: University of California Press.

Giroux, H. A. (1983). *Theory and resistance: A pedagogy for the opposition.* Westport, CT: Bergin & Garvey.

Graff, J. (2010). Countering narratives: Teachers' discourses about immigrants and their experiences within the realm of children's and young adult literature. *English Teaching: Practice and Critique, 9*(3), 106–131.

Haddix, M. (2010). No longer on the margins: Researching the hybrid literate identities of Black and Latina preservice teachers. *Research in the Teaching of English, 45*(2), 97–123.

Halliday, M. (1994). *Introduction to functional grammar* (2nd ed.). London: Edward Arnold.

Hodge, B., & Kress, G. (1988). *Social semiotics*. Ithaca, NY: Cornell University Press.

Janks, H. (2005). Language and the design of texts. *English Teaching: Practice and Critique, 4*(3), 97–110.

Kress, G. (2009). *Multimodality: A social semiotic approach to contemporary communication*. London: Taylor & Francis.

Labov, W., & Waletsky, J. (1997). Narrative analysis: Oral versions of personal experience. *Journal of Narrative and Life History, 7*(1), 3–38.

Ladson-Billings, G. (1994). *The dreamkeepers: Successful teachers of African American children* (1st ed.). San Francisco: Jossey-Bass Publishers.

Luke, A. (2004). Notes on the future of critical discourse studies. *Critical Discourse Studies, 1*(1), 149–152.

Macgilchrist, F. (2007). Positive discourse analysis: Contesting dominant discourses by reframing the issue. *Critical Approaches to Discourse Across the Disciplines, 1*(1), 74–94.

Martin, J. (2004). Positive discourse analysis: Solidarity and change. *Revista Canaria de Estudios Ingleses, 49*, 179–200.

Martínez-Roldán, C. (2005). Examining bilingual children's gender ideologies through critical discourse analysis. *Critical Inquiry in Language Studies, 2*(3), 157–178.

Mosley, M., & Rogers, R. (2011). Inhabiting the "tragic gap": Preservice teachers practicing racial literacy. *Teaching Education, 22*(3), 303–324.

New London Group. (1996). A pedagogy of multiliteracies: Designing social futures. *Harvard Educational Review, 66*(1), 60–92.

Norris, S. (2004). *Analyzing multimodal interaction: A methodological framework*. New York: Routledge.

Orellana, M. (1996). Negotiating power through language in classroom meetings. *Linguistics and Education, 8*(4), 334–365.

Pecheux, M. (1975). *Language, semantics and ideology*. New York: St. Martin's Press.

Rex, L., Bunn, M., Davila, B., Dickinson, H., Carpenter-Ford, A., Gerben, C., McBee-Orzulak, M. & Thompson, H. (2010). A review of discourse analysis in literacy research: Equitable access. *Reading Research Quarterly, 45*(1), 94–115.

Rogers, R. (2011/2004). *An introduction to critical discourse analysis in education*. (2nd ed.). New York: Routledge.

Rogers, R. & Mosley, M. (2010). Read alouds as spaces for the deliberation of public sphere issues. *National Reading Conference Yearbook, 59*, 102–116.

Rogers, R. & Mosley Wetzel, M. (2013). Studying agency in teacher education: A layered approach to positive discourse analysis. *Critical Inquiry into Language Studies, 10*(1), 62–92.

Rogers, R. & Schaenen, I. (under review). *Critical discourse analysis in language and literacy research: A critical review of the literature, 2004–2012*.

Scollon, R. & Wong Scollon, S. (2004). *Nexus analysis: Discourse and the emerging Internet*. New York: Routledge.

Solórzano, D. & Yosso, T. (2002). Critical race methodology: Counter-storytelling as an analytical framework for education research. *Qualitative Inquiry, 8*(1), 23–44.

Wohlwend, K. (2007). Friendship meeting or blocking circle? Identities in the lamanated space of playground conflict. *Contemporary Issues in Early Childhood, 8*(1), 73–88.

Woodside-Jiron, H. (2003). Critical policy analysis: Researching the roles of cultural models, power, and expertise in reading policy. *Reading Research Quarterly, 38*(4), 530–536.

Young, J. P. (2000). Boy talk: Critical literacy and masculinities. *Reading Research Quarterly, 35*(3), 312–337.

3

TEMPORAL DISCOURSE ANALYSIS

Catherine Compton-Lilly

Across a recent ten-year study, Jermaine's mother consistently re-articulated her belief that Jermaine's difficulties were not due to a lack of intelligence. As she reported, he was simply stubborn.

> [He's] probably just stubborn.
> *(January 4, 1996)*

> He can be stubborn sometimes, very stubborn.
> *(May 12, 1997)*

> He's stubborn at times ... because he thinks he's missing something outside.
> *(July 17, 1997)*

> Actually she [the teacher] said he's a good boy; he's just stubborn.
> *(July 20, 2000)*

> He's kind of stubborn.
> *(April 12, 2001)*

> But the teacher said he can do it he just stubborn. He just sits there. He do it when he want to do it.
> *(May 30, 2004)*

> Jermaine, he's a good child. He's just stubborn at times but Jermaine is really good ... he's just stubborn. I know he can do it.
> *(May 30, 2004)*

This compiled set of remarkably similar comments and many others collected across this ten-year study intrigued me. Repeated discourses inspired me to wonder about how meaning is constructed across time and how these constructions contribute to the ways students become literate, and construct literate identities.

What is Temporal Discourse Analysis?

Temporal discourse analysis is an analysis of discourses across time, and highlights time as a constitutive dimension of experience that people use to conceptualize their experiences with literacy, schooling, and identity. To explore time as a contextual dimension of meaning construction as well as other aspects of temporality, I have identified what I call "temporal discourse analysis." Temporal discourse analysis provides insights into how people make sense of their experiences across and within time. This analytic method can be used to examine discourses over both long and short periods of time – a ten-year school trajectory or a 45-minute class period. Not only does temporal discourse analysis attend to the temporal language used by participants (e.g., "Last week," "when I was four," "when my mom was little," "When I grow up"), but it also examines the ways participants situate themselves within historical accounts (e.g., "Dr. King said...," "Frederick Douglas lived nearby") and draw upon both the past and possible futures to construct meanings in the present. While time is sometimes invoked by particular words that reference "when" things happen, temporal discourse patterns are also evident as discourses and stories are repeated, revised, and revisited across time. In this chapter, I identify five types of temporal discourse and draw on examples from a recent research project to illustrate the five categories of temporal discourse and explore the affordances of each: (1) the language people use to situate themselves in time; (2) references to the pace of schooling and the timelines that operate in schools; (3) comments and practices that reflect long social histories; (4) repeated discourses over time; and (5) repeated stories that present changing or consistent meanings. Attention to temporal discourses allows researchers to explicitly investigate the ways participants situate themselves in time and to the ways they use language across time to construct meanings.

Considering Discourses across Time

Attention to temporal dimensions of discourse provides rich insights into issues related to literacy learning, identity construction, and trajectories through school. This is admittedly not a new idea (e.g., Rommetveit, 1974). A wide range of scholars have used analysis of language and/or discourse to attend to temporality. These efforts can be understood as contributing to an emerging methodological tool, temporal discourse analysis, that highlights time as a constitutive dimension of learning and becoming.

Drawing on his work in the 1960s, Labov (2006) highlighted how temporal language is used to organize narratives. Among other temporal dimensions, he explores how narratives generally open with the presentation of a significant "reportable event" (p. 38) and then backtrack to present a series of causal events that use temporal language to link events to their outcome(s) of the narrative. In Labov's analysis, temporal language is key to the constructing, framing, and recounting of past experiences as people tell stories and construct narratives.

The widely used concept of "Discourse" (Gee, 1999) has significant temporal dimensions. As Gee (1999) argued, Discourses (with a big "D") involve ways of "acting-interacting-thinking-valuing-talking-(sometimes reading-writing) in the 'appropriate way' with the 'appropriate' props at the 'appropriate' times in the 'appropriate' places" (p. 17). Thus Discourses draw upon pre-existing cultural models that contribute to the ways people understand their worlds. These models are, to a significant degree, shared by people within particular sociocultural groups and contribute to the recognition of particular types of actors and activities. As Gee notes, "the key to discourses is 'recognition'" (p. 18) of both the type of actors and the types of activities involved in a given practice. References to both pre-existing cultural models and acts of recognition imply temporality as people draw on past experiences and understandings.

Gutierrez (2008) explored how the temporal "grammar of third spaces" (p. 157) could be used by educators to invite students to envision possible futures while simultaneously creating transformative instructional spaces "where the potential for an expanded form of learning and the development of new knowledge are highlighted" (Gutierrez, 2008, p. 152). Specifically, she called attention to the frequent use of auxiliary modal verbs (e.g., may, will, could) and language that expresses possibilities for students' futures. Her analysis highlights words such as "hope," "imagine," "try," and "raise." These verbs focus on the future and support student efficacy and agency. Thus, third spaces are created through the use of temporal language that suggests new possibilities and possible futures.

Other educational researchers (Bloome, Beierle, Grigorenko, & Goldman, 2009; Mercer, Dawes, & Starrman, 2009; Nystrand, Wu, Gameron, Zeiser, & Long, 2009) have highlighted the role time plays in classroom micro-interactions. Nystrand et al. (2009), drawing on Saussure's (1959/1915) concern with the heterogeneous ways in which discourse unfolds across time, introduced *event history analysis* (p. 135), a quantitative method to explore classroom discourses in terms of the antecedents and consequences of various discoursal moves in English and social studies classrooms. Their analysis focused on identifying discoursal sequences that led to open-ended discussions among students and teachers and dialogue characterized by engaged student questioning. By tracking the evolution of classroom discourses over time, Nystrand and his colleagues (2009) were able to construct event history models that identified critical features of talk that led to valued types of classroom discourses. Discoursal event history analysis treats time as a central dimension of interest as discoursal moves are situated and understood as acts occurring within time.

In their analysis of dialogic teaching in science classes, Mercer et al. (2009) highlighted how teacher talk was used to situate students within time relative to the content they were studying. They observed teachers using language to link new learning to previous lessons and experiences helping students to recognize and draw upon the temporal organization operating within and across lessons. Bloome et al. (2009) described the process of intercontextuality in which individuals remember or restate "particular utterances of language-based interactions in the present context, building on these reinstated (recalled) events, and creating new events in the moment" (p. 319). Their micro analysis of the ways students and teachers collectively drew on past learning and events involved a discoursal analysis of temporal language used in classroom interactions words (e.g., "memory," "first," "start," "right now," and "today").

Other researchers have tracked changes in discourses over time which have shown to reflect changes in perspectives and understandings. These changes can create opportunities for teachers and learners to construct and assume new identities and positionalities relative to schooling. Lewis and Ketter (2011) explored how the discourses used by teachers in a teacher/researcher study group evolved over time as teachers drew upon the discourses, genres, and perspectives used within the group to construct new spaces to explore learning and develop novel teaching selves. Wortham (2001) explored the language used by teachers and students across time to track how students were positioned and the classroom identities they assumed.

Each of these studies points to the ways understandings of the world are situated in time. Narratives rely on temporal language to convey both the sequence of narratives and to connect the events of the story. Temporal language can also be used to rewrite lives – referencing and simultaneously constructing possible futures. Temporal language operates within classrooms providing clues to the sequences that contribute to various discoursal patterns and the intertextual experiences that students draw upon to make sense of current learning in relation to past shared learning and experience. While attention to temporality in discourses related to school and literacy learning is not new, the possibilities for using temporal discourse analysis as an analytical tool has not yet been systematically explored.

Temporal discourse analysis is particularly well suited for exploring research questions that explore either the ways people situate themselves relative to their lived pasts and conceivable futures. What stories do people tell to make sense of their lives and how do they draw on both their past and their dreams for the future to make sense of who they are and who they could become? Temporal discourse analysis also invites questions that highlight expectations related to development and achievement. For example, passing the fourth grade ELA test, graduating high school at age 18, and reading books at one's grade levels are all markers of adequate progress; not meeting these temporal benchmarks suggests failure and often a need for remediation. Temporal discourse analysis can also explore how people situate themselves within larger social histories. When an African American mother reports that she stayed up all night watching episodes of *Roots* (Haley & Lee, 1977) and describes her interest in African American history, this is a temporal positioning that relates not only to her own memories of watching *Roots* as a young adult and her own experiences growing up in the South, but also situates herself and her family within a larger social history. Finally, when temporal discourse analysis is applied to qualitative longitudinal data, researchers can observe change and/or stasis over time as participants draw on particular discourses across time and tell and retell stories. Temporal discourse analysis highlights aspects of people's experiences related to the "invisible temporal" (Adam, 2008, p. 1) – the temporal dimensions of experience that affect the ways we make sense of our worlds and craft identities

Temporal Discourse Analysis: An Exemplar Study

Like many qualitative researchers, I have routinely used coding and constant comparison methods (Strauss & Corbin, 1990) to identify themes and findings in my data sets. For the longitudinal study that included Jermaine and his family (Compton-Lilly, 2011, 2012), data was collected when the children were in grades one, four/five, seven/eight, and ten/eleven. Each phase of the study included interviews with children and parents, student writing samples, and a reading assessment. I initially developed separate sets of grounded codes for each of the four phases of the study. Across the ten-year study, I conducted a grounded coding of phase one data and separate grounded codings for data in phases two, three, and four. This allowed me to identify themes and patterns that were salient for each phase of the project.

However, by focusing on themes present in the data at particular points in time, these traditional coding processes distracted me from recognizing and attending to longitudinal discourse patterns from across the phases of the study. In fact, sorting data into categories that were unique to each phase of the project obfuscated long-term patterns. It was only through my continual re-readings of the data across the various phases of the study that long-term temporal patterns became visible. As I reread the data, I heard the voices of participants using similar, and in some cases, identical language at various points in the project. Discourses recurred and participants repeated stories that they had told during earlier phases of the study. Over time, I became increasingly aware of the temporal expectations related to literacy and schooling, and the challenges that some students faced in fulfilling these expectations and meeting official benchmarks.

These experiences and insights drew my attention to the temporal language used by participants as they situated themselves within time. During the third phase of the project, when I had been working with the families for eight years,

I identified a set of codes related to time (e.g., "change," "future," "now and then") and I began to attend to participants' explicit use of temporal language (e.g., "now," "then," "someday," "next week," "after," "fast"). At this point, I had also begun to theorize about how participants recursively and selectively drew on their experiences across time, repeatedly returning to some stories while neglecting and forgetting others, and framing some stories as examples of larger patterns. Some books and literacy practices were mentioned at multiple interviews; others were forgotten. I found that discourses, sometimes using identical words and phrases, could be tracked across time. It became clear that meanings were not constructed within simple, linear, and chronological landscapes but that people judiciously drew on past events as they made sense of literacy, schooling, and themselves. Some events contributed significantly to participants' accounts of themselves as readers, writers, and students; others did not. Particular recollections of the past, as well as perceived possibilities for the future converged as students identified and re-identified themselves relative to school expectations, literacy practices, and potential identities. Five temporal manifestations of discourse became visible through my analysis of data from this ten-year study (Compton-Lilly, 2011, 2012):

1. the language that people use to situate themselves within time;
2. references to the pace of schooling and the timelines that operate in schools;
3. comments and practices that reflect long social histories;
4. repeated discourses over time; and
5. repeated stories over time.

Summary of Ten-year Study

The data that I draw on to illustrate various dimensions of temporal discourse analysis comes from the longitudinal study mentioned above in which I followed seven of the children from my first grade class through grade 11 (see Table 3.1). All of the children presented in this chapter are African American. When they were in my first grade class, they attended Rosa Parks Elementary School where 97% of the students qualified for free or reduced-price lunch. The school is located in a city in the Northeastern United States that continues to struggle with unemployment, substandard housing, a lack of quality physical and mental health care, the closing of local libraries, gang violence, and a proliferation of illegal businesses, including drug trafficking. Despite these challenges, residents of this community consistently demonstrated high levels of resilience, agency, and hope for their children's futures. By high school, seven of the original ten families remained in the study and attended schools in the district.

TABLE 3.1 Participants

Focal children	Family members
Marvin	Mr. and Ms. Sherwood – grandparents and legal guardians
Peter	Ms. Horner – mother
Jermaine	Mr. and Ms. Hudson – parents
	Jermaine's aunt
Bradford	Ms. Holt – mother
Alicia	Ms. Rodriguez – mother
	Leon – Alicia's brother
David	Ms. Johnson – mother
Javon	Ms. Mason – mother

The Language that People Use to Situate Themselves within Time

People constantly use temporal language. Phrases such as "last week," "when I was in school," "when I grow up...", or "when my mom was little" are common dimensions of everyday speech. People use these words to draw on events across time as they respond to interview questions and explain events in their lives and in the lives of others. Stories from the past are used to illustrate and substantiate their claims about schooling and literacy. In this longitudinal project, participants, including Mr. Sherwood and Ms. Horner, told stories of the parents and their grandparents, stories that indicated temporality.

When Marvin was in first grade, his grandfather, Mr. Sherwood, told a story that I originally interpreted as a simple illustration of the challenges he had faced with learning to read during the 1950s. I later came to understand this story as an illustration of the role Mr. Sherwood viewed himself as playing in the literacy learning of his grandson, Marvin. In this account, Mr. Sherwood explained that when he first learned to read, his teachers were doing little to help – "They wouldn't teach you anything. They just gave you the book."

> I was just mumbling through the whole thing [when I read in class] ... that's when I told my mother about it ... She said '**It's time for** you to get a library card and I'll help you out with that.' **Every Saturday morning** ... we [Mr. Sherwood and his twin brother] had to go to the library and **we stayed at the library** until we picked up on our reading.

In this flashback, extending into his own youth, Mr. Sherwood identified the library as an icon of possibility. It was a resource that his mother accessed to address the failure of his teachers to teach him to read. In years to come, I witnessed Mr. Sherwood, like his mother, treating the library as a resource when he repeatedly described visiting the public library so that Marvin could learn about computers. Eventually, Marvin himself used the library in high school after being released from incarceration not only to complete school assignments but also to affiliate with more studious peers and to work toward a new future.

Significantly, Mr. Sherwood situated his account within time referencing the potency of the moment and the repetition of the library. His mother reportedly highlighted the moment saying, "It's time for you to get a library card" and Mr. Sherwood pointed to the repeated nature of the visits "every Saturday morning" and the fact that they "stayed" until Mr. Sherwood and his brother learned to read. Mr. Sherwood's mother is credited with both agency and persistence that eventually extended across four generations – Marvin, his grandfather, and his great grandmother.

In another example of both the use of temporal language and the sharing of intergenerational knowledge across time, Ms. Horner described her grandmother giving her advice on how to help Peter to be successful when he got to school.

> Ms. Horner: [Learning to read] definitely start at home. My grandmother told me [Ms. Horner laughs as she remembers] **when Peter was a little baby,** she says, "You say the ABC's to him and you count to him one to twenty **every single day, even a couple times a day** so that when he gets older he will be up a little you know. He'll be familiar with the letters and the numbers.... So that's what I did with him.

Like Mr. Sherwood's account, this story highlights both the potential of a particular time period ("when Peter was a little baby") and repeated nature of the literacy practices ("every single day, even a couple times a day"). Like Mr. Sherwood, Ms. Horner highlights agency and persistence and her account is equally remarkable; the advice she shared has also extended across four generations.

The voices of these women, their acts of agency, and their persistence, while voiced and enacted in the past, operate in the present and present possibilities for the future. Attending to temporal language allows speakers in the space of the present – within the ongoing interview – to draw on the past helping researchers to access the ways participants make sense of their lives as they illustrate the points that they strive to make. Temporal discourse analysis allows researchers to view how participants situate themselves in the present relative to the past. These examples highlight language that places significance on agency in the moment and perseverance across time as well as illustrating the operation of intergenerational knowledge that contributes to how meanings are made in the present.

The Pace of Schooling and the Timelines that Operate in Schools

Temporality was also manifested in the ways participants spoke about schooling and the temporal expectations that accompanied school success. Jermaine focused on the pace of instruction and his inability to keep up. He identified teachers as contributing to his difficulties. In fourth grade, he complained about teachers who, "only give us five minutes to do something." Three years later he noted:

> When they teach you so fast, **you don't pick up that fast**.... They do like a week of this and then next week ... [they] do something that's different.... Cause **I don't pick up stuff fast** like the other kids ... **you gotta wait**. Like do two weeks of it.

Jermaine's inability to keep up with the pace of instruction was confirmed by him failing the fourth and eighth grade state ELA tests and his multiple retentions in middle school. He eventually repeated grade seven twice and grade eight three times. At our final interview, he was 17 years old and anticipated being retained yet again in grade eight.

The pace of instruction was a challenge for other students in the sample. Ms. Holt worried that Bradford's teachers moved too quickly through the curriculum and did not take the time needed to help Bradford. As she reported:

> The teacher's not explaining it to him. They don't even teach how to [do it or] explain it to you. [Ms. Holt assumes Bradford's voice saying] 'He's [the teacher's] making me **go too fast**.' When **they do it too fast** he don't understand. He gets disgusted and it's over with. It's a wrap.

In both of these examples, temporal language not only marks the overly fast pace of instruction but also reflects how students view themselves relative to their ability to keep up ("I don't pick up stuff fast like the other kids," "It's a wrap").

When Jermaine was initially retained in grade eight, he had hopes of catching up to his peers. His school enrolled him in a computerized reading program and assured him that the program would help; as Jermaine explained, he could be in his "right grade." Jermaine was assigned to a computer lab every afternoon where he worked with *Fast ForWord*, a computerized reading intervention described on the company's website as developing and strengthening "memory, attention, processing rate, and sequencing – the cognitive skills essential for learning and reading success" (Scientific Products Learning, 2009). Jermaine believed that if he completed this compensatory program that he could be promoted to a higher grade, "They let me know they had a program I could join and they could skip me up [to a higher grade]." As he explained, "I was like in 8th grade class. They gave me 8th grade work and everybody else 7th grade work ... I'm in the 9th or 10th grade now."

The summer following his participation in *Fast ForWord*, Jermaine assumed he would be promoted to high school.

I passed that program. I took the test for them, passed it and they put me in ninth and tenth grade and into another program where I could take it again and I could be in my right grade. **My right grade is eleventh grade.**

However, when school commenced in the fall, Jermaine was again placed in grade eight.

Temporal discourse analysis can help researchers to focus on how participants are located with institutions that bring temporal constraints and impose judgments based on meeting official criteria at particular points in time. Locating students within institutions and attending to the consequences of benchmarks, retentions, and the pace of instruction provide clues about the messages they receive from schools and how they make sense of their capabilities, identities, and potential.

Comments and Practices that Reflect Long Social Histories

Larger social histories that extended beyond the lives of participants and their families also influenced the ways participants made sense of their worlds. As members of low-income African American families, histories related to oppression, language variation, the civil rights movement, Jim Crow, and slavery appeared in interviews across the sample.

When Alicia was in first grade, her mother drew on historical meanings related to the "ghetto" to describe her children's teachers:

> A lot of teachers in a lot of schools ... **say this is the ghetto**, right? And they say a lot of people is in the ghetto so they **assume everybody is on welfare**. And they'll say "When your mother get her check tell her to buy you so and so." And that's embarrassing for the kid.

In Ms. Rodriguez's account, teachers identified the community as a "ghetto;" they made assumptions about the families in the school community many of whom were recipients of welfare. The term "ghetto" carries a significant history. Decades ago, it was used to refer to segregated parts of European cities that housed Jewish people before and during the Holocaust. In America, the word "ghetto" was used extensively during the civil rights era to identify segregated parts of cities that housed African American people and other economically struggling social and cultural groups. In particular, Ms. Rodriguez's story references the assumptions that have been historically made about African American parents – specifically mothers.

Historically constructed meanings are also apparent in the critique Ms. Sherwood, Marvin's grandmother, articulated about African American children and special education. She viewed his special education classification as highly problematic and offered her critique of the school policy, "I've been reading up on it and **they mostly put Black kids in** them kind of classes and then they sunk them. And that's **how you all** [gesturing at Marvin who was sitting nearby] **get behind.**" While special education was presented to Ms. Sherwood as an opportunity for helping Marvin to catch up with his peers and reverse past failures, Ms. Sherwood ultimately blamed special education for leaving Marvin behind.

Ms. Rodriguez's critiques about teacher assumptions and living in the ghetto and Ms. Sherwood's concerns about race and special education both have long social histories. These critiques were not constructed on the basis of Alicia and Marvin's experiences in school. Their critiques are grounded in discourses and histories that pre-date this study. They are situated within long legacies of racism, prejudice, and deficit views of African American children and families. Temporal discourse analysis invites researchers to attend to social histories referenced by participants that are significant to the ways people make sense of their worlds.

Repeated Discourses over Time

This chapter opened with a repeated discourse voiced by Ms. Hudson about her son Jermaine and his proclivity to be what she described as "stubborn." Several recurring discourses were voiced across this data set. Several participants repeatedly drew upon the discourse of the "paycheck." Below is a sampling:

JERMAINE: They [teachers] **just want the money**, they're not trying to teach you.

MS. RODRIGUEZ: So we're saying that when we used to go to school, it's like the teacher was there to teach, **not just get her paycheck**. And it seem like they [teachers today] just **get their paychecks**.

MS. JOHNSON: But a lot of these teachers are **just there for the paycheck**.

MS. MASON: Because we've had people that really care, that you know that they want to see the kids. Then you have the one that's **just there for the paycheck**.

Not only are discourses about teachers and paychecks repeated over time, in the above examples, they are often framed as "now and then" discourses. Discourses in which elders compare current situations to the past with the past often being deemed superior.

While the "paycheck" discourse involved repeating particular words and phrases, other recurring discourses were conceptual rather than verbatim. A recurring conceptual discourse for Alicia and her family was what I have labeled the "golden rule discourse." This discourse advocated that people treat others in the way they wish to be treated. While this discourse was rearticulated by various family members at various points in time, it was consistently applied to authority figures (e.g., teachers, police officers). For example, Ms. Rodriguez worried that her children's teachers often expected respect from their students while failing to demonstrate respect for those same students.

> **They want the respect from the kids, but they don't want to give that respect.** So they want to talk to you all [addressing her children who were in the room] any kind of way and then expect you all to sit back and say, "Okay," and then you got to be [okay with that]. Kids that are practically grown, that is looking at you like, "My Mama don't talk to me like that."

Later in the same interview, after we had moved on to discussing other topics, Leon, Alicia's brother, described an incident of police profiling in which police officers stopped him for walking down the street after dark wearing a backpack. The police had mistakenly assumed that he was involved in a nearby robbery. Leon recounted his interaction with the police officer as he was taken to the police station.

LEON: You can put me in the cop car if you want to. **I'm gonna treat you like you're treating me.** You're treating me like a little kid. So I'm going to treat ya'll like one. It doesn't matter to me.

Two and three years later Alicia made similar comments about teachers:

ALICIA: They [teachers] should be respectful if they want the kids to be respectful to them.

ALICIA: [reported that whether she was polite to her teacher depended on] how the teacher be acting towards you. **If you act mean towards me, I'm acting mean back.** If you act nice I'm acting nice back.

Discourses repeated over time provide a lens into the ways meanings are constructed and maintained within families. In this case, rearticulated discourses related to fairness and authority presented a space where people who lack authority were validated in their reluctance to display respect for authority figures that did not accord them the same respect. Repeated discourses can be traced over time and provide clues about how people make sense of their situations and their worlds.

Repeated Stories over Time

In other cases, participants in this study recounted particular stories at different points of time. In this first example, Ms. Rodriguez tells the same story three years apart and, interestingly, the story has changed. Rather than a friend reportedly identifying a connection between the book's protagonist and Ms. Rodriguez, in the second version, Ms. Rodriguez describes herself as making this connection. Ms. Rodriguez had borrowed the book *Mama* (McMillan, 1987) from her girlfriend.

> My girlfriend said, "She [the protagonist] **reminds me of you** in some ways," and I was like, when I started reading that, I called her up and I said "Roneta, no, uh-uh. She don't remind you of me. Home girl [the main character in the story] is a whore." [Roneta responded] **"No, I am talking she got five kids."** I am like "Oh okay. That part, yeah, but you know, a whore?"

Three years later, Ms. Rodriguez spoke again about reading *Mama* and this time she claimed an affiliation with the book's protagonist,

> Ohhh, that [book] was good ... when I read it I was like, this book **reminds me of me.... This woman got five kids and [is] struggling, and she's all on her own. I got six. I got more than she do.**

Perhaps the most rearticulated story across the study involved Jermaine and Carl in grade school. This story was repeated in various versions throughout the research study. As Jermaine explained, he was a "good boy" until fourth grade when Carl repeatedly got him in trouble.

JERMAINE: When I was in fourth grade, me and Carl got in an argument...
CCL: Tell me about Carl.
JERMAINE: I used to be a good boy and then, but...
MS. HUDSON: You still is good.
JERMAINE: Carl, he just used to pick on people – like he the bully of the class. Right? Now **he not no bully of me no more** because I am not scared of him no more because I beat him up too many times now.

It was later during Jermaine's fourth grade that I again heard about Carl. I have used Jermaine's words to craft the following account of a memorable incident.

> When we went outside, Carl told me to meet him. I was like "yeah whatever. I am not going to fight because I don't want to get suspended" and I waited for somebody so I went up to the park ... the girl in his class cause she wanted to talk to me but she set me up. She set me up with Carl ... All the people was right there and Carl was right there behind him. Carl jumped out [of] the crowd.

And he, then he said "One day Jermaine give me a fair one." I was like "Who you talking to? I don't want to hurt you" so I turned back my back. I came back turned around pushed him and then he grabbed my hair. He grabbed it so tight, man it was hurting me and then just he just had like a thing that scratched me, it scratched me right in my face and my arm. [A] pin, something like that.

I didn't see it. I felt something stinging my face, so he grabbed me, pushed me against the wall. I punched him in his eye and I slammed him and I pushed him up and throwed him into the gate. And he swung at me and I swung at him and I punched him in his his mouth. And now his teeth are like this [shows with his finger].... He started [talking about] this – his two teeth was knocked out.

Throughout the interviews that followed, Jermaine and members of his family often referenced the story of Carl. In grade seven, Jermaine's mother spoke of Carl when I asked whether Jermaine missed his old friends when he moved to a new school.

CCL: He doesn't seem to miss his old friends?
MS. HUDSON: No. That was the trouble. Carl, boy, **he used to always get into fights with all the time was Carl**.

Three years later, Jermaine's father similarly recalled Jermaine's altercations with Carl:

MR. HUDSON: You remember Carl don't you?... You [Jermaine] **used to fight him every day**. Every day those two used to fight. They couldn't go to sleep at night until they [fought] ... Carl was a bad boy. They'd fight every day.

Later that year, Jermaine's aunt and mother both recounted the earlier incidents with Carl.

CCL: What do you remember about Jermaine back when he was in elementary school?
MS. HUDSON: Trouble.
JERMAINE'S AUNT: Well me, what was that boy's name?
JERMAINE: Carl.
MS. HUDSON: Carl. Everyday.
JERMAINE'S AUNT: **Every day Carl was get[ting] whooped.**

From a temporal discourse analyst's perspective, these repeated discourses are seminal – not only in terms of how people positioned Jermaine, but also to the ways Jermaine made sense of himself. Stories that are recounted over time are significant in terms of the ways meanings are constructed in this family. The ways these stories recur and circulate across time contributes to the ways Jermaine makes sense of himself and his experiences. Temporal discourse analysis that attends to the recounting of events at multiple points in time allows researchers to view both stasis and change in the ways the past is interpreted and used to make sense of the present.

Conclusion

The discourse analysis techniques illustrated in this chapter reveal some of the ways people make sense of their experiences and themselves across and within time. While this analytic method can be used to examine discourses over both long and short periods of time, in this chapter, I have explored the ways temporality is embedded in language across a ten-year longitudinal study. Temporal discourse analysis can be used to explore how people situate themselves in time, view themselves relative to institutional expectations – including those operating in schools – draw upon larger social histories so they make sense of their experiences, and repeat and revisit discourses and stories over time. These five dimensions are directly related to the ways people make sense of their experiences, and students make sense of literacy practices and schooling. Temporal discourse analysis has the potential to help researchers to understand and appreciate time as a constitutive dimension of experience that people use to conceptualize their experiences with literacy, schooling, and identity.

References

Adam, B. (2008). The timescapes challenge: Engagement with the invisible temporal. In R. Edwards (Ed.), *Researching lives through time: Time, generation, and life stories.* Timescapes working paper series no. 1. Leeds, UK: University of Leeds. Retrieved at www.timescapes.leeds.ac.uk/resources/publications on April 1, 2013.

Bloome, D., Beierle, M., Grigorenko, M., & Goldman, S. (2009). Learning over time: Uses of intercontextuality, collective memories, and classroom chronotopes in the construction of learning opportunities in a ninth-grade language arts classroom. *Language and Education, 34(4)*, 313–334.

Compton-Lilly, C. (2011). Time and reading: Negotiations and affiliations of a reader, grades one through eight. *Research in the Teaching of English, 45(3)*, 224–252.

Compton-Lilly, C. (2012). *Reading time: The literate lives of urban secondary students and their families.* New York: Teachers College Press.

Gee, J. (1999). *An introduction to discourse analysis: Theory and method.* New York: Routledge.

Gutierrez, K. (2008). Developing sociocritical literacy in the third space. *Reading Research Quarterly, 43(2)*, 148–164.

Haley, A. & Lee, J. (1977). *Roots* [screenplay]. ABC Miniseries.

Labov, W. (2006). Narrative pre-construction. *Narrative Inquiry, 16(1)*, 37–45.

Lewis, C. & Ketter, J. (2011). Learning as social interaction: Interdiscursivity in a teacher and researcher study group. In R. Rogers (Eds.), *Discourse analysis in education.* (pp. 128–153). New York: Routledge.

McMillan, T. (1987). *Mama.* New York: Houghton Mifflin.

Mercer, N., Dawes, L., & Starrman, J.K. (2009). Dialogic teaching in the primary science classroom. *Language and Education, 23(4),* 353–369.

Nystrand, M., Wu, L., Gameron, A., Zeiser, S., & Long, D. (2009). Questions in time: Investigating the structure and dynamics of unfolding classroom discourse. *Discourse Processes, 35(2),* 135–198.

Rommetveit, R. (1974). *On message structure: A framework for the study of language and communication.* New York: John Wiley and Sons.

Saussure, F. (1959/1915). *Course in general linguistics* (A. Riedlinger, Ed.; W. Baskin, Trans.). New York: Philosophical Library.

Scientific Products Learning. (2009). *Fast ForWord.* Downloaded on March 20, 2009. Available at www.scilearn.com/products/index.php.

Strauss, A. & Corbin, J. (1990). *The basics of qualitative research: Grounded theory procedures and techniques.* Newbury Park, CA: Sage Publications.

Wortham, S. (2001). *Narratives in action: A strategy for research and analysis.* New York: Teachers College Press.

4

MEDIATED DISCOURSE ANALYSIS

Tracking Discourse in Action

Karen Wohlwend

Mediated discourse analysis, sometimes called nexus analysis (Scollon & Scollon, 2004), is an action-oriented approach to critical discourse analysis that takes sociocultural activity as its primary focus, looking closely at a physical action as the unit of analysis rather than an ethnographic event or a strip of language (e.g., utterance, turn of talk). In this way of thinking about activity, every action is simultaneously co-located within a local embodied community of practice (Lave & Wenger, 1991) and a far-reaching nexus of practice, the expected and valued ways of interacting with materials among people. The purposes of MDA are

1. to locate and make visible the nexus of practice—a mesh of commonplace practices and shared meanings that bind communities together but that can also produce exclusionary effects and reproduce inequitable power relations;
2. to show how such practices are made up of multiple mediated actions that appropriate available materials, identities, and discourses;
3. to reveal how changes in the smallest everyday actions can effect social change in a community's nexus of practice.

To accomplish these goals, the analyst locates a rich site for ethnographic study, which eventually leads to close discourse analysis of core actions with most significance to the people participating in that site. These actions must also be situated in their pertinent histories, global trends, cultural studies, and current news and media. Mediated discourse analysis opens up

> the circumference around moments of human action to begin to see the
> lines, sometimes visible and sometimes obscured of historical and social

process by which discourses come together at particular moments of human action as well as to make visible the ways in which outcomes such as transformations in those discourses, social actors, and mediational means emanate from those moments of action.

(Scollon & Scollon, 2002)

For example, let's consider a moment of play with a popular iPad app.

A one-year-old in a pink fuzzy sleeper bends intently over an iPad that wobbles on her lap. She bounces and coos as she swipes her finger across the screen, an action which launches an animated "Angry Bird" from a large slingshot. She launches another and another, giggling when each bird explodes into a mass of feathers. What are the cycles in and out of practices, materials, and discourses that come together in this moment? How do these cycles shape our interpretation? Is she precocious or just playing? An innocent at risk from over-exposure to games and media? Or a technotoddler with a digital headstart in the race to learn more faster and earlier?

In this chapter, I demonstrate methods of mediated discourse analysis (Scollon, 2001; Norris & Jones, 2005) as a way of unpacking and tracking how the smallest actions, like a baby's wordless swipes and taps on a tablet, constitute key meaning-making practices (e.g., talking, reading, writing, playing, viewing, designing, filming, computing) that signal literate abilities and identities. This action orientation distinguishes mediated discourse analysis from other types of critical discourse analysis through a recognition that:

- Activity is often neither narrated nor accompanied by text or talk; however, such activity is still packed with discourse that is invisible and submerged in familiar practices that have become routine, expected, and unremarkable.
- The ways we use everyday materials are shaped by discourses and histories of practices that underlie our shared expectations (e.g., who may use an object and how it should be used).
- Such tacit expectations influence what seems possible, affecting future actions with artifacts and potential identities in the cycles that flow into and emanate from a single action.

To explain how actions with things create meanings, Scollon (2001) drew upon theories that situate literacy and language in sociocultural histories of practices and identities that are shared among members of a culture. This theory of mediated discourse merges constructs of mediation and situated learning in cultural-historical activity theory (Leont'ev, 1977; Vygotsky, 1935/1978) with constructs of social practice and habitus in Bourdieu's practice theory (Bourdieu, 1977). For example, Scollon's foundational work came from an ethnographic study of a one-year-old learning intercultural meanings attached to physical actions in the practice of handing. He micro-analyzed actions in the video data to understand how she learned to reciprocate in handing interactions: taking an object from and/or giving an object to another person. Depending upon the surrounding cultural-historical context, the same action of handing over a toy could be interpreted as different social practices: giving a gift, cleaning up a play area, or sharing with a friend. The meaning of an action signals something different within particular trajectories of histories or emanations across a lifetime: for example, this trajectory can travel from a baby's handing to an adult handing out flyers on a street corner or handing in assignments in a university classroom:

> This little practice of handing, seen within the very wide circumference that includes a timespan from the first year of life through to being a teacher or a student, remains a pivotal means of organizing an inter-agentive human contact, and—this is the point—this inter-agentive human contact serves as a very important enabling practice upon which further social interactions and discourse are built. In summary, a traditional classroom is constructed as the physical trajectories of teachers and students (and books and other objects) which converge in a suitable place which they then progressively transform from being simply a place with people in it to being a university class through such inter-agentive practices as handing objects, showing joint and mutual attention to the smooth flow of the talk which is directed to the point of the syllabus or the teacher-determined topic. While the discourses of text and topic are visible and focal for this type of social encounter, the discourses of inter-personal social interaction are deeply submerged in a life history of practice.
>
> *(Scollon & Scollon, 2002)*

In my research on the nexus of literacies, play, and technologies in early childhood (Wohlwend, 2009, 2011; Wohlwend & Handsfield, 2012), I look closely at the mediated actions in children's handling of toys, literacy materials, and digital technologies. However as suggested by Scollon and Scollon, the analytic potential of mediated discourse analysis extends far beyond early childhood research. Mediated discourse analysis provides excellent tools for examining issues from critical sociocultural perspectives (Lewis, Enciso, & Moje, 2007); it has been used to reveal strengths in an African-American family's literacy practices with technology (Lewis, 2009), to support collaborative writing practices in secondary English education (Rish, 2011), and to reconstruct critical literacy practices and racial power relations in teacher education (Mosley, 2010a, 2010b; Rogers & Mosley, 2008) and graduate classes (Rogers, 2011).

Mediated discourse analysis aligns with the turn toward embodiment in interdisciplinary linguistic and multimodal approaches to the study of social practices, including interactional sociolinguistics (e.g., Goffman, 1983), linguistic anthropology (e.g., Gumperz & Hymes, 1964; Scollon & Scollon, 1981; Scribner & Cole, 1981), and critical discourse analysis (e.g., Gee, 1999). For example, Scollon and Scollon's study (1981) of intercultural communication pioneered an interactional approach to the analysis of multimodality in literacy, aligning with ethnographic work in New Literacy Studies (Heath, 1983; Street, 1995; Gee, 1996) that reconceptualized literacy as ideological practices that can reproduce or remake extant power relations.

Like critical discourse analysis, mediated discourse analysis recognizes the mutually constitutive relationship between language and power. Critical discourse theory posits that discourse (as language) is always doing something, a *discourse as action* perspective. By contrast, mediated discourse analysis examines *discourse in action*, that is, the focus is on activity in a material sense that puts practices with artifacts on equal footing with discourses. Second, the analytic goal is not only to deconstruct but to reconstruct the activity in a place or community. Social action is at the forefront as researchers' work with participants to promote social change. Mediated discourse analysis makes visible the ways that everyday actions realize power relations and identify those actions that have potential for remaking identities, discourses, and institutions (Norris & Jones, 2005).

Questions for Mediated Discourse Analysis

Here's a set of questions I've adapted to track literacy practices in a nexus of practice:

Site of Engagement

1. What is the mediated action of interest used by social actors with this set of materials?

Social Histories of Practices

2. Which social practices for meaning-making (semiotic practices) seem routine (natural, expected) and necessary for participation? Which valued and typically backgrounded practices are foregrounded so they can be explicitly taught to novices so that they can participate?
3. How do social actors wield these routine practices? How do they combine actions with other actions to show expertise and exert power over others?
4. How do these actions and semiotic practices fit into cycles of histories and anticipated futures of social practices in this culture? For example, how did these practices become routine?

Cultural Meanings in a Community of Practice and Discourse

5. Who belongs here? What past identities are expected? What future identities are imagined?
6. Which identities are valued in this discourse? How do identities relate to each other?
7. Who decides what matters? Who authorized the rules and roles that operate here?

Material Histories of Use and Access

8. Who gets access? Which identities get access to the materials needed for this mediated action? How?
9. Who produces what? How are expert/novice relationships established through artifact production?
10. How did these materials get here?

In the next section, I use these questions to follow cycles in and out of a nexus of mediated actions—pressing and swiping—to examine the issue of young children's relationships to technologies and participatory social media cultures. It is important to point out that the current analysis is an illustration; a complete mediated discourse analysis requires researchers to personally engage the nexus in order to deeply understand how discourses, practices, and artifacts mold people's lives and everyday practices (including our own practices).

Illustrating Mediated Discourse Analysis: A Baby Thinks a Magazine is a Broken iPad

Despite rapidly changing technologies, burgeoning social media (e.g., Facebook friends, Twitter followers, chat groups), and widespread availability of mobile technologies, early childhood education remains a digital desert, or perhaps an oasis, depending upon your discursive perspective. Although very young children's direct and independent engagement with digital cultures appears restricted in school or after-school settings, babies and toddlers are highly visible on YouTube as subjects in productions, created with and posted by their families to the digital video-sharing site. In fact, infants are featured in a large portion of "cute" videos, which is arguably the dominant genre on YouTube where clips of babies, kittens, or puppies go viral and prompt thousands of likes, "lol"s, and smiley face emoticons. You can easily find similar technotoddler (Luke, 1999) videos through a YouTube search; the term "iPad baby" recently returned over 16,000 results. Often in these amateur videos, the producers add text, in the form of subtitles or adult narration that describes what the children are doing. A common trope in such narration is to provide script that imagines what the child might say.

Currently, the top result for *iPad baby* is the meme "A Magazine is an iPad That Does Not Work" which at the time of this writing has had 3,484,116 views since it was posted on October 6, 2011 (www.youtube.com/watch?v=aXV-yaFmQNk). In this video, a toddler uses her fingers to press, tap, swipe, and pinch on the screen on an iPad. Next, she tries using the same finger movements on several magazines and appears puzzled when nothing happens, stopping to test her finger by pressing on her knee. The final scene returns to iPad apps that respond instantly to her finger touches. The subtitles imagine her monologue as she babbles, squeals, and interacts with the two texts. Figures 4.1–4.3 show screenshots with parental captions from the video:

How does mediated discourse analysis of this viral video that foregrounds one mediated action—a toddler's finger tapping an iPad, a magazine, and a pudgy knee—unpack dense aggregates of taken-for-granted discourses and

FIGURE 4.1 "This One Works" caption follows baby pressing one finger on an iPad to open an app

FIGURE 4.2 "Useless" caption follows baby pressing down on print on fashion magazine

commonplace practices cycling into this onscreen nexus of practice? The toddler's action with the iPad and the magazine is a *mediated action*: a concrete, here-and-now physical handling of materials to make sense of and participate in the physical, social, and cultural environment. Pressing an icon or swiping a finger across the screen changes the image and constitutes the mediated action *turning a page*. Here, several mediated actions—gazing at a lighted glass screen, pressing down on an icon to open it, pinching and spreading thumb and fingers to size a page—combine to create a recognizable pattern that we can interpret as online reading, a *social practice*: a set of mediated actions that become categorized as a recognized way of behaving and interacting. The social practice of online reading is a way of accessing and making sense of a text by using a *mediational means*: the material artifacts as well as the semiotic systems (Wertsch,

FIGURE 4.3 "Yet My Finger Does Work" caption follows baby pressing one finger on own knee

1991) that provide us with meaningful words, gestures, images, and so on; in this case, the meditational means is literacy. This depiction of a baby using an iPad happens in a real-time moment or *site of engagement*: a social space where practices come together along with meditational means to make a mediated action the focus of attention (e.g., a baby swiping an iPad screen sitting at home on a wooden deck). Every site of engagement occurs in a moment, a point in time, located in a convergence of histories but also trajectories of discourses, materials, identities that gel in this action in this place: a baby playing with an iPad at home is a moment made durable and transportable through filming in a video captured by a parent, that was uploaded to YouTube, viewed by millions, and commented upon by thousands. For the analyst, the challenge of examining a mediated action as one point in the intersection of multiple dynamic

> For my 1-year-old daughter,
> ## a magazine is an iPad that does not work.
>
> It will remain so for her whole life.
>
> Steve Jobs has coded a part of her OS.

FIGURE 4.4 Final caption

trajectories means that one must follow these cycles in and out of the present moment. We examine a mediated action in the context of overlapping cycles to locate opportunities to open up access and create far-reaching transformative practices through small changes in ordinary activity.

> these nexus are constructed out of a very large and diverse number of discourses and practices (as submerged discourses) and any change of either the discourses or of the mechanisms by which they are linked in the physical world brings about a new set of affordances and constraints which constitute a change in the activity itself.
>
> *(Scollon & Scollon, 2002)*

Figure 4.5 illustrates how I've adapted an activity system as a map for analyzing the interaction among key elements in a particular mediated action: the top triangle represents the real-time site of engagement, a moment that focuses on some *who-doing-what-with-which-materials* in order to make a meaningful *artifact*. In the model, mediated discourse analysis expands the focus from examination of this here-and-now moment to consider three simultaneously social, ideological, and material forces: (1) practices and their social histories/possibilities; (2) discourses and identities; and (3) use of and access to artifacts and their material trajectories. Each of the smaller triangles along the bottom of the model provides an entry point for examining practices, discourses, or artifacts to analyze the site of engagement and trace the circumferences of the focal mediated action.

Tracking the Circumferences of an Action Through Discourses, Practices, and Artifacts

To track the circumferences (past and potential affordances and constraints) of a baby's finger swipes in the iPad video, we must look beyond the moment of filming that captured a toddler's emergent digital reading to consider the context of a video-sharing site: the captions and the following written

FIGURE 4.5 Activity model for nexus of practice

description that accompany the clip explicitly situate this moment in a shift between past/future, mind/technology, and paper/touch screens.

> Technology codes our minds, changes our OS. Apple products have done this extensively. The video shows how magazines are now useless and impossible to understand, for digital natives. It shows real life clip of a 1-year old, growing among touch screens and print. And how the latter becomes irrelevant. Medium is message. Humble tribute to Steve Jobs, by the most important person: a baby.

Contestation is evident in the contrasting number of likes (6,385) and dislikes (3,303) and in the content of viewers' comments (2,853). To connect these data to discourses, it is helpful to consult cultural studies and critical discourse analyses to identify the range of discourses prominent in technology, early childhood, and literacy. A sampling of viewer comments shows discourses of developmentalism (Burman, 2008), nostalgia (James, Jenks, & Prout, 1998), childhood innocence (Jenkins, 1998), and the risk of alienated techno-subjects (Luke & Luke, 2001).

How is the action of touching images on a page interpreted variously through conflicting and overlapping histories and discourses in ways that

TABLE 4.1 Discourses of developmentalism

Sample comment	Discourse
Blaming Steve Jobs for your child doing something that is average for her age is ridiculous. Along with blaming him for you presenting the iPad to your child as a toy. It's not his creation that created behaviour you are identifying as bad when it's normal.	Developing organism
Oh … and come to think about it, why would you expose your precious baby's eyes and brain to the radiation of an iPad – it's literally 10 cm away from her face. You have shown nothing here but really bad parenting and a really weird point of view. Terrible.	Vulnerable innocent
Oh the terror! The children of today will tomorrow read and educate themselves through devices instead of having to cut down billions of trees to do so!	Digital future
I thought I said (about 4 lines in) that I didn't play with computer stuff UNTIL I was almost 12 years old. I think most of what seems wierd [sic] to me is that old era toys (what my 60 year old mom played with) basically were my childhood toys and those seemed to be getting dropped out of toys stores because some new computer thing will make learning innovative. So much for coloring books and crayons and lite brites and simple outside toys. Apparently those aren't cool enough anymore.	Nostalgia

influence who gets access to social practices with valued materials and which ways of acting matter in this site? Here, whether a baby handling an iPad is viewed as dangerous or precocious depends upon discourses that circulate assumptions about the safety or developmentally appropriateness of technology or the aptitude of a new generation of digital natives (Prensky, 2001). Further comments refer to viewers' own reading and computing histories, marketing and manufacturing safety specifications for mobile technology, the histories of paper books, and some viewers' beliefs that books will and should persist into the future. Whether or not the emanations of this swiping action lead to better preparation for the future pits "headstarts and accelerated skills" against "natural" interactions with picture books.

Close analysis of the moment-by-moment actions in the video reveals the practices and identities that are submerged through routine practices or "frozen" in artifacts through regular use. In this case, the iPad evokes reading practices with page-turning taps and swipes that simply won't work with a glossy magazine page: a swipe to search or scroll, a pinch to size, a tap to select. There is an expectation that a one finger touch should be the primary mode for interacting with text and that a screen will respond to this touch. These are the tacit expectations that make up the "intuitive" skills of a "digital native" identity. The expectation of independent exploration in this technoliteracy nexus of practice conflicts with the expectation of a need for close monitoring and protection for a "developing organism" to prevent overexposure to screens (e.g., as in a recent prohibition by the American Association of Pediatricians) or the scaffolding for an "emergent reader" within developmentally appropriate nexus of practice. Mediated discourse analysis uncovers the roots and trajectories of these tensions so that other interpretations are visible and possible. This analysis is recursive and generates further questions for ethnographic study: who is privileged by discourse in this nexus of practice? Who gets early and easy access to 24/7 mobile devices? What builds on—or becomes difficult without—these early literacy experiences? Exploring these timescales may be a career long endeavor when we consider the time it takes to follow multiple cycles of relevance spinning out from one tiny mediated action.

Clearly, mediated discourse analysis provides useful inquiry tools for tracking complexity in digital literacies in overlapping contexts of online sites such as YouTube. In addition, this approach offers new ways to analyze a range of embodied and spatialized literacies that converge in face-to-face contexts. Finally, this approach to sociocultural inquiry is productive as well as critical. In the current example in this chapter, I use mediated discourse analysis to emphasize action over speech (e.g., tapping images rather than naming alphabet letters) as a critical move away from dominant print literacy and skills mastery discourse. This shift reveals the embodied literacies in a toddler's play that would be typically backgrounded in linguistic transcription and identifies the mediated actions with potential for reconstructing the nexus of practice. This analysis links the taps and sweeps of tiny fingers to issues of wider access to touchscreens for young children that could produce far-reaching ripples in their life-long literacy practices.

References

Bourdieu, P. (1977). *Outline of a theory of practice*. Cambridge, UK: Cambridge University Press.

Burman, E. (2008). *Deconstructing developmental psychology*. New York: Routledge.

Gee, J. P. (1996). *Social linguistics and literacies: Ideology in discourses* (2nd ed.). London: RoutledgeFalmer.

Gee, J. P. (1999). *An introduction to discourse analysis: Theory and method*. London: Routledge.

Goffman, E. (1983). The interaction order: American Sociological Association, 1982 presidential address. *American Sociological Review, 48*(1), 1–17.

Gumperz, J. J., & Hymes, D. (1964). The ethnography of communication. *American Anthropologist, 66*(6) (Special issue).

Heath, S. B. (1983). *Ways with words: Language, life, and work in communities and classrooms*. Cambridge, MA: Cambridge University Press.

James, A., Jenks, C., & Prout, A. (1998). *Theorizing childhood*. New York: Teachers College Press.

Jenkins, H. (1998). Introduction: Childhood innocence and other. In H. Jenkins (Ed.), *The children's culture reader* (pp. 1–40). New York: New York University Press.

Lave, J., & Wenger, E. (1991). *Situated learning: Legitimate peripheral participation*. Cambridge, MA: Cambridge University Press.

Leont'ev, A. N. (1977). *Activity and consciousness, philosophy in the USSR, problems of dialectical materialism*. Moscow: Progress Publishers.

Lewis, C., Enciso, P., & Moje, E. B. (2007). *Reframing sociocultural research on literacy: Identity, agency, and power*. Mahwah, NJ: Lawrence Erlbaum.

Lewis, T. Y. (2009). *Family literacy and digital literacies: A redefined approach to examining social practices of an African-American family*. Unpublished doctoral dissertation, State University of New York, Albany, NY.

Luke, A., & Luke, C. (2001). Adolescence lost/childhood regained: On early intervention of the techno-subject. *Journal of Early Childhood Literacy, 1*(1), 91–120.

Luke, C. (1999). What next? Toddler netizens, Playstation thumb, techno-literacies. *Contemporary Issues in Early Childhood, 1*(1), 95–99.

Mosley, M. (2010a). Becoming a literacy teacher: Approximations in critical literacy teaching. *Teaching Education, 21*(4), 403–426.

Mosley, M. (2010b). "That really hit me hard": Moving beyond passive anti-racism to engage with critical race literacy pedagogy. *Race Ethnicity and Education, 13*(4), 449–471.

Norris, S., & Jones, R. H. (2005). *Discourse in action: Introducing mediated discourse analysis*. London: Routledge.

Prensky, M. (2001). Digital natives, digital immigrants. *On the Horizon, 9*, 1–2.

Rish, R. (2011). *Engaging adolescents' interests, literacy practices, and identities: Digital collaborative writing of fantasy fiction in a high school English elective class*. Unpublished Dissertation, Ohio State University, Columbus, OH.

Rogers, R. (2011). Becoming discourse analysts: Constructing meanings and identities. *Critical Inquiry in Language Studies, 8*(1), 72–104.

Rogers, R., & Mosley, M. (2008). A critical discourse analysis of racial literacy in teacher education. *Linguistics and Education, 19*(2), 107–131.

Scollon, R. (2001). *Mediated discourse: The nexus of practice.* London: Routledge.

Scollon, R., & Scollon, S. W. (1981). *Narrative, literacy and face in interethnic communication.* Norwood, NJ: Ablex.

Scollon, R., & Scollon, S. W. (2002). Why do we need nexus analysis? Talk given at the PARC Forum, December 12, 2002. Palo Alto, CA.

Scollon, R., & Scollon, S. W. (2004). *Nexus analysis: Discourse and the emerging internet.* New York: Routledge.

Scribner, S., & Cole, M. (1981). *The psychology of literacy.* Cambridge, MA: Harvard University Press.

Street, B. V. (1995). *Social literacies: Critical approaches to literary development.* Singapore: Pearson Education Asia.

Vygotsky, L. (1935/1978). *Mind in society* (A. Luria, M. Lopez-Morillas, & M. Cole, Trans.). Cambridge, MA: Harvard University Press.

Wertsch, J. V. (1991). *Voices of the mind: A sociocultural approach to mediated action.* Cambridge, MA: Harvard University Press.

Wohlwend, K. E. (2009). Early adopters: Playing new literacies and pretending new technologies in print-centric classrooms. *Journal of Early Childhood Literacy, 9*(2), 119–143.

Wohlwend, K. E. (2011). *Playing their way into literacies: Reading, writing, and belonging in the early childhood classroom.* New York: Teachers College Press.

Wohlwend, K. E., & Handsfield, L. (2012). Twinkle, twitter little stars: Tensions and flows in interpreting social constructions of the technotoddler. *Digital Culture and Education, 4.* www.digitalcultureandeducation.com/uncategorized/dce_1058_wohlwend/.

5

MULTIMODAL (INTER)ACTION ANALYSIS

Sigrid Norris

Multimodal (Inter)action Analysis: Purpose, Origin, and Description

Multimodal (inter)action analysis originated from mediated discourse theory (Scollon, 1998, 2001), interactional sociolinguistics (Goffman, 1974; Gumperz, 1982; Tannen, 1984), and social semiotics (Kress and van Leeuwen, 1996, 2001). The method has taken mediated discourse (Scollon, 1998) as its theoretical underpinning, has built upon the notion of pragmatic meaning unit (particularly the utterance) taken from interactional sociolinguistics (Tannen, 1984), and incorporates modes of communication beyond language as exemplified in social semiotics (Kress and van Leeuwen, 2001).

While multimodal (inter)action analysis squarely grew out of these three fields of study, the method is most strongly connected to mediated discourse through its theoretical linkage, continuously not only developing the method (Norris, 2011), but also the theoretical underpinnings within mediated discourse (Norris, 2013). Thus, multimodal (inter)action analysis does not differ from, but rather extends mediated discourse. Further, the method incorporates a pragmatic view due to its pragmatic meaning units such as the utterance, thereby following in the footsteps of interactional sociolinguistics (Tannen, 1984). However, while sociolinguistics mostly remains a study of naturally occurring language, multimodal (inter)action analysis is the study of a vast number of naturally occurring modes including verbal and non-verbal. In the multimodal respect, the method is closer to social semiotics (Kress and van Leeuwen, 2001); however, with its detailed naturally occurring interactional aspect, it is closer to interactional sociolinguistics (Tannen, 1984). In other words, multimodal (inter)action analysis is tightly connected to mediated discourse and at the same time, and to an equal amount, closely connected to interactional sociolinguistics and social semiotics.

Multimodal (inter)action analysis is a methodology that allows the researcher to analyze video and other multimodal data on the micro, intermediate, and macro level, or from micro to intermediate to macro, or vice versa depending upon the focus of the study. With a strong theoretical underpinning in mediated discourse theory (Scollon, 1998, 2001), this methodology offers a variety of tools that a researcher can use together or can choose from and use in connection with other methodologies. The methodological tools guide the researcher in *how to begin* a multimodal (inter)action analysis and *how to investigate* the micro, the intermediate, and the macro of the (inter)action. In the example below, I illustrate how a micro analysis leads to new discovery; and in order for the reader to view an intermediate and macro analysis using multimodal (inter)action analysis, the reader may wish to have a look at Norris (2011). As explained in Norris (2013):

> Multimodal (inter)action analysis has antecedents that made its development possible. The primary antecedent is mediated discourse analysis (Scollon, 1998, 2001), other antecedents are interactional sociolinguistics (Goffman, 1959, 1963, 1974; Gumperz, 1982; and Tannen, 1984) and semiotics (Kress and Van Leeuwen, 2001; Van Leeuwen, 1999).
>
> As the primary antecedent, mediated discourse analysis has had the strongest influence on multimodal (inter)action analysis (Norris, 2004, 2011), which has kept the primary features, building upon them and expanding them into a direction of a primarily qualitative multimodal methodology.

Multimodal (inter)action analysis incorporates all relevant modes within the (inter)action that is being examined such as language, gesture, furniture, posture, proxemics, and music in a theoretically founded way by taking the mediated action as the unit of analysis (Scollon, 1998, 2001; Wertsch, 1998). In this view, an utterance is a mediated action as is a gesture, the arrangement of furniture, a postural shift, the proxemics that an individual takes up to another, and the music that is played and listened to. With the mediated action as unit of analysis, multimodal (inter)action analysis focuses each study on *what* social actors do (the action that is performed) and *how* the action is performed (the mediational means/cultural tool used to perform the action). This focus on social actors as they perform an action highlights three interconnected elements: the social actor, the action itself, and the tools that are being used. While none of these elements can be viewed independently from the other two, an analyst can begin their analysis with any of them; starting the analysis either by investigating a social actor, or by looking at an action, or by examining a tool that is used. No matter what the analyst's primary focus of study, multimodal (inter)action analysis as a method always brings the analyst back to engaging in a deeper analysis of the social situation, of which the initial focus (the social actor, the action, or the tool) is always only a part. With its draw into deep levels of analysis, multimodal (inter)action analysis allows for a new and novel investigation of social interactions from classroom discourse to intercultural communication and literacy to name but a few.

Applying Multimodal (Inter)action Analysis: (Inter)action, Unit(s) of Analysis, Transcription

Applying multimodal (inter)action analysis, a researcher may wish to ask some basic questions about reading such as 'What makes reading possible?', 'How is reading embedded in other (inter)actions?', and 'How can a distinction between various levels of action allow us to better understand the process of reading?' or 'What do these levels of action allow us to understand about the process of learning to read?'

In the following paragraphs, the term *(inter)action* is written with parentheses rather than the usual interaction written without the parentheses; then I define and give examples for the units of analysis; and offer some guidelines for multimodal transcriptions. With these tools in hand, the reader will have a basic understanding of the method and will be able to begin engaging in multimodal (inter)action analysis.

(Inter)action

In multimodal (inter)action analysis, researchers recognize that social actors not only interact with one another, but also interact with the environment and the objects within (we call these mediational means or cultural tools). When a child is reading a book, for example, the child (the social actor) is interacting with the book (mediational means or cultural tool). This action is viewed as an (inter)action in multimodal (inter)action analysis. The parentheses in (inter)action signify that we do not differentiate between a social actor (inter)acting with the environment or objects within or a social actor (inter)acting with other social actors. Our focus is always the action that is being performed: in the above case *a child reading a book*; and every action is made up of a social actor(s) + mediational means or cultural tool(s) (Scollon, 1998, 2001; Wertsch, 1998).

The Unit of Analysis

Our unit of analysis is the mediated action (social actor acting with/through a mediational means or cultural tool) (Norris and Jones, 2005; Scollon, 1998, 2001; Wertsch, 1998). However, because as such, the unit of analysis was too broad for a micro analysis and because it did not incorporate actions embedded in objects, the unit of analysis was differentiated and defined in the following ways in Norris (2004):

1. Lower-level Action

A lower-level action is a mode's smallest meaning unit. Leaning on discourse analysis, researchers in MIA use the utterance (Chafe, 1994) as the smallest meaning unit for spoken language. A gesture unit (a fully articulated gesture including pre-, post-stroke hold (if present) and retraction) is the smallest meaning unit for the mode of gesture. A postural shift (often a one-two shift) is the smallest meaning unit for the mode of posture, etc. In the above case of the reading child, the picking up of the book, the turning of a page, and so on are all lower-level actions.

Important for the researcher is that each lower-level action is defined by an analyzable starting and an ending point. Lower-level actions build chains in (inter)action that interweave at points in higher-level actions while simultaneously forming the higher-level actions.

2. Higher-level Action

A higher-level action is the coming together of multiple chains of lower-level actions. Thus, while a social actor utilizes a particular mode when performing a lower-level action (i.e., the lower-level action of pointing draws on, creates, recreates, and changes the mode of gesture), a social actor always utilizes multiple modes when performing a higher-level action.

The actual definition of the higher-level action under scrutiny is always defined by the researcher. For example, one may wish to investigate the higher-level action of the child reading. This higher-level action may start when the child walks to a shelf to choose a book; and the higher-level action may end when the child drops the book on the floor and moves on to a different higher-level action. Everything between these two points can be analyzed in minute detail by investigating the lower-level actions (and chains thereof) that the child performs. Now, we can see (through analysis of facial expression, posture, and gesture for example) when the child is getting interested in a particular part (or aspect) of the book. We can analyze which stories and pictures are of interest; how the child (inter)acts with particular pages in a book; and whether particular colors draw the child's attention. Or, taking a wider focus (another level of higher-level action), investigating the child's reading over time, we can analyze what motivates the child to choose particular books.

But the higher-level action can again be defined differently if we have yet a different focus: The higher-level action of interest to the researcher may in fact be a reading class in which children may go away, chose a book, and read on their own. Now, with this wider focus, we may want to investigate how children (inter)act with the books, with the environment and with each other. Here, we may ask: which books are chosen, where do the children go to sit and read, and do they show each other pages and/or tell the stories they are reading to each other?

Taking an even broader view-point, we may wish to analyze the higher-level actions of teachers and/or librarians to see which books are chosen and made available to the children in the first place. In an analysis such as this one, we would learn much about the cultural expectations that are embedded in the teachers' and/or librarians' actions and in the cultural tools (the chosen books). Here, we would be interested in the actions that produce the practices of schooling in a particular society and culture.

Thus the level of the higher-level action is determined by the researcher and by the questions that are being investigated. The important factor for the researcher is to determine the opening and ending of the chosen higher-level action, allowing the researcher to make sense of a certain level of higher-level actions. By doing this, the researcher will find that there are many different layers of higher-level action embedded when investigating the broader levels.

3. Frozen Action

Frozen actions are embedded within objects and the environment, as we can often tell from the environment and from objects within which actions social actors have engaged in. Taking a reading class as an example we could say that the children are all beginning readers. Then, we can imagine that the class is on break and the children and the teacher have left the classroom to go to the play-ground. If we now imagine walking into the empty classroom, we could see books on tables and on the floor and we would have a pretty good idea of the actions that had been going on just a moment before the break. The books, the chairs, the pillows on the floor all *tell* of the actions; they tell us where the children were sitting, which books were being read, where little groups had formed, how many children were reading alone, and much more. These are the actions that are now *frozen* in the environment, visible to the observer. Some-times, taking pictures of environments allows us to analyze those aspects that are usually not taken into account when investigating classroom discourse. Again, frozen actions, which are often higher-level actions embedded in objects and the environment, can be analyzed on various levels. Thus, we can for example also examine the types of books chosen by the children out of the ones available to them.

Attention/Awareness Levels of a Social Actor: Simultaneous Performance of Higher-level Actions

In multimodal (inter)action analysis, we are interested in the attention/aware-ness levels of social actors. Through analyses of many different (inter)actions (Norris 2004, 2011), we have come to know that social actors often produce several higher-level actions simultaneously. For example, a woman may (inter)act with her friend and be engaged in conversation at the same time as she watches several children play together and at the same time as she is preparing dinner. Sometimes, the woman may pay more attention to the conversation with her friend, sometimes she may pay more attention to the children, and sometimes she may pay more attention to the cooking. While each higher-level action continues, and while there always can only be one focus, she pays different amounts of attention to any one of these higher-level actions at different moments.

Attention levels can be analyzed through the notion of modal density (Norris, 2004), which describes the modal intensity and/or complexity of lower-level actions (which always draw on, develop, and create the modes) to produce a higher-level action. The higher the modal density of a higher-level action is, the more attention a social actor pays. Attention/awareness levels of social actors are heuristically visualized on a continuum. The higher-level action that a social actor focuses on occurs in the focus (or the foreground) of a social actor's (heuristically depicted) attention/awareness continuum. The higher-level action that the social actor pays medium attention to/is aware of to some medium degree, resides in the mid-ground of the (heuristically depicted) attention/awareness continuum. While the higher-level action that the social actor pays very little attention to/is very little aware of is positioned in the background of the heuristic depiction of the social actor's attention awareness continuum. Thus in the example above, the woman will construct more intense and/or complexly intertwined lower-level actions when she focuses upon the higher-level action of cooking (such as stirring a pot, turning down the heat of the burner, saying something about the cooking, looking at the ingredients, and reading a recipe), than when she pays very little attention and is backgrounding the higher-level action of cooking (such as keeping an eye on the time, only). Thus, modal density and the foreground–background continuum of attention/awareness are heuristic notions that allow us to analyze simultaneously constructed higher-level actions.

Transcribing Multimodal Data

Without going into more detail than this short chapter allows, I would like to point out that transcription in multimodal (inter)action analysis is a large part of the data analysis. We use a flexible transcription system (Norris, 2011) in order to analyze and describe our data in detail. The transcription system, as you will see in the example below, is image based with an overlay of spoken language, arrows, circles, and/or numbers as needed for a data piece. These kinds of multimodal transcripts are ideally compiled qualitatively by taking screen grabs and adding them to make up a figure. By doing this, the analyst is leading the transcription-analysis based on the data, allowing for the possibility of new discoveries about (inter)action (if one was to use tier-based transcription software [such as ELAN], the analysis is led by the software, not the data). In these multimodal transcripts, researchers embed their analysis within each screen grab, making tedious transcription an exciting process. Part of this process is the embedding of images (also of frozen actions and mediational means) and transcribed dialogue/sound that allow the reader to follow the analysis. By using this transcription system, a viewer of the actual data can understand how the researcher arrived at his/her conclusion

Using Multimodal (Inter)action Analysis: An Example

In the following example, we see Andrea (an artist, here in her role as art teacher) in an art supply store buying various materials for a project that she is leading at a school and in the example buying a size two paint brush for herself. The data piece was selected as a representative sample from an ethnographic study investigating Andrea's identity production, which I conducted over three months in 2010 (a continuation of my one-year longitudinal ethnographic study of Andrea conducted in 2000/2001). The data piece presented here are frames extracted from a 2.58 minute long video taken in the art store in Germany. The language spoken is German and the translation is given in textboxes on the transcripts. In the following analysis, I am particularly interested in Andrea's actions related to reading a number on a paint brush. Thus, here I view the action of reading differently than in the examples in the beginning of the chapter. Here, I focus on the actual reading of one number, only.

Background

One morning, Andrea needed to buy art supplies for her school project that she was leading. We drove to an art supply store located about 50 km (about 30 miles) away from her home. While she was driving to the store, she decided to also buy some art supplies for herself. We had been at the store for about ten minutes before the particular video, from which the transcript was created, was taken. The video begins when she enters an aisle with paint brushes and ends when she leaves the aisle.

In the beginning of the clip she was looking for a specific fine size two paint brush for herself. However, she first saw and picked up a flat paint brush and decided to buy that one as well, keeping it in her left hand. She then began to look for the fine brush that she needed. In this example, Andrea is looking for this particular size two paint brush, but, as illustrated in Figure 5.1, is unable to read the size as Andrea is far sighted and the writing is very small. As soon as she realizes that the writing is too small for her to read, even when extending her arm to lengthen the distance between her eyes and the paint brush, she begins to put on her glasses. At first glance, this action may seem to be quite irrelevant to literacy and the actual reading of a number (or in other cases of letters and words). However, when we remember that Andrea needs to read the information in order to be able to pick out the correct paint brush, the relevance of putting on glasses and the embeddedness of the various actions that Andrea performs in the action of reading become apparent.

When investigating the higher-level action of Andrea looking for a size two paint brush, we can examine the many chains of lower-level actions such as her gaze, head movements, postural shifts, or spoken utterances, all of which are involved in the very mundane action of reading a number on a paint brush. Here, I am particularly interested in the time and the intricacy of the actions and will therefore also refer to the times in the following paragraph.

In Figure 5.1, first row first image (at 1:03 of the clip), we see that Andrea is trying to read the number on the brush that she is holding in her right hand. As she is unsuccessful in this action of reading, she says 'wesste watt' (you know what), moves the flat brush, which she had been holding in her left hand, into her right hand (1:06), saying 'Andrea zieht jetzt' (Andrea will once) and puts her left hand into her purse (1:06), feeling for her glasses. She turns her body away from the shelves (1:06–1:11), continuing her utterance 'erst mal wieder die Brille an' (again put her glasses on). While feeling for the glasses (1:03–1:11), she changes her facial expression and presses her lips tightly together (1:07); she

FIGURE 5.1 Looking for a size two paint brush: lower-level action of reading a number turns into a higher-level action

looks down, squinting and almost closing her eyes (1:07–1:11); she raises both shoulders and her upper body as she takes a long in-breath and then produces a loud out breath first through her mouth and then continues the out breath noisily (but not as loudly) through her nose (shown in 1:11, but occurring at 1:09–1:10), shaking her head three times (1:10–1:12) while turning her upper body further away from the shelves (occurring simultaneously with shoulder and head movements 1:09–1:11) and then back toward the shelves (1:15) in order to open her glasses case and take out her glasses. She then puts her glasses case back into her purse (1:19) and puts on her glasses (1:22). Only at this point, can Andrea read the number on the paintbrush (1:24). She now realizes that she is holding a size four paint brush in her hand, as she is reading it out loud, followed by gazing up at the shelf to find a number two paint brush in the last image of the last row (1:26).

In this excerpt, Andrea is speaking with the researcher, who is standing (and filming) only a few paces away from Andrea. She refers to herself by name, which may be a result of her thinking of her young students for whom she went to the store to buy supplies; or it may be a sign of her speaking to the camera. However, no matter why she refers to herself by name, she clearly turns to the researcher (or camera), engaging in (inter)action with her. When analyzing Andrea's attention levels, we find that they shift in this example. The graph in Figure 5.2, illustrates Andrea's attention levels in the first image of Figure 5.1, where she foregrounds the higher-level action of buying a size two paint brush and mid-grounds the higher-level action of (inter)acting with the researcher.

Then, the begun lower-level action of reading the number on the paint brush balloons into a higher-level action and Andrea foregrounds this new higher-level action of reading. She continues mid-grounding the interaction

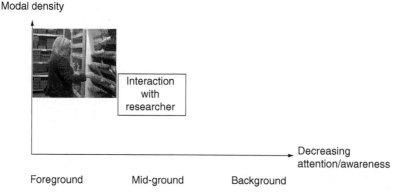

FIGURE 5.2 Andrea foregrounds the higher-level action of buying a size two paint brush and mid-grounds the higher-level action of (inter)acting with the researcher

with the researcher, actually paying a bit more attention to her now. Heuristically speaking, however, even though Andrea is clearly paying more attention to the researcher than she had been just a moment earlier, we still place the higher-level action on the mid-ground in the graph (illustrated in Figure 5.3) as Andrea is paying much more attention to the higher-level action of reading (which can only be performed by her through putting on glasses), focusing on this higher-level action and not upon the higher-level action of (inter)acting with the researcher. At the same time, the higher-level action of buying a size two paint brush has moved further back in Andrea's attention/awareness. The foreground, mid-ground, and background of Andrea's attention can be determined by looking at the modal density that she employs for each of these higher-level actions. Thus, we see that the methodological tool (the modal density foreground–background continuum) is a heuristic tool that allows the illustration of simultaneously performed higher-level actions in relation to the amount of attention/awareness that the social actor, who is performing the particular higher-level actions, pays to each at specific moments in time.

As mentioned above, the placement of higher-level actions on the graph in Figure 5.3 can be delineated when we investigate the modal density that Andrea utilizes: For the new higher-level action of reading, Andrea turns to better place her hand into her purse to take out the glasses; looks at her purse and then the glasses case to first open it and then to put it into her purse again; she opens the glasses while gazing at them then places them on her nose and then reads the number on the paint brush, saying 'vierer' (size four). The multitude of these actions produce a modally dense (or a chain of lower-level action-dense) environment, illustrating that she is paying most attention to this higher-level action at this moment.

Modal density

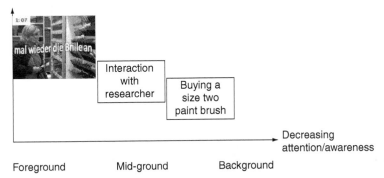

FIGURE 5.3 Andrea foregrounds the higher-level action of reading, mid-grounds the higher-level action of (inter)acting with the researcher, and backgrounds the higher-level action of buying a size two paint brush

As illustrated in Figure 5.1, it takes Andrea 21 seconds to put on her glasses before she can read the number on the paint brush: from 1:03 (first row first image) to 1:24 (last row, middle image). Besides the time that passes between the moment when Andrea first tries to read the number and when Andrea actually does read the number, there are many chains of lower-level actions that she performs, building the higher-level action of reading the number on the paint brush.

Discussion

Let us now imagine that Andrea either did not need glasses or wore bifocals on a continuous basis. This imaginary Andrea is setting out to buy a size two paint brush much like Andrea does in the example above (in Figure 5.1). When you now look at Figure 5.4, which is a shortened transcript of the one in Figure 5.1 (without the multitude of actions to put on her glasses), you will realize that our imaginary Andrea would gaze at the paint brush in a similar way as Andrea actually does in Figure 5.1 (first image first row). She would read the number (Figure 5.4), and continue the higher-level action of buying a size two paint brush – similarly as Andrea actually does in Figure 5.1 after 21 seconds (last row middle and last image).

In the case of our imaginary Andrea (Figure 5.4), reading the number '4' on the paint brush is a lower-level action, building a chain, interconnected with other chains of lower-level action that all together build the higher-level action of buying a size two paint brush. Here, the social actor gazes (part of the chain of gaze shifts) at the paint brush, reads the number (part of the chain of reading), looks at the shelf (part of the chain of gaze shifts) to find the next paint brush, pick one out (part of the chain of object handling), gazes at this paint brush (part of the chain of gaze shifts), reads the number (part of the chain of reading), and so on. These chains of lower-level action intersect with one another and are also dependent upon one another. Besides the chains of lower-level actions such as the chain of gaze shifts, reading, and object handling, we also find others such as the chain of head movements, hand–arm movements, and postural shifts. Figure 5.4, reading the number '4' would be embedded in, and at the same time helps produce, the higher-level action of buying a size two paint brush.

FIGURE 5.4 (Imaginary) lower-level action of reading a number on a paint brush

However, in the actual (inter)action shown in the example above (Figure 5.1), where Andrea is the social actor, who in fact does need glasses and does not wear bifocals on a continuous basis, at the moment of buying a size two paint brush, reading the number '4' is not a smoothly integrated lower-level action that also builds part of the higher-level action. In the actual example of Andrea (Figure 5.1), the lower-level action is begun as a lower-level action (Figure 5.1, image 1). But this lower-level action of reading a number then balloons into the higher-level action of reading. This higher-level action is performed through a multitude of other chains of lower-level actions from object handling (purse, glasses case, and glasses) to spoken language (speaking about glasses and complaining about the size of print, long in-breath, and loud out-breath) to postural shifts (away from and back toward the shelf), head movements (shaking her head three times), and facial expression (pressing her lips tightly together and squinting her eyes).

In Figure 5.1, the reading of a number on a paint brush thus begins at minute 1.03 as a lower-level action that balloons into a higher-level action, which ends at minute 1.24. For these 21 seconds, this new higher-level action interferes with the higher-level action of buying a size two paint brush, resulting in Andrea's annoyance (apparent in her facial expression, loud out breath, and spoken language).

Conclusion

Analyzing minute details of reading can give us insight into actual literacy practices. In the example illustrated in Figure 5.1, reading the number is only possible for Andrea once she has taken out her glasses and put them on. Rather than taking a second to gaze at the paint brush and read the number as one lower-level action, Andrea has to produce the reading of the number as a higher-level action. This higher-level action comes about through multiple chains of lower-level action from spoken language, head movements, shoulder movements, postural shifts, gaze, facial expression, and object handling.

Here, reading a number on a paint brush, something that would be a lower-level action for someone who is not far sighted or someone who wears bifocals (Figure 5.4) that is embedded within the higher-level action of buying a size two paint brush, turns into a higher-level action for Andrea. While she is performing this action, she turns her body, expresses some frustration or annoyance through her facial expression, upper body movements, head shaking, and noisy out breath, as well as through her spoken language. All of these chains of lower-level actions are part of the higher-level action of reading the number on the paint brush that she is holding in her right hand.

When we look at the above example, we find that Andrea was foregrounding the higher-level action of buying a size two paint brush until she needed to read a number and could not do so. At that point, she needed to construct the reading of the number as a higher-level action. Because this new higher-level action inter-feres with the higher-level action of buying paint brushes, which she had been focused upon, and because Andrea has not always been far sighted and remembers the reading of a number as a lower-level action that she could accomplish without interference in the higher-level action that she was focused upon, this new higher-level action causes frustration. This frustration is expressed to the researcher (or the camera), paying more attention to the higher-level action of (inter)acting with the researcher than to the higher-level action of buying paint brushes. Thus, Andrea now foregrounds the higher-level action of reading, mid-grounds the higher-level action of (inter)acting with the researcher, and backgrounds the higher-level action of buying paint brushes (as illustrated in Figure 5.3). While reading a number would have usually been embedded in the higher-level action of buying a size two paint brush, this lower-level action of reading takes on weight and increases in modal complexity (through the many other chains of lower-level actions that Andrea has to perform), thus turning into a higher-level action, which Andrea has to pay much attention to.

This example brings with it some interesting insight: A simple lower-level action of reading even just one number for Andrea, who is fully literate, turns into a complex higher-level action that needs to be focused upon. When we now think about the teaching of literacy skills, we will find that we are trying to teach the learner the opposite. We are trying to teach the very beginning reader to move from the higher-level action of deciphering the written word to engaging in reading as a chain of lower-level actions, which is embedded in the higher-level action of understanding the text. Or, to say it another way, to move from focusing on the higher-level action of reading the letters and words (or images) to perform-ing these skills as lower-level actions, making it possible for the reader to fore-ground the content and complexities presented in the text.

By conducting a micro analysis of readers in various settings and with various abilities, we can begin to understand the action of reading. Such concrete actions of readers then allow us to gain knowledge about literacy practices, which are concrete actions with a history (Scollon, 1998). Therefore, investigating the micro leads us to a discovery of practices, which are the intermediate level between micro and macro. Moving further once we have gained a true understanding of the micro actions and the intermediate practices of literacy, we can also begin to derive new knowledge about the macro societal levels of literacy.

The strength of multimodal (inter)action analysis is that the researcher always begins by studying the concrete micro actions performed by social actors.

Literacy Settings: Some Project Ideas using Multimodal (Inter) action Analysis

When taking multimodal (inter)action analysis as the methodological frame-work, the researcher will be able to gain knowledge of how the shift from reading as a higher-level action to reading as a chain of lower-level actions which is embedded and builds a part of the higher-level action of understanding a text is achieved by new readers. Thus, were a researcher to study a young beginning reader, the researcher could determine which chains of lower-level actions such as sounding out the words, pointing at the words, moving the feet and legs, and many more, make up the higher-level action of reading. Following the young reader's learning, the researcher will likely see how there are fewer chains of lower-level actions employed by the child when reading. For example, foot movements will diminish and so will the elaborate sounding out of words or syllables. Eventually, reading will no longer be made up of many chains of lower-level actions, but will be integrated as a chain of lower-level actions of reading that will be embedded in the higher-level action of sense-making. However, without a detailed study, we cannot be sure how exactly a young reader develops. A multimodal (inter)action analysis is needed to allow us to not just assume (as I have done here) what is likely to happen, but to illustrate exactly how learning to read progresses. Even some case studies would broaden our sketchy knowledge greatly. Such understanding would be useful in the development of new teaching strategies to make this change from higher- to lower-level action easier for the reader.

Multimodal (inter)action analysis is well suited to qualitative research utilizing observational data such as video. By providing the necessary tools to examine multimodal data on the micro, the intermediate and the macro levels, it enables the researcher to investigate a broad range of research questions. My earlier discussion of units of analysis provides examples of research questions appropriate for a focus on analyzing lower-level, higher-level, and frozen actions.

References

Chafe, W. (1994). *Discourse, consciousness, and time: The flow and displacement of conscious experience in speaking and writing.* Chicago: University of Chicago Press.

Goffman, E. (1959). *The presentation of self in everyday life.* New York: Doubleday.

Goffman, E. (1963). *Behavior in public places.* New York: Free Press of Glencoe.

Goffman, E. (1974). *Frame analysis.* New York: Harper & Row.

Gumperz, J. (1982). *Discourse strategies.* Cambridge, UK: Cambridge University Press.

Kress, G. and van Leeuwen, T. (1996). *Reading images: The grammar of visual design.* London: Routledge.

Kress, G. and Van Leeuwen, T. (2001). *Multimodal discourse: The modes and media of contemporary communication.* London: Edward Arnold.

Norris, S. (2004). *Analyzing multimodal interaction: A methodological framework.* London: Routledge.

Norris, S. (2011). *Identity in interaction: Introducing multimodal interaction analysis.* Berlin, Germany: Mouton de Gruyter.

Norris, S. (2013). Multimodal (inter)action analysis: An integrative methodology. In C. Müller, E. Fricke, A. Cienki and D. McNeill (eds), *Body—language—communication.* Berlin, Germany: de Gruyter Mouton

Norris, S. and Jones, R.H. (eds). (2005). *Discourse in action: Introducing mediated discourse analysis.* London: Routledge.

Scollon, R. (1998). *Mediated discourse as social interaction.* London: Longman.

Scollon, R. (2001). *Mediated discourse: The nexus of practice.* London: Routledge.

Tannen, D. (1984). *Conversational style: Analyzing talk among friends.* Norwood, NJ: Ablex.

Van Leeuwen, T. (1999). *Speech, music, sound.* London: Macmillan Press.

Wertsch, J.V. (1998). *Voices of the mind: A sociocultural approach to mediated action.* Cambridge, MA: Harvard University Press.

6

VISUAL DISCOURSE ANALYSIS

Peggy Albers

Visual Discourse Analysis: Origins and Traditions

Within the past decade more attention has been paid to visual literacy. This is particularly exciting, especially with the proliferation of visual messages that we encounter daily. Burnaford and her colleagues reviewed research (2007) on the arts and literacy and concluded that while these two disciplines had obvious connections, the idea that literacy instruction and research should help students develop frames for talking about visual texts is new in all too many schools (Albers, Harste, Vander Zanden, & Felderman, 2008; Marsh, 2006; Rowsell & Pahl, 2007; Vasquez, Albers, & Harste, 2010). Ann Hass Dyson (2006) has gone so far as to argue that the ability to understand how visual literacy influences and constitutes one's cultural and linguistic experiences must be part of the school's everyday literacy practices.

For the past 20 years, I have studied how visual texts do the work they do from the perspectives of semiotic and critical literacy. My work has positioned visual texts, especially those created in literacy and language arts classes, as significant to understanding the literacy practices of students, and supported teachers and researchers in designing and developing projects that attend to how visual information works in text. In this chapter, I review the work that has been done in the analysis of visual texts, demonstrate through data how visual discourse analysis works, and forward its significance as a research theory and method in literacy research.

Within the past three decades, a great deal of work around art as a language system emerged in literacy and language arts instruction and practice. In the late 1980s and up through today, there has been wide integration of art in language arts and literacy instruction, largely positioning art as a catalyst to improve comprehension and/or writing. Collectively, this work demonstrated links between how art as a language system informed, and often elicited, stronger and more descriptive writing (Cowan, 2001; Ehrenworth, 2003; Frei, 1999; Olshansky, 1995), improved comprehension and writing (Carger, 2004; Dyson, 1988), and connections to creativity (Pahl, 2007). In the early part of the 2000s, researchers interested in art as a language system were greatly influenced by Kress and van Leeuwen's (1996) grammar of visual design, a way of studying more systematically how objects and elements in visual texts mean.

A review of the literature reveals that a number of researchers, including myself, began to study more systematically, and within a critical perspective, picturebook illustrations as well as visual texts created by children. These researchers found links between children's identities and beliefs and their visual texts (Albers & Murphy, 2000; Evans, 2004; Marsh, 1999, 2000; Moss, 2001; O'Brien, 1994; Rowsell & Pahl, 2007). In O'Brien's (1994) well-known study, five- to seven-year-old students critically analyze and re-design junk mail— advertisements—focused around Mother's Day. These children analyzed catalogs and flyers which led to discussions of how mothers are perceived and presented in image and text, and who benefits from these days of recognition. Other research placed importance on grammatical knowledge for critical readings of texts included that by Janks (2005) and the advertisement, "Spot the Refugee." Serafini (2010, 2011), Marshall (2011), and Albers (2008) studied how illustrations in picturebooks operated on viewers to position them to read in particular ways, and establish concepts about markers of social identity including gender, race, culture, religion, and so on. Vasquez (2004), Vasquez and Felderman (2012), and Lewison and Heffernan (2008) began to develop practices that supported children as they learn to read, interpret, and interrogate a range of texts critically. Vasquez's work in particular (2000, 2004) focuses on supporting students as they develop a critical stance toward literature, media, social issues, everyday texts such as candy wrappers and cereal boxes, and issues that arose in their own community and school.

As children learn and use language they learn different literacies. Embedded in the knowledge that literacies bring are learners' ways of doing and acting, what Gee (1997) refers to as "big 'D' discourse." In classrooms, children are only able to speak from the perspectives that are offered by the Discourses that have been made available to them. These ways of doing and acting are manifested in one's attitudes, actions, learning processes, and everyday life. They comprise forms of power that shape who one can be in a community. Another set of studies offered insight into how visual texts made visible traces of textmakers' identities. In 2010, Pahl and Rowsell forwarded the concept of artifactual literacies, or the stories, beliefs, and values that underpin the objects that comprise children's visual texts. Our work in 2009 (Albers & Frederick) also studied how visual texts revealed traces of identity in images created across time. These studies show that visual texts can provide information about the textmaker regarding her/his interests, beliefs, and values—information that guides theory and practice in literacy. This move toward more systematic analysis of visual texts led to significant insights into the intentionality behind the production and interpretation of visual images.

Guiding Tenets of Visual Discourse Analysis

The aforementioned studies, especially those in the late 1990s and early 2000s led to my own work in Visual Discourse Analysis (VDA) (Albers, 2007). Although a number of methods have been applied to professionally generated artworks (see Banks, 2001; Kress & van Leeuwen, 2006; Pink, 2001; Rose, 2003), I systematically studied student-generated visual texts, the discourses that emerged within the text, the text itself, the macro and micro conversations surrounding the making and viewing of texts, and the visual text as a communicative event. VDA is grounded in semiotics, a theory that explores the nature and function of signs as well as the systems and processes underlying signification, expression, representation, and communication. Semiotics offers a way of thinking about meaning in which language and visual texts work in concert, and in which language is not the primary source through which meaning is mediated and represented. For Hodge and Kress (1988), text is "a structure of messages or message traces which has a socially ascribed unity" (p. 6), and *discourse* "refers to the social process in which texts are embedded ... text is the material object produced in discourse" (p. 6). A visual text, then, is a structure of messages within which are embedded social conventions and/or perceptions, and which also present the discourse communities to which the visual textmaker identifies. The text, as Halliday (1985) noted, is in a dialectal relation with context; the text creates the context as much as the context creates the text. Meaning arises from the friction between the two. VDA is also informed by discourse analysis (Gee, 2005), and the grammar of visual design (Kress & van Leeuwen, 2006). VDA is a general term for an approach to analyzing visual language use, especially as it naturally occurs within classrooms, not as invented texts. It is concerned with a theory and method of studying visual language that identifies how certain social activities and social identities get played out, how visual language enables literacy and language arts educators to identify genres of visual texts and what this signifies, and how art as language positions this sign system more significantly in the messages that learners communicate. More specifically, visual discourse analysts are concerned and interested in analyzing the marks on visual texts within the constructs of art as a language system, and the situations in which art as a language is used.

Visual discourse analysis focuses not only on how visual elements relate within a text (Kress & van Leeuwen, 2006), but also for how language is used to communicate and acts as a force on viewers to encourage particular actions or beliefs. Four principles guide visual discourse analysis. First, visual language is reflexive in that it both has the capacity to create and reflect the context and reality in which it was created. Second, language allows for situated meanings to occur, images or texts that are "assembled on the spot" (Gee, 2005, p. 94) in a given context (schools) and informed by learners and their interaction with other texts and conversations. Third, language is composed of many different social languages (Bakhtin, 1982). How students express their thoughts visually differs from how artists speak; students often have less knowledge about art as a discipline, and often default to structures and visual elements and objects that carry messages that society has defined and have become an accepted part of the social collective (Albers, 2007). Fourth, there are cueing systems within visual texts, structural, semantic, artistic, tactile, and visual, that provide information regarding how, why, and what students draw upon as they construct meaning (Albers, 2007). Students often communicate more than what their oral or written narratives about a literary text say, and visual discourse analysis allows educators to understand what else students say about texts visually. This encourages a critical perspective, one that helps with the identification of political and social injustices and how social communities condone such inequalities, and to theorize our own visual productions of meaning and analyses of visual texts we see in public and/or in schools. Examined within a larger context, situated meanings, discourses, intertextuality, and structural features, VDA offers insights into the beliefs, thoughts, and practices of the textmaker that otherwise lay hidden as "art."

Questions that guide visual discourse analysts include the following: how is language used to communicate (use of technique, design, color, and so on), how do (or might) viewers respond to the context of the text (composition), what is revealed about the textmaker through the image (attention to discourses and systems of meaning that underpin the visual text), and how does art act as a force on viewers to encourage particular actions or beliefs (use and organization of image; discourses that underpin the text)?

Visual Discourse Analysis: A Demonstration and Exemplar Study

Albers, Frederick, and Cowan (2009) conducted an interpretive study that involved the production and close readings of the visual texts of 38 fifth grade students (female n = 20, male n = 18) in two classes, created at the end of a unit of study in which students studied stereotypes, including race and gender. Two questions guided our investigation: What does a close analysis of visual elements suggest within and across visual texts? and What messages do elementary children send about boys' and girls' experiences and interests through their visual texts created in English language arts classes?

Students were enrolled in a small rural school that lay outside a large metropolitan area, and represented a range of socioeconomic backgrounds. Given the problems that often occur when students from diverse socioeconomic groups are merged, students were engaged in units of study that addressed gender and racial stereotypes. The students in this study had completed a unit had explored gender stereotypes within the contexts of fiction (e.g., particularly fairytales), and nonfiction. We invited students to take on the perspective of the opposite sex: we asked boys to visually represent what they believed were girls' interests and experiences, and we asked girls to visually represent what they believed were boys' interests and experiences. Literacy and language arts educators often ask children to figuratively walk in the proverbial shoes of and imagine themselves as the characters in stories, regardless of the character's gender; we invited students to do this through art.

Initially, we divided the visual texts into gender sets; that is, we studied images created by girls and those created by boys to see how gender was represented through these images. We read each text holistically in each set in terms of semantics, noting which picture subjects (what the picture was about) were represented and how many times they were represented. We then read the structures within each text (Kress & van Leeuwen, 2006), paying particular attention to the graphic and syntactic information. We identified and analyzed size and volume of objects, placement of objects on the paper canvas (four quadrants, effective center of attention), colors used, and the intensity with which color was applied onto the paper (light pastel lines vs. thick dark lines), orientation of the canvas (vertical/horizontal). We also coded written text as part of the visual text. This close study of elements enabled us to note the text-maker's perception of the significance of the activity or object to the opposite sex; for example, Figure 6.1a and b, two images created by Anthony and Karl, who, along with their classmates, visually expressed their beliefs about girls' interests and experiences after completing a unit of study that explored gender and racial stereotypes. Upon closer and side-by-side readings, Anthony's and Karl's images show remarkable similarity in composition, structure, and discourse. Compositionally, both boys draw specific objects that they associate with girls (unicorns, castles, rainbows, flowers), both include spaceships in the upper left hand quadrant, both use graphite (pencil) as their primary medium; Karl added yellow and orange to his rainbow. Structurally, both centralize objects that discursively represent fantasy (unicorns, castles) and love (flowers, curved lines, boy and girl holding hands), objects that occupy the largest part of the text.

We also studied the graphic information in light of Koch's concept of "recurrent pictorial elements" (cited in Sonesson, 1988, p. 38) or visual elements repeated within a text, or elements that cut across texts. For example, within his text, Anthony used flowers as a recurrent visual element, curved lines to represent a rainbow, three turrets on the castle. Karl also represented similar content, and used recurrent visual elements of curved lines (rainbow), three turrets, and flowers. Across texts, we noted the graphic and structural similarity and differences of visual elements from one child's text to another. For example,

a

b

FIGURE 6.1a, b Anthony and Karl's visual texts: boys' representation of girls' interests

both Anthony and Karl placed their castle with three turrets on the left hand side of the canvas, both of which have spaceships, viewed from below, atop one turret. Both included rainbows, flowers, smiling unicorns, objects associated with fantasy. When we noted that two texts contained a number of similar visual elements, we called this a visual conversation, and coded this using directional lines that linked elements between texts.

To corroborate this finding, we looked at the seating arrangement and organized the visual texts to reflect where children sat for this experience. This enabled us to consider how and to what extent students related to the content and to each other's texts (Cazden, 2001). The more visual elements that were shared, the stronger the conversation was between textmakers. Further, we noted to what extent we could determine who started the conversation and who took it on. The more arrows that led to and away from a text, the more we saw this textmaker as starting the conversation This analysis of visual elements also helped us understand the extent to which these students integrated cultural information associated with objects (flowers = love), and which objects, concepts, and/or actions they associated with the opposite sex. When three or more texts contained similar elements and objects and/or picture subjects, we coded this as a discourse.

Two key findings emerged from our analysis of these images: recurring elements indicated that visual conversations occurred between and across texts, and that particular and unified discourses of gender visually emerged in their use of color and objects, and their organization of objects in the image. For example, Figure 6.2 demonstrates how Anthony and Karl shared similar objects, ideas,

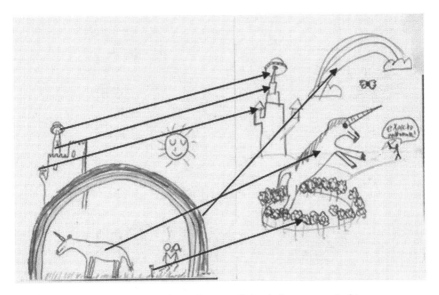

FIGURE 6.2 Directional arrows show sharing of visual elements and objects

and organization in their texts. Proximity—how close students sat near each other—informed the extent to which students integrated objects, colors, ideas from other surrounding texts. We also found that visual conversations were controlled by one or two textmakers evidenced by the way in which others took up objects, elements, and organization in their own texts. When we noted that three or more texts expressed similar ideas, we saw this as a discourse, a unified expression of a social collective.

In terms of the second finding, we noted that clear discourses of gender emerged, and these discourses fell along traditional ideas often associated with boys and with girls. That is, girls engaged in visual conversations around six distinct interests that they believed boys had: video games, sports, cars, monsters/dragons, violence/war, and animals (reptiles). Boys visually shared conversations around five distinct areas they believed girls had: romance, fantasy, domesticity, beauty, and caricature. Figure 6.3 represents one of the strongest visual conversations that emerged in this study centered on fantasy and romance.

Across this visual conversation, boys repeated or integrated objects often associated with girls: flowers, unicorns, rainbows, romance, and dreams. All seven of these contained flowers and unicorns, were set in castles or meadows, and five contained rainbows. Clear conversations around what girls like emerge across these texts, and where these boys sat determined to what extent elements were taken up. We noted that Textmaker 1 and 2 led the discourse of fantasy/romance with their highly detailed drawings of objects often found in fantasy as a genre; the other five textmakers integrated similar elements and objects in

FIGURE 6.3 Strong visual conversations that emerged in this study centered on fantasy and romance

their own texts, only shifting slightly the conversations in their own way. We found two distinct discourses within this set of images, fantasy as traditional and protective and fantasy as love and romance. Textmaker 1 traditionally locates his captive female in the castle as the male shouts to her, "expecto patronum!" ("I await a protector!"), and then moves in to save her. Objects like flowers, unicorns, and rainbows serve as cultural markers of romance, the imagined and happy life, and happy relationship. The castle, placed in the upper left hand quadrant, represents what we culturally know. They symbolize strength (constructed of sturdy materials), and protection (tall and strategically located on hills), places where women can feel safe. In close proximity to these two textmakers, Textmakers 4 and 5, in particular, took up this discourse through their choices and placements of objects very similar to that of Textmaker 1. Textmaker 5's visual text is a near replication of Textmaker 1's, as is Textmaker 4; however, he shifted this conversation slightly by representing the balcony scene from *Romeo and Juliet* rather than Textmaker's 1 allusion to Harry Potter. The clear, visible, and multiple integration of Textmaker 1's visual elements and objects into Textmakers 4 and 5's visual texts suggests that they align strongly with Textmaker 1's more normative discourse of romance and fantasy. We suggest that such acute observation and attempt to replicate the objects in another text indicated not only an interest in what these objects symbolized, but also the discourses around which these objects have been culturally defined.

Textmaker 2's visual text led a conversation around the discourse of fantasy focused on love and romance. The objects within his text—couple holding hands, to the single flower, smiling sun, and unicorn, orange and yellow rainbow—serve not so much to protect but to protect their love. As a cultural symbol of purity, elegance and charm, the unicorn, a central object in this visual text, is on equal plane with the couple, and because of this position, the couple takes on this symbolism. Noticeable is the unicorn's turn to the left side of the image, or the real/known, while the couple, hand-in-hand, walk away and toward the unknown. This organization of elements signified for us Textmaker 2 walking away from childhood and into young adulthood and the expectations placed on girls and boys in their move from elementary school to middle school. Textmakers 3 and 6 more closely align with the discourse of romance and love. Textmaker 6's female is central, encircled in flowers, accompanied by her unicorn, and finds this setting "Cool." Textmaker 3's free-floating flowers, the unicorn, and the sun, in combination, focus on the house, where apparently the female resides. The flowers in this loving scene caress the home much like the singing birds circling Snow White in the Disney movie.

Although some elements were shared, others were not. None of the other five boys took up Textmakers 1 and 2's addition of the spaceship on top of the castles. We suggest that this inclusion of this object was a way for these two boys to masculinize the feminine, and thus participate freely in the conversation of romance/love, and could do so as boys, rather than as boys representing girls.

As for the other five boys, we suggest their not including the spaceship may be related to maturity level and the possibility that they were not as ready to participate in this conversation. Rather, they chose to go along with Textmakers 1 and 2 in order to maintain solidarity; they had less to contribute to the conversation and may simply have been in agreement with the topic and willing listeners.

In conducting this study, we suggested that children dynamically engaged in both gendered and discursive visual conversations. Not only did they share elements and objects, but took up the cultural symbolism associated with them (flowers=love), a sharing that became an issue of critical literacy and power (Lewison, Leland, & Harste, 2008). Even though they had studied issues of gender in a six-week unit prior to this engagement, experience in this study was not defined by engagement with a topic but by how they gendered subjects. In essence, they were taking up available discourses of gender, and visually representing the selves that they were taking each other to be. At the same time, art as a language allowed these children to put on a gendered performance—they vicariously put themselves in the proverbial shoes of the opposite sex. In terms of the visual representation, gender was performed, but in terms of the context, that we asked students to draw what they considered the interests of the opposite sex, we positioned them to see how this performance would look. We believe exploration of beliefs through art allows for such play and performance. From a critical perspective, this study provides some evidence that visual conversations raise questions about power relations that exist within the classroom—who has the power to start the conversation, who takes it up, and who is the subject of how representations are made. As a sign system, art afforded them space to take up traditional discourses in ways that they might not otherwise do. This study suggests that visual representations make visible the complex interplay among signifier (the form the sign takes) and signification (the concept represented), and the social and discursive practices that are part of classroom practices. This study also provides evidence that children's pictures are artifacts of their beliefs, values, and ideas around such issues that involve social markers of identify. By helping children read, analyze, and talk about the visual texts they create and, especially about size, volume, color, design layout as well as context, they can learn to read their own as well as professionally generated texts with a more critical eye.

Conclusion

With the proliferation of visual information that passes by us at incredible rates, critical and systematic analysis of this information is crucial. From the thousands of advertisements that we encounter daily in magazines, Internet, sides of busses and buildings, to the billboards that line every road and highway, these images teach us—across time and across messages—to think, act, behave in particular ways. These public pedagogies (Shannon, 2011) act on us subtly or consciously to encourage particular behaviors and beliefs. Consider how McDonald's yellow arches and happy meals have influenced children's eating habits, or how companies like Ralph Lauren or Calvin Klein products have shaped bodies and minds to desire particular body types. Or consider the messages that continue to position the interests of girls and boys in particular ways, ways that emerge in the visual texts of children like those whom I have describe in our study.

Visual discourse analysis offers a way to study how texts work, and to understand that reading is not only about print-based texts, but becomes essential in interpreting and understanding information generated through other texts like candy wrappers, cereal boxes, sports equipment, catalogs, and flyers. From a visual discourse analysis perspective, visual texts—like written texts—contain structures that can be analyzed both in how something is said (grammar of visual texts: media, object placement, space, color, etc.), and within critical literacy or what is said (composition: messages conveyed and discourses). Identification and location of these compositional and structural marks on a text—candy wrappers, menus, promotional materials—offer insight into how we figuratively and literally buy into these messages, and thus shape our social practices.

Ultimately, reading is about agency—understanding from where the choices that we make about how we act, think, or value arise—and how we can react, interrogate, or critique messages—written, spoken, visual, gestural, musical—with insight and the methods to do such analysis. As I have argued, analysis of visual texts, or a study of the relationships between and among objects within a visual text, along with a holistic and critical reading of visual texts, provide information about the backgrounds and experiences of the textmaker, and also make visible discourses that emerge in visual texts (e.g., photographs, drawings, sculptures, digital).

This chapter encourages literacy researchers and educators to consider the role of analysis of visual texts as information that encourages a deeper discussion of what constitutes literacy. By knowing the role that Discourses play in the reading, interpreting, and analysis of visual texts, researchers and educators, alike, can more thoughtfully understand to what extent very young children through adults internalize messages that comprise these texts. Making critical the role of visual analysis significantly implicates the textmaker and the viewer as active and critical makers and readers of visual texts, rather than as passive makers and viewers whose primary stance is aesthetic. The forms through which knowledge and understanding are constructed, remembered, and expressed must be wider than verbal or written language alone. If students, and educators, are to understand written, visual, musical, and dramatic texts (and so on) and be more able to express what they know through a range of media, they need to have the opportunity both to study structures, purposes, and qualities within their own visual texts, and to learn to read said texts.

References

Albers, P. (2007). Visual discourse analysis: An introduction to the analysis of school-generated visual texts. In D. W. Rowe, R. T. Jiménez, D. L. Compton, D. K. Dickinson, Y. Kim, K. M. Leander, & V. J. Risko (Eds.), *56th yearbook of the National Reading Conference* (pp. 81–95). Oak Creek, WI: NRC.

Albers, P. (2008). Theorizing visual representation in children's literature. *Journal of Literacy Research, 40*(2), 163–200.

Albers, P., Frederick, T., & Cowan, K. (2009). Features of gender: A study of the visual texts of third grade students. *Journal of Early Childhood Literacy, 9*(2), 243–269.

Albers, P., Harste, J. C., Vander Zanden, S., & Felderman, C. (2008). Using popular culture to promote critical literacy practices. In Y. Kim, V. J. Risko, D. L. Compton, D. K. Dickinson, M. Hundley, R. T. Jiménez, K. M. Leander, D. W. Rowe (Eds.), *57th yearbook of the National Reading Conference* (pp. 70–83). Oak Creek, WI: NRC.

Albers, P., & Murphy, S. (2000). *Telling pieces: Art as literacy in middle school classes.* Mahwah, NJ: Lawrence Erlbaum Associates.

Bakhtin, M. (1982). *The dialogic imagination.* Austin, TX: University of Texas Press.

Banks, M. (2001). *Visual methods in social research.* London: Sage Publications.

Burnaford, G., Brown, S., Doherty, J., & McLaughlin, H. J. (2007). *Arts integration frameworks, research & practice: A literature review.* Washington, DC: Arts Education Partnership.

Cazden, C. B. (2001). *Classroom discourse.* Portsmouth, NH: Heinemann.

Cowan, K. (2001). *The visual-verbal connections of literacy: An examination of the composing processes of the fifth- and sixth-grade student.* Unpublished dissertation, Georgia State University, Atlanta, GA.

Dyson, A. H. (1988). *Drawing, talking, and writing: Rethinking writing development. Occasional Paper No. 3.* Center for the Study of Writing. Berkeley, CA: University of California Press.

Ehrenworth, M. (2003). *Looking to write: Students writing through the visual arts.* Portsmouth, NH: Heinemann.

Evans, J. (2004). *Literacy moves on: Popular culture, new technologies, and critical literacy in the primary classroom.* London: David Fulton Publishers.

Gee, J. (2005). *An introduction to discourse analysis: Theory and method* (2nd ed.). Abingdon, UK: Routledge.

Gee, J. P. (1997). Meanings in discourses: Coordinating and being coordinated. In S. Muspratt, A. Luke, & P. Freebody (Eds.), *Constructing critical literacies: Teaching and learning textual practice* (pp. 273–302). Creskill, NJ: Hampton Press.

Halliday, M. A. K. (1985). *An introduction to functional grammar.* London: Arnold.

Hodge, R., & Kress, G. (1988). *Social semiotics.* Cambridge, UK: Polity Press.

Janks, H. (2005). Language and design of texts. *English Teaching: Practice and Critique, 4*(3), 97–110. Accessed from http://education.waikato.ac.nz/research/files/etpc/2005v4n3art6.pdf.

Kress, G., & van Leeuwen, T. (2006). *Reading images: The grammar of visual design* (2nd ed.). New York: Routledge.

Lewison, M., & Heffernan, L. (2008). Rewriting writers workshop: Creating safe spaces for disruptive stories. *Research in the Teaching of English, 42*(4), 435–465.

Lewison, M., Leland, C., & Harste, J. C. (2008). *Creating critical classrooms: K-8 reading and writing with an edge.* Philadelphia: Lawrence Erlbaum Inc.

Marsh, J. (2006) Popular culture and literacy: A bourdieuan analysis. *Reading Research Quarterly, 46*(2), 160–174.

Marshall, E. (2011). Stripping for the wolf: Rethinking representations of gender in children's literature. *Reading Research Quarterly, 39*(3), 256–270.

Moss, G. (2001). Seeing with the camera: Analysing children's photographs of literacy in the home. *Journal of Research in Reading, 24*(3), 279–292.

O'Brien, J. (1994). Show mum you love her: Taking a new look at junk mail. *Reading, 28*(1), 43–46.

Olshansky, B. (1995). Picture this: Image-making within the writing process. *Thrust for Educational Leadership, 25*, 14–16.

Pahl, K. (2007). Creativity in events and practices: A lens for understanding children's multimodal texts. *Literacy, 41*(2), 86–92.

Pink, S. (2001). *Doing visual ethnography: Images, media, and representation in research.* London: Sage Publications.

Rose, G. (2003). *Visual methodologies.* Thousand Oaks, CA: Sage Publications.

Rowsell, J., & Pahl, K. (2007). Sedimented identities in texts: Instances of practice. *Reading Research Quarterly, 42*(3), 388–404.

Serafini, F. (2010). Reading multimodal texts: Perceptual, structural and ideological perspectives. *Children's Literature in Education, 41*(2), 85–104.

Serafini, F. (2011). Expanding perspectives for comprehending visual images in multimodal texts. *Journal of Adolescent and Adult Literacy, 54*(5), 342–350.

Shannon, P. (2011). *Reading wide awake: Politics, pedagogies, and possibilities.* New York: Teachers College Press.

Sonesson, G. (1988). *Methods and models in pictorial semiotics.* Report 3 from the Semiotics Project. Lund, Sweden: Lund University.

Vasquez, V. (2000). Our way: Using the everyday to create a critical literacy curriculum. *Primary Voices, 9*(3), 8–13.

Vasquez, V. (2004). *Getting beyond I like the book: Creating space for critical literacy in K-6 classrooms.* Newark, DE: International Reading Association.

Vasquez, V., Albers, P., & Harste, J. C. (2010). From the personal to the worldwide web: Moving teachers into positions of critical interrogation. In B. Baker, (Ed.), *The new literacies: Multiple perspectives on research and practice* (pp. 265–284). New York: Guilford Press.

Vasquez, V., & Felderman, C. (2012). *Technology and critical literacy in early childhood.* New York: Routledge.

PART II

Methods in Arts-based and Autoethnographic Research

7

AUTOETHNOGRAPHY

PS I Love You[1]

Jodi Kaufmann

I want to think differently. Sought with passion to create the world anew, autoethnography allows me to work toward "writing a world to come" (Deleuze, 1995). Drenched in trauma or permeated with beauty, autoethnography is a story of self in society (Reed-Danahay, 1997). It is not a new practice: Ethnographers have long written personal accounts of their experiences in the field. Malinowski, for example, shared his thoughts, passions, and reflections in *A Diary in the Strict Sense of the Word* (1967). But such accounts were considered superfluous, external to "real" research, and self-indulgent. Since the postmodern turn and the paralleled crises of an absolute in research – the crisis of Truth, representation, and identity – self-narratives for some have moved from margin to center. Comprising a methodology in its own right, autoethnography after the postmodern turn is a methodology and a text that is literally a sum of its parts: writing [graphy] that moves back and forth between self [auto] and culture [ethno] (Ellis & Bochner, 2000).

In the following, I will note the predominate frameworks of autoethnography. This will be followed by a discussion of methods of data generation and representation used in poststructural autoethnography in particular. I conclude with a few thoughts for using this methodology in the field of literacy.

Autoethnographic Frameworks

All research is grounded in a theoretical perspective, a philosophical stance (Crotty, 1998) that informs how one makes meaning. These philosophical stances or paradigms have been categorized by Lather (2006) as predict, understand, emancipate, deconstruct and next?. Fitting nicely on paper, in practice paradigms are convoluted and fluid. Simplistically speaking, autoethnography predominately emerges from the paradigms of understand, emancipate and deconstruct (Lather). The primary focus of autoethnographies grounded in the paradigm of understand is to share and make sense of life experience. Texts in this paradigm rely on a variety of interpretive theories – symbolic interactionism, hermeneutics and (variations of) phenomenology (Crotty, 1998). Within this paradigm, the works of Carolyn Ellis (1995) are exemplar. In Ellis's book *Final Negotiation*, she tells, often in graphic detail, how the love, anger and guilt of caring for her dying husband functions to understand self in culture.

Autoethnographies grounded in the paradigm of emancipate attempt to equalize power relations and/or promote social justice in society. This paradigm is beautifully illustrated in "On being a white person of color: Using autoethnography to understand Puerto Ricans' racialization" (Vitdal-Ortiz, 2004). Weaving theory and personal narratives of being Puerto Rican and gay in the States, Vitdal-Ortiz brings to the fore structural inequities based on race, ethnicity and sexual orientation.

Autoethnographies grounded in the paradigm of deconstruct focus on how experience functions rather than what it means. Using a variety of poststructural theories, such as the works of Butler (1993), Derrida (1997/1974), Deleuze and Guattari (1987/1980) and Foucault (1980), autoethnographers who work in this paradigm often seek difference rather than similarity, absence rather than presence, the local rather than the universal and the fragmented rather than the whole. Rollings (2004) in "Messing around with identity constructs: Pursuing a poststructural and poetic aesthetic," deconstructs his identity in the wake of the death of his father. In this piece he wants to "mess up" normal constructs and "tell of new poststructural possibilities – to restore the agency that allows [him] to disembowel a discourse of sublimation rather than be disembodied, classified, and delimited by it" (p. 552).

Paradigms are not absolute. Often autoethnographers use what Stinson (2009) calls theoretical eclecticism, drawing on multiple paradigms in writing texts. This can be seen in such work as last year's winner of the American Education Research Association (AERA) Qualitative Special Interest Group (SIG) Dissertation Award. Laura (2011) situated her inquiry in both the paradigms of understand and emancipate as she sought to understand how her brother dropped out of school. While seeking to understand the experience, she also inquired into the structural inequities faced by Black males in urban America. Because of the theoretical disjuncture/s between seeking to understand, where a meaning emerges, and desiring to deconstruct, where meaning disintegrates, work bridging these paradigms is scarce, in fact I know of none. However, several autoethnographers work simultaneously from the paradigms of emancipate and deconstruct. Spry, for example, explicitly does so in her piece "Performing autoethnography: An embodied methodological praxis" (2001). Weaving theory, personal poetry and narrative, Spry illustrates and discusses the personal, professional and emancipatory potential of autoethnography while simultaneously revealing the "fractures, sutures, and seams of self interacting with others" (p. 712).

There are numerous paradigms and paradigmatic combinations from which to situate autoethnography. Many paradigmatic spaces, however, remain as of yet unthought. With spans of uncharted territory, imaginations may wander, passions may engage and one may get lost in possibilities to come.

Generating Data and Meaning

What something means differs according to the epistemology one employs. Traditionally, grounded in a postpositivism, qualitative researchers thought meaning was inherent in the object. Using the correct methods, a researcher believed s/he could discover or ever more closely approximate the truth (Crotty, 1998). Thus, for example, Malinowski could discover the systems of exchange on Trobriand Island (1922). Later the epistemology of constructionism was utilized more frequently by qualitative researchers. Constructionists believe that meaning is constructed between the subject and the object (Crotty, 1998). Although some think Truth can be found, others put ontology aside and settled for closer and closer approximations of socially contextualized experience (Schwandt, 2000). This is the epistemology grounding most autoethnographies situated in the paradigms of understand and emancipate.

Recently, some qualitative researchers have been grounding their work in a poststructural epistemology, aligned with a poststructural theoretical perspective. Along with focusing on difference, absence and the local, poststructuralism troubles everyday concepts. Thus, concepts on which we often rely without thought are no longer understood to be stable. For example, the self, rather than being an inherent individual that has a material body that ends at the skin, a mind that is essentially rational and a natural agentic capacity, generally speaking, is understood as fragmented, discursive, fluid and performative. Because poststructuralists often rely on deconstruction – seeking the questions beneath the answers in a text or tradition (Ricoeur as cited in Klein, 1995), meaning is considered ephemeral and/or delusional and focus shifts to function.

This is the place I like to play, imagining possibilities and seeking an explosive passion of living differently. In this space, data is generated from anything that can be read. Understanding reading as making meaning from any actual or virtual object, event or intensity, I understand data as any actual or virtual object, event or intensity which can be read. Some examples of the possibilities of data are as follows: emotional, dream, sensual and response data (St. Pierre, 1997), literature (Brinkman, 2009), music (Snead, 2010), email, chatrooms and game rooms (Markham, 1998), social networking sites (Kaufmann, 2011a; Marcus, Machilek, & Schultz, 2006) videos, movies, art work (Bal, 1999), buildings, graveyards, documents (Prior, 2003), photographs (Harper, 2003; Kaufmann, 2011a; Pink, Kurti, & Afonso, 2004) and performance (Jones, 2010).

As data has proliferated, meaning has deceased. Here, meaning is not something waiting to be found; it does not exist prior to being named. Therefore, in poststructural autoethnography one cannot search for themes; there are no commonalities to be found. In fact, there is nothing to be found; there is nothing there before one looks. In this space, I understand that meaning emerges in the relations between the actual and virtual elements of an event (Deleuze, 1994). Actual elements are material and perceptible things, a person, a building, an animal, a behavior. The virtual is pure difference and pure becomings (Williams, 2004). I visualize virtual elements as energy, flows of possibility. Unseen and imperceptible, virtual elements and relations are sensed. Meaning emerging in the relations between the actual and the virtual is ephemeral, constantly changing as one intensity, or difference, envelops another. These envelopments make clear some virtual ideas, while obscuring others. Williams (2004) gives the following example: *"As jealousy covered love the idea of humanity as conflict grew clearer and the idea of humanity as trusting receded into the depths"* [italics in the original] (p. 8). The constant flow of meaning, the emergence and disappearance of virtual elements in actual objects, is usually stabilized by being organized, in habit or memory, according to the concepts available (Deleuze & Guattari, 1987/1980). Braidotti (2006) argues that this trapping of meaning in the concept is a force of habit that is "socially enforced and thereby a 'legal' type of addiction … [that] engenders forms of behavior that can be socially accepted as 'normal' or even 'natural.'" Thus, the concept, habitually used over and over, reifies experience, constitutes normality and constricts possibility within the bounds of the signifier. This is because that which does not fit under the concept, although always there, is ignored and made invisible. For example, when I conceptualize myself as an agentic, human female, those elements of myself that resonate most closely with male and animal are ignored, the testosterone that is produced in my body, the low growl I make when I am frustrated. And, when the process of jealousy envelops love and functions to make humanity appear as conflict, I understand this to be an outcome of my rational thought based on empirical evidence – He is late; "What is he doing that is more important than I am?" I am ready to argue. Thus, when we construct meaning we allow or force some intensities, pure differences, to move to the fore while others become enveloped (Deleuze, 1994) and imperceptible. Consequently, constructing meaning has the propensity to limit the possibilities of experience and knowledge by erasing that which is there, always already existing as possible becomings.

Situated in this space, I seek to bring to the fore that which remains obscure but exists as potential clarity. To do this I often experiment with thinking data through diverse concepts. To experiment is to creatively connect and disrupt different intensities in order "to introduce thoughts and acts that change an individual perspective on the whole, and thereby, to change it for all individuals" (Williams, 2004, p. 30). By analyzing myself through the concept of wolf, for example, I can begin to understand and manifest my wolfness, my becoming wolf (Deleuze & Guattari, 1987/1980). Or through conceptualizing participants as haeccities, individuations that are not a person but relations of intensities, I can recognize how a human is not necessarily a self, but an event that is not an individual subject (Deleuze & Guattari, 1987/1980). In other words, by experimenting with consciously applying different concepts to analyze empirical matter, it is possible to bring into view that which is erased by the concepts that are habitually applied. Intensities that were enveloped in other intensities and relations are allowed to come to the fore, functioning to constitute different meanings and change the whole.

Playing with Possibilities: A Demonstration

I like to play with paradigms, theories, data and autoethnography, allowing them to join and break free, becoming in ways unexpected. Such play, for me, does not begin with a question, but emerges from tensions between stories. Poststructural autoethnographies erupt from the pinch of stories I am told and tell myself on my fabulas of absolute – those narratives I hold with white knuckles out of fear if I let them go, my world will fragment into absence. In this space, there are no questions; there are no answers to be found. There is only the pushing/breaking of narration of self and society in order to become differently. So, as one begins to play with poststructural autoethnography, it is not enough to merely rehearse an experience. One breaks open the narrative tensions, cracking the fabulas of that which we cannot live without. One writes (Richardson, 2000), gets lost (Lather, 2007) in order to become differently (Deleuze, 1987/1980).

In the following I share a few long excerpts from several of my autoethnographies in order to illustrate the following: (1) how poststructural autoethnography emerges not with a question, but in the tension between narratives, (2) how in this methodology data is played against/with each other in order to create an opportunity to think differently and (3) how theoretical perspective functions in the construction of autoethnography. Each of the following excerpts began as a sadness that jumped on a passion, but not all autoethnography need begin this way. Yet for me, it primarily does.

Playing Between Emancipate and Deconstruct

"Learning to be an American" (Kaufmann, 2009) is an autoethnographic text of my experiences with American and Iranian culture. In this piece, there is no question, nor is an explicit concept by which to construct meaning given. There is, however, an underlying political critique which emerges in the unstable relations between data – poetry, personal experience, published history and media reports. This instability is intended to illustrate the ineffable absence of meaning and violence of identity (personal, cultural, political) narratives. Thus, my political intent is critical, but my theoretical perspective is

poststructural, situating this autoethnography in the fissures between the paradigms of emancipate and deconstruct. An excerpt follows:

Seattle, Washington, August 12, 1978: Me, a young white woman, sun stream-
ing through stained glass windows, Mendelssohn's wedding march, and a man
who resembles Omar Sharif. My world collapses open.

> In the silence of the temple of desire
> I am lying beside your passionate body;
> My kisses have left their marks on your shoulders
> Like fiery bites of a snake.
> *(Forough Farrokhzad as cited by Kianush, 1997)*

Published history: In 1901 Englishman William Knox-D'Arcy bought oil
exploitation rights from the Iranian government. Seven years later he discovered
oil and the Anglo-Persian Oil Company (AIOC), later known as British Petro-
leum (BP), was formed. With the discovery of oil, "Iran became a strategic
interest of great importance to Britain, and the European penetration into both
state and society was accelerated" (Ansari, 2006, pp. 10–11). When many in
Iran became disenchanted with the inequitable distribution of profits, approximately 2:1, nationalization efforts emerged. The British response to these efforts
was "an air of disbelief at the 'ingratitude' of the Iranians" (Ansari, 2006,
p. 132). This arrogant response fueled nationalization efforts and in 1952, under
the leadership of Mohammed Mosaddeq, Iranian parliament unanimously voted
to nationalize the oil fields, and the British were expelled from the country.
One month later, Mossadeq, hailed as a national hero and defender against
Western Imperialism, was democratically elected Prime Minister. He was for-
cibly removed from office in a coup backed by the United States and Britain
and remained under house arrest for the remainder of his life (Albright, 2000;
Ansari, 2006; Keddie, 2006). It was Kermit Roosevelt, grandson of President
Theodore Roosevelt and senior CIA agent, who carried the coup agreement to
the Shah and gave him, upon receipt of his signature, the equivalent of US$15
million. In the decade following the coup, U.S. military aid topped $500
million, the armed forces increased from 120,000 to 200,000, and SAVAK,
Iranian intelligence, was created (Ansari, 2006).

> No one thought of love any longer
> No one thought of triumph any longer
> No one
> Thought of anything any longer
> In the caves of loneliness
> Futility was born.
> *(Baraheni, 1977)*

MaShar: Iran, 1987: I walk down the dirt road to buy myself morning bread. Everyone else has long been up, but as the American wife, I sleep in. In a little hut, closed on three sides and roofed, sits a wooden table. Behind the table is a large, open, upright wood stove. Above the fire propped up on rocks is a rack. One man flattens the dough, patting it between his hands, and throws it down toward the second man who picks it up with a long wooden spatula. With an in-stroke the man standing in front of the fire tosses the flat bread on the left side of the rack. With a side-stroke he flips the browning dough, moving the bread from left to right, and with an out-stroke he pulls the cooked bread from the kiln and piles it on the right end of the table. Mostly it is his body I remember: a thin, gnarly wrist bone, ankles bones long and triangular. He has no shoes. The heels are cracked, jagged crevices filled with dust. A light beige cotton dress shirt and dark brown cotton trousers drip. He is saturated with sweat. I walk home with my bread. I sit on the Persian carpet in front of a table cloth that has been prepared for me, a white cloth set with strawberry jam, butter, tea, sugar cubes, and feta.

Seattle, Washington, 1989–2000: A single mother focused on survival, I await my earned income credits and occasional child support payment. Violin lessons, gas bills, laundry mats, and public transportation. I love my daughter with a passion. Thoughts of politics vanish.

January 29, 2002: "States like these [Iran, Iraq, and North Korea], and their terrorist allies, constitute an axis of evil" (Bush, 2002).

Playing In/With Deconstruct

The next example is an autoethnography of stories that live in my body. Here, I rely on the poststructural theories of Deleuze and Guattari (1987/1980), Butler (1990) and Caputo (1993). The data represented in this piece is literally (or imaginatively) texts that live in my body and theories from the above authors. Meaning is ephemeral as it emerges and dissipates in the representation of its parts. Following is a snippet of "I Spit to Meet You on a Line Unfolding" (Kaufmann, 2012):

> I collect stories in my body. Each stuffed in tissue, wrapped in muscle, packaged for oblivion. Oblivion is a lie. Each story sings a continuously repeating cacophonous melody at full volume without sound – vibrating, coagulating my body, pulling my neck, tightening my shoulders, twisting my back. Sometimes one breaks through. I shiver "Ah and you too." I love my stories. I must because I protect them diligently. But, they are getting heavy. So I have begun to lay them down, one by one, with a breath or when I am being contrary, a tantrum.
>
> Breath. I breathed stories all week, pulling visions from my body. Practicing on the bus and in the bathtub, I solidified the story I would

tell. I sat at the southeastern corner of the table in my Women Studies course and waited my turn to present my rendition of what it means to be a woman. At the opposite end of the table, next to the window, sat a white woman with long brown hair, pulled loosely and clipped. Light from the window glistened on misguided tendrils. I can see her out of the corner of my left eye. Most of the words I shared that afternoon are gone; I dropped a few on 81st Street in Ballard, Washington, several disappeared in the sand of Puget Sound, a few were swallowed and later shat. What remains of my fabula are unconnected signifiers that mean more than they should and the last line "To be a woman is to live with maggots on my breath." Silence too long. And then I peripherally see brown tendrils move, a slow twitch followed by a jerk forward. In a voice beginning in a broken whisper and shallowly inhaled to a halted hysteria, the woman with the glistening tendrils said, "How dare you. How dare you! How dare you tell me that story? You had no right to tell me that story without warning me." Energy from my throat chakra, frayed and scared, reached across the table and surrounded her words, bound them tightly, and pulled them in, lodging maggots on my breath.

And:

My stories of you are my stories of me denied. Blaming, judging, healing you is my diversion from the pains of my folds. You, without a face, allow me to plug my ears from the howling of my own body and propel us toward demise. May I take my stories out of your body in search for the status of the same.

And... And... And...:

I savor stories like pebbles in my mouth. I suck them dry and produce saliva to swallow. With a mouth full of spit, I have begun to wonder how my stories influence my capacity for life – to breathe, to eat, to move – and also my capacity to work – to use qualitative research as a tool to make a better world to come (Deleuze, 1995). I am wondering if the cacophonous vibration of my stories instigates a repetitive performance which may have the capacity for variation (Butler, 1990), but alters little in amplitude in each repetition, thus performing the relatively same. Collecting stories, housing them in my body, I am beginning to think, allows me little space to become a world to come (Deleuze, 1995). My stories fold you and me.

To become a humanity I must chew the pebbles in my mouth, unwrap the tales in my tissue, and spit them onto the earth so they can be transformed to loam. I spit to meet you on a line unfolding.

Playing More With/In Deconstruct

The final example represents my struggle with the ethics of representing others. I ask myself: Do I have the right to write you? Is there a me to write without an/other? If there is no me without an/other and I am barred by my ethics to write you, how do I write (live?) at all? Challenged by these issues, I played with the possibilities of writing an autoethnography without an/other. Data is generated from my imagination, theory and pencil drawings. Imagination data are stories in my head and in my body, or if one is esoteric, perhaps in the ethers. They may appear as vivid photographs, which I attempt to paint with words. Other times they hum behind a fog, and I search with blind fingertips to find them, whole or torn. Often, these data are not there at all, but emerge in the writing, coming to form as I stare at my computer and allow my fingers freedom. Theory data are bits of structured thoughts of others, philosophies of the way we construct our world that I use to help me think differently. Pencil drawings are etchings, done in moments of sadness, I keep in an old Mac box. (I seem to only feel the passion to generate data when I am sad, when the world breaks my heart.) In the following, I interrupt imagination data and pencil drawings with theory data, specifically the thoughts of Deleuze and Guattari (1987), in an attempt to disrupt the notion of myself as a subject. This attempt to represent a desubjectification of self is situated in the paradigm of deconstruct, and meaning is understood as delusional. An excerpt of "An Autoethnography of a Face" (Kaufmann, 2011b) follows:

> I know myself. Do I dare tell? You, I fear, will think I am crazy. Not just silly, but delusional. And I don't want you to go away; a-loneliness-stalks-my-body.
>
> I am a haeccity (Deleuze & Guattari, 1987). Formed by a collection of ever changing elements that fold into a nodal point – biological matters, discourses, energies, bodies … swirling, connecting, and coagulating. Lines, only lines without direction, signified by a proper name that desig-nates not an individual, but "an instantaneous apprehension of a multi-plicity" (p. 37). As a haeccity, I have my semiotic of expression: "Proper names, verbs in the infinitive and indefinite articles or pronouns," which are to be read without pause (p. 264). Jodi-to-become-a-face.
>
> Lines of words spill from my tongue. A sentence on a line in an assem-blage of the face on my cheek. I know by your silence I spoke with the wrong face. Invitations not answered. Text message box empty. Watch-ing your back walk away, I pick the syllables off the floor. A-depression-becomes-the-body.
>
> I am faces. I walk the lines of their assemblages, existing in multiple bodies at once. I fold my bodies within a singular face. The howls of becoming an organism less agonizing than the sight of your back.

FIGURE 7.1

A Conclusion or And, And, And

How one ends depends on how one begins. The structure of a conclusion shifts according to the paradigm grounding the work. So how do I end as I have written in and between paradigms? Do I follow my assumption of your desire and conclude within the structure of understand and emancipate? Or do I embrace my desire and stop my writing in the paradigm of deconstruct? Neglecting neither of us, not wanting to be co-dependent or narcissistic, I offer both:

Understand/Emancipate: A Conclusion

Autoethnography is a respected methodology. From its emergence as side notes and diary entries to its current position as a methodology of award winning dissertations and books, autoethnography is a methodology that is not only respected, but has the capacity to give us insight into our pedagogical practices and the power to change the structures of our world. For the literacy scholar

FIGURE 7.2

and practitioner, the possibilities for autoethnography are endless, as she examines the relations of self and culture in the practice of literacy: How does my White privilege function in the literacy of my students? How does my dismissal of popular culture inhibit a literacy connection with my students? Where do I constitute my student/s as unworthy to read? These questions are important, and require deep personal reflection and honesty. Autoethnography is not for the timid. The journey is often painful as one uncovers pieces of self that are ugly – racial prejudice, misogyny, apathy. But the journey is worth it, as one works to create a just and equitable world.

Deconstruct: And... And... And...

There is no ending. Conclusions are artificial; I might even say violent. They cut a signifying boundary, tossing the remainder to absence. There is only difference and middles and...

I closed my eyes to read the world and he died. They found him floating in an eddy. The upper left corner of my heart dried, dehydrating into cracks. I breathe panic because I forgot to live... and... and...

Sculpting my experience with words, I become differently. And in this becoming I desire to un/fold a world to come. This world is not of being, there already waiting my arrival; it is only potential that un/comes as I write ... and... and... and...

Generate data from anywhere; constitute it with joy. Write the self and the other with kindness, seeking to realize possibilities unthought. Be willing to not know (Lather, 2007), and play with abandon. Poststructural (PS) autoethnography I love you ...

Note

1. I am grateful to Norman Denzin, Editor and Chief of *Qualitative Inquiry* and *International Review of Qualitative Research*, for his permission to use modified versions of previously published works in this chapter.

References

Albright, M. (2000). *Remarks before the American-Iranian Council*. Retrieved March 25, 2008, from www.fas.org/news/iran/2000/000317a.htm.

Ansari, A. (2006). *Modern Iran*. Harlow, UK: Pearson Longman.

Bal, M. (1999). *Narratology: Introduction to the theory of narrative*. Toronto, Ontario: University of Toronto Press.

Baraheni, R. (1977). *The crowned cannibals: Writings on repression in Iran*. New York: Vintage Books.

Braidotti, R. (2006). *Transpositions: On nomadic ethics*. New York: Polity Press.

Brinkman, S. (2009). Literature as qualitative inquiry: The novelist as researcher. *Qualitative Inquiry, 15*(8), 1376–1394.

Bush, G. (2002). President's State of the Union Address. Retrieved May 2, 2008, from www.whitehouse.gov/news/releases/2002/01/20020129-11.html.

Butler, J. (1990). *Gender trouble: Feminism and the subversion of identity*. New York: Routledge.

Butler, J. (1993). *Bodies that matter: On the discursive limits of "sex."* New York: Routledge.

Caputo, J. (1993). *Against ethics: Contributions to a poetics of obligation with constant reference to deconstruction*. Bloomington, IN: Indiana University Press.

Crotty, M. (1998). *The foundations of social research: Meaning and perspective in the research process*. Thousand Oaks, CA: Sage Publications.

Deleuze, G. (1994). *Difference and repetition* (P. Patton, Trans.). New York: Columbia University Press. (Original work published 1968.)

Deleuze, G. (1995). *Negotiations* (M. Joughin, Trans.). New York: Columbia University Press.

Deleuze, G. & Guattari, F. (1987/1980). *A thousand plateaus: Capitalism and schizophrenia* (B. Massumi, Trans.). Minneapolis, MN: University of Minnesota Press.

Derrida, J. (1997/1974). *Of grammatology* (Gayatri Chakravorty Spivak, Trans.). Baltimore, MD: Johns Hopkins University Press.

Ellis, C. (1995). *Final negotiation.* Philadelphia, PA: Temple University Press.

Ellis, C. & Bochner, A. (2000). Autoethnography, personal narrative, reflexivity: Researcher as subject. In N. Denzin and Y. Lincoln (Eds.), *Handbook of qualitative research* (pp. 733–768). Thousand Oaks, CA: Sage Publications.

Foucault, M. (1980). *Power and knowledge: Selected interviews and other writings: 1972–1977* (C. Gordon, L. Marshall, J. Mephar & K. Sopher, Trans.). New York: Panteon.

Harper, D. (2003). Framing photographic ethnography: A case study. *Ethnography, 4*(2), 241–264.

Jones, K. (2010). *Bournemouth University Centre for qualitative research, master class in theoretical improvisation of research data.* Retrieved January 25, 2010, from www.bournemouth.ac.uk/cqr/rescqrmc.09.html.

Kaufmann, J. (2009). Learning to be an American. *International Review of Qualitative Research, 1*(4), 461–470.

Kaufmann, J. (2011a). Heteronarrative analysis: Examining online photographic narratives. *International Journal of Qualitative Studies in Education, 24*(1), 7–26.

Kaufmann, J. (2011b). An autoethnography of a face. *Qualitative Inquiry, 18*(4), 913–916.

Kaufmann, J. (2012). I spit to meet you on a line unfolding. *Qualitative Inquiry, 18*(1), 16–19.

Keddie, N. (2006). *Modern Iran: Roots and results of revolution.* New Haven, CT: Yale University Press.

Kianush, M. (1997). Forugh Farrokhzad. Retrieved March 23, 2008, from www.artarena.com/forugh.htm.

Klein, C. (1995). *Meeting the great bliss queen: Buddhists, feminists, and the art of the self.* Boston: Beacon.

Lather, P. (2006). Paradigm proliferation as a good thing to think with: Teaching research in education as wild profusion. *International Journal of Qualitative Studies in Education, 19*(1), 35–57.

Lather, P. (2007). *Getting lost: Feminist efforts toward a double(d) science.* New York: SUNY Press.

Laura, C. (2011). *Being bad: My baby brother and the social ecology of discipline.* Unpublished doctoral dissertation, University of Illinois, Chicago, IL.

Malinowski, B. (1922). *Argonauts of the Western Pacific.* London: Routledge.

Malinowski, B. (1967). *A diary in the strict sense of the word.* New York: Harcourt, Brace and World.

Marcus, B., Machilek, F. & Schutz, A. (2006). Personality in cyberspace: Personal websites as media for personality expression and impressions. *Journal of Personality and Social Psychology, 90*(6), 1014–1031.

Markham, A. (1998). *Life online.* Lanham, MD: Alta Mira.

Pink, S., Kurti, L. & Afonso, A. (Eds.). (2004). *Visual research and representation in ethnography.* London: Routledge.

Prior, L. (2003). *Using documents in social research.* Thousand Oaks, CA: Sage Publishers.

Reed-Danahay, D. (1997). *Auto/ethnography: Rewriting the self and the social.* New York: Berg.

Richardson, L. (2000). Writing as a method of inquiry. In N. Denzin and Y. Lincoln (Eds.). *Handbook of qualitative research* (pp. 923–943). Thousand Oaks, CA: Sage Publications.

Rollings, J. (2004). Messing around with identity constructs: Pursuing a poststructural and poetic aesthetic. *Qualitative Inquiry, 10*(4), 548–557.

Snead, T. (2010). *Dichotomous musical worlds: Interactions between the musical lives of adolescents and school music-learning culture.* Unpublished doctoral dissertation, Georgia State University, Atlanta, GA.

Spry, T. (2001). Performing autoethnography: An embodied methodological praxis. *Qualitative Inquiry, 7*(6), 706–732.

St. Pierre, E. (1997). Methodology in the fold and the irruption of transgressive data. *International Journal of Qualitative Studies in Education, 10*(2), 175–189.

Stinson, D. (2009). The proliferation of theoretical paradigms quandary: How one novice researcher used eclecticism as a solution. *Qualitative Report, 14*(3), 498–523.

Schwandt, T. (2000). Three epistemological stances for qualitative inquiry: Interpretivism, hermeneutics, and social constructionism. In N. Denzin and Y. Lincoln (Eds.), *Handbook of qualitative research* (pp. 189–214). Thousand Oaks, CA: Sage Publications.

Vitdal-Ortiz, S. (2004). On being a white person of color: Using autoethnography to understand Puerto Ricans' racialization. *Qualitative Sociology, 27*(2), 179–201.

Williams, J. (2004). *Gilles Deleuze's difference and repetition: A critical guide.* Edinburgh, Scotland: Edinburgh Press.

8

TEXTS, AFFECTS, AND RELATIONS IN CULTURAL PERFORMANCE

An Embodied Analysis of Dramatic Inquiry

Carmen Medina and Mia Perry

> Acting people are acting bodies.
> *(Shilling, 2003, p. 8)*

For a number of years in our collaborative work as drama and theatre educators, we have been exploring the question of how to analyze the complex landscape of performance pedagogies and student engagement in performative experiences (Medina, 2006, 2004a, 2004b; Perry, 2011; Perry & Medina, 2011; Weltsek & Medina, 2007). Classroom-based dramatic inquiry (within language arts curricular experiences amongst others) is often the center of these experiences. Through collaboration we have spent significant time wrestling with questions of approach and method to the analysis of dramatic inquiry. We have considered the practice in relation to performance and cultural studies (Diamond, 1996), social semiotics (Franks, 2004), feminist and gender perspectives (Butler, 1990, 2005; Cruz, 2001; Grosz, 1994), social theory (Ford & Brown, 2005; Shilling, 2003), and affect theory (Leander & Rowe, 2006; Ling, 2009; St. Pierre, 1997). During the course of our work in this field, we have found the notion of embodiment to be essential to a methodology that is concerned with teaching and learning. We understand embodiment in education to

> [describe] teaching and learning in acknowledgement of our bodies as whole experiential beings in motion, both inscribed and inscribing subjectivities. That is, the experiential body is both a representation of self (a "text") as well as a mode of creation in progress (a "tool"). In addition, embodiment is a state that is contingent upon the environment and the context of the student.
> *(Perry & Medina, 2011, p. 63)*

Moving through theoretical and methodological positionings in this field, we have searched for frameworks that may support our understanding of performance as a set of signs as well as a site for action and creation in meaning making and becoming. What we aim to share in this chapter is how we perceive the learner to be simultaneously inscribing and inscribed by social codes and cultural performances that get created, reproduced, and recontextualized in particular moments in time. This inscription occurs through engagement in activities and in relation to the multiple histories and subjectivities that performers bring to a creative moment (Pineau, 2005). In addition, we consider the affective dimension in these performance-based encounters. In this way, we consider the participant as a relational body/mind/self who through sensing, responding, and expressing is always becoming or "in motion" (Ellsworth, 2005) and creating new forms of participation. Therefore both the cultural-historical social performance and embodied engagement of the participant are at the core of how we approach analysis in dramatic practices in education.

Moving forward, we propose a theoretical model that helps us consider the discursive in relation to cultural production; embodiment in relation to identity and practices; and representations in relation to affect and interrelation. In this chapter we share our approach to, and method of, data analysis of these aspects focusing on the multiple layers of performance engagement (which we will summarize here as texts, affects, and relations). Our intention is to share the ways in which an embodied analysis of performance in education can encompass a rich and nuanced process of consideration, affording both clear narratives of interpretation as well as an attention to affect, relation, and contingency in our "findings."

The next section of this chapter will further unpack the theoretical context of our proposed analytical model. From there we will describe our process of analysis. Based on data generated with second-grade students in an urban elementary school in Puerto Rico, we proceed in this chapter to demonstrate an analysis of the experiences constructed by the students and teachers as they negotiate media discourses, improvised content, and their own subjectivities to co-create a short performance dealing with violence in their society.

Situating the Field

In developing new possibilities for analysis in the field of drama/theatre/ performance in education, it has been important to look at the trajectory of this evolving field. Although an historical analysis is beyond the scope of this chapter, it is significant to reflect on how much of the research in this field has taken place in social constructivist and phenomenological paradigms. Over its relatively short history, the field has predominantly moved between descriptive accounts of practice, reflective practitioner research, and more recently critical ethnographic inquiries. Taking from this both rich and complicated history of research in the field, we have ventured into other fields of scholarship in order to develop a methodology that allows space for, if not answers to, the complexity of performance-based inquiry in education. Specifically, we draw from embodiment studies, cultural performance studies, and theories of affect, and we will touch on each of these areas below.

Embodiment and Social Inscriptions

Scholarship in embodiment studies reflects a notable advocacy in relation to the absence of the body. The notion of the absent body, particularly in phenomenology (Merleau-Ponty, 1962; van Manen, 1997), and the social theory (Leder, 1990; Shilling, 2012), emerges as a critique of Cartesian dualism between mind and body that positions the mind at the center of who we are and how we come to "know" things. The critique of the absent body, particularly from a gender and feminist perspective (Cruz, 2001; Grosz, 1994) and from cultural performance theory (Diamond, 1996), can then be understood as a form of political action in relation to what counts as knowing, where and how it is produced and experienced. This context became informative as we wrestled with the challenges and objectives of embodied analysis that works toward shifting a dominant paradigm within social science research.

An important element in understanding the historical and theoretical context of embodied methodologies is the multiplicity of perspectives that have been put to use, perspectives that have in most cases been seen to be working in opposition to one another. Much work on embodiment points to the limits or glorification of a particular theoretical or analytical perspective and not necessarily in dialogue with each other. Table 8.1 lists some of these perspectives along with corresponding claims to help readers situate our analysis in the context of the range of approaches to embodied theories and methodologies that are available.

It seems that scholarship on embodiment is acquiring relevance across disciplines. Bryan Turner in his work on body and society speaks of a "somatic society" to describe how the body in modern social systems has become "the principal field of political and cultural activity" particularly through media and new technologies (cited in Shilling, 2012, p. 1). Despite the influence of media and technologies, bodies and embodiment are at the core of how we engage in complex social systems as learners, and indeed as consumers, producers, and participants of networks of images that portray lifestyles and ways of being. These narratives trigger particular desires that become complex dynamics of longing and belonging (Pugh, 2009), and where new embodied subjectivities emerge as people play and enact identities. According to Grosz (1994) these subjectivities emerge within the complex embodied landscape of "social inscriptions" where:

> the body, or bodies, cannot be adequately understood as ahistorical, precultural, or natural objects in any simple way; they are not only inscribed,

marked, engraved, by social pressures external to them but are the products, the direct effects, of the very social constitution of nature itself.

(p. 15)

This notion of social inscriptions guides our analysis as we examine how the
body is inscribed and produced within a particular dramatic inquiry moment.
We are interested, as we will share in the data analysis section, on the mapping
of cultural performances and the social inscriptions that mark the body and that
emerge from the body as new forms of embodiment as it interacts, relates, feels,
and creates in dramatic inquiry.

Social Inscriptions in Cultural Performance

Performance theorist Judith Butler (1990, 2005; Butler, Laclau, & Zizek, 2000)
perceives the study of performativity as a lens to interpret social relations, particularly in the ways it allows us to see "performativity as a cultural ritual, as the
reiteration of cultural norms, as the habitus of the body in which structural and
social dimensions of meaning are not finally separable" (Butler et al., 2000,

TABLE 8.1 Embodiment: perspectives on theory, analysis, and key claims

Embodiment: perspectives on theory and analysis	Key claims
Biological body (naturalistic)	The body "is" when it is born. Its finalized physiology determines who we are and how we behave.
Body as sign (semiotics)	The body as a site for the production of meaning. The body as representational, as text.
Body as unity (phenomenology)	The body as a part of the conscious self, affecting perception and experience accordingly. Every experience is therefore considered as embodied, and every self as a unity present only to itself. In this way, there is no "other" accounted for.
Experiential, relational, and sensational body (poststructuralism, affect theory)	Bodies as a fluid and unfinished entity, always becoming in relation to forces of affect.
Embodiment as cultural practice (social theory, cultural performance, critical feminist)	The body is completed in engagement with cultural practices. History and cultural discourses are reproduced and recontextualized in/through our bodies (the gendered body, racial body, popular culture body, etc.)
Discursive body (Foucault)	The body as discourse embedded with, and positioned by, structures of power.

p. 29). In her work, similar to other scholars in performance studies, "actors" are perceived to take stances, enact discourses and social actions in relation to the multiple positionings that reiterate particular cultural norms and expectations (for other perspectives on social theory and action see Wohlwend's chapter in this book). Identity then in cultural performance, as Butler (1990) suggests, works constructed and constructing and within and against the regulatory practices and discourses that aim to create a false or fictional stable self through "culturally intelligible grids" (p. 184) such as gender, race, socioeconomic status. In performance from a sociocultural perspective bodies, language, images, movement, and all the complex range of textual practices that make a performative moment to emerge, could be traced to normative discourses and ways of being that get recreated, recontextualized, and reinvented in any improvisational moment. Nevertheless, within the making of any performative moment the possibility for emergence and ruptures for new embodied discourses exists. In her later work Butler (2005) is concerned with a perspective on performance that questions and acknowledges the role of emergence, improvisation, and thinking beyond reproduction. She challenges social theorists and asks: "How would the new be produced from an analysis of the social field that remains restricted to inversions, aporias, and reversals that work regardless of time and place?" (p. 29). The performative, then, is not only grounded on what gets reproduced within larger social norms, but also a means to maintain, disrupt, and improvise identities within these dynamics in ways that

> certain practices of recognition or, indeed, certain breakdowns in the practice of recognition mark a site of rupture within the horizon of normativity and implicitly call for the institution of new norms, putting into question the givenness of the prevailing normative horizon.
>
> *(2005, p. 24)*

When identities are understood as such, we are able to see the political constitution and the fabricated notions that frame hierarchies of power in identity constructs and how these are made visible in the performative moment in relation with the emergence of new social inscriptions. Dolan (1993) believes these new social inscriptions that are possible emerge in experiences such as dramatic inquiry, as "social subjects perform themselves in negotiation with the delimiting cultural conventions of the geography within which they moved" (p. 419). Performing, learning, and embodiment then are marked by context and environment where the histories and cultural inscriptions that allow us to participate in particular social contexts could be not only reproduced but also improvised, reframed, and for new contexts, ways of being and participating to emerge. This is a major focus in our data analysis as we engage in the process of tracing the trajectory of what social norms are recontextualized but also what emerges as new embodied knowledge in interactions with the complex histories and geographies participants bring to create an improvisational moment.

Introducing Affect

Looking back in our field, from the enlightenment philosophy of Kant, to contemporary paradigms in education, there is a strong conviction that experience is more than that which is represented or representational. Lyotard's aesthetic of the sublime draws directly from Kant, "The region of the sublime [being] the distance between [the] faculties of conception and presentation" (Quick, 1994, p. 30). Phenomenology (Merleau-Ponty, 1962; van Manen, 1997), complexity theory (Mason, 2008; Sumara, 2000), feminist theory (Braidotti, 1993; Grosz, 1994; Grumet & McCoy, 2000), and poststructural theories in education (Ellsworth, 2005; St. Pierre & Pillow, 2000) are among the contemporary bodies of work that address, to varying degrees, non-representational concepts in education. Experience beyond that which is represented is very often accepted as real, yet underexplored as an element of pedagogy or art practice.

In order to make sense of embodiment and performance studies as applied to research in dramatic inquiry in education, we have found it essential to consider experience beyond representation terms. We turn, therefore, to registers of affect, sensation, and interrelation. Affect is succinctly described by Leander and Rowe (2006) as "the change that occurs when bodies come into contact" (with other forces); they explain, "affective intensities are the forces between bodies through their contact or collision rather than an expression of their qualities as things" (p. 433). A sensation is a similar force but it implies the involvement of the bodily senses; it is an affect that is visceral, physical, and results in embodied change. Put in other words, "Sensation is the affect, which is neither subjective nor objective; rather it is both at once: we become in sensation and at the same time something happens because of it" (Boundas, 2005, p. 131).

Considering affect in relation to, and in addition to, critical models of social, cultural, or discourse-based analyses has been demonstrated in research for at least the past decade (Ngai, 2002, 2005). Indeed, Patricia Clough (2010) suggests that the turn to affect in critical theory and cultural criticism provided the opportunity for expansive and exploratory work due to the fact that it allowed a consideration of experience both in terms of "what is empirically realised and in terms of the philosophical conception of the virtual" (p. 208). Said another way, this analytical endeavor takes up experience not only in terms of its representational indicators (signs, texts, images, etc.), but in terms of the affects, sensations, and relations that it prompts the consideration of. Reminiscent of many poststructural thinkers in research, we look at data in terms of what is happening (empirically and conceptually), as opposed to what is done, or what is meant (Conquergood, 2002; Deleuze & Guattari, 1987; Sontag, 1999; St. Pierre, 1997). This shift in focus moves us beyond a consideration of the represented.

Developing a Framework for Analysis

When analyzing cultural performance we develop a set of questions grounded on the key concepts we discussed above—embodiment, performativity, and affect—as well as the data in question. We carefully read, watch, and reflect on the data in order to generate responses to the guiding questions. Across this work, common considerations relate to the explicit and implicit forces, the relationships, and the multiple social, political, and historical contexts that are always at play. In the case of the research that we share in this chapter, the following questions guide embodied performative analysis.

Questioning Embodied Performance in the Classroom

1. What is represented through texts (spatial, physical, verbal, etc.) in relation to emerging narratives, identity constructs (such as gender, race, class), and relationships (between peers, between content and curriculum, between instruction and activity)?
2. How are cultural norms, histories, and knowledges inscribed or disrupted in a particular performative moment?
3. What relationships and dynamics (affects and forces) can be observed between bodies, between positions, material and immaterial contexts, instruction and action?
4. What is happening in this process (as seen through all the above mentioned foci)? What and how are changes, events, creations occurring?

The following section provides an introduction to, and background of, the data in question. From this basis, we will return back to the four guiding questions and proceed to illustrate an analytic process.

Embodiment, Cultural Performance, and Affect: Analyzing the Embodiment of Violence

Background

A group of second-grade students in Puerto Rico worked on the creation of a performed video with the fictional objective of generating a media campaign that makes visible the consequences of violence on the island; particularly, they decided to focus on the violent murder of innocent bystanders to a crime. The video project was embedded in a larger student-led inquiry unit developed on the theme of "tolerance." The unit was triggered by a violent episode children witnessed through the local news involving a women at a local pub who was waiting to use the restroom and who shot another woman who did not want to wait her turn in line. This violent event made it to the headlines of national media and was part of a larger Puerto Rican media culture of "prensa amarillista" (yellow press) that feeds into highly emotional and sensational representations of local violence. While violence is a tangible complex reality in contemporary Puerto Rico (approximately 1,000 violent crimes were reported in 2011), it is presented and manipulated by media as a normalized lifestyle, and used as a resource to create fear and dependence. This materializes through, for example, sensationalized representations of dead bodies, live performed shootings, and emotional attachments. What becomes interesting in the analysis we take on here is the children's enactment of a mediatized performance and the improvised, relational and social meanings that are constructed.

Here we share three images and the corresponding script including a description of actions to give a sense of the kind of work the students produced. Nevertheless, in the process of analysis we worked with the entire video rather than these specific three photos. It is significant to acknowledge the importance of developing an analysis in relation to the whole improvisational experience. A performance event is never produced in a vacuum or in isolation from its contexts and it should always be contextualized as a whole and in relation to the multiple locations, people, and artifacts that exist materially in that moment (school, hallway, girls, boys, second graders, chairs, etc.) and the ones that are evoked within the improvisation (the street, a house, prison, woman bystander, robber, guns, cell phones, etc.).

FIGURE 8.1 Niñas pillo/Girl robbers' complicity in justifying and strategizing robbery

FIGURE 8.2 Niña pillo #1/Girl robber #1 shooting a man

FIGURE 8.3 Boys shooting a bystander

The violence in this scene is represented in the context of, or in the service of, a socially oriented message to eradicate this type of behavior. This approach to current and local affairs is one that can be seen as expected, and supported in schools and within the critical literacy inquiry that was taking place at that moment in the classroom. The children are performing an example of a tragic consequence of this type of violent behavior (e.g., the death of two innocent people as a result of one person's need/desire for money) in order to support a final choral message of "No usar armas" (Don't use weapons) as a strategic expression of a solution to the problem presented.

Table 8.3 indicates the points of interest and relevance that we took from the data in line with the four guiding questions (above).

Using Table 8.3 as a stepping-stone, the narrative of analysis that follows represents the results of our review of the data informed and framed with the theoretical lens taken up in the process. In this way, what you will find below is an interwoven text that includes specific data references, consequent ideas, propositions, and questions, all contextualized transparently in relation to a theoretical perspective. With the objective of organizing the analysis narrative, we have divided the following section into three areas, each articulating a different treatment of the subject of violence.

Knowing Violence

Considering and interacting within the above set of relationships and affects makes visible ways of doing and knowing violence. Children in school uniforms, engaging in dramatic inquiry as instructed by the teacher, actively play with their roles as classmates and their knowledge and ideas of violent and innocent activities. Students bring unsanctioned knowledge (also, limited and contingent knowledge) into the space of school that brings coherence to the

TABLE 8.2 Improvisation transcript

Spanish (original text)	English (translation)
Dos pillos parados una frente a la otra. Ambas son niñas.	[Two robbers facing each other. Both are girls.]
niña/pillo #1: *Chica, no tenemos chavos ¿que vamos a hacer?* [Manos abiertas. Recostando la cabeza hacia un lado y haciendo un movimiento ligero de "no."]	girl/robber #2: *Girl, we don't have any money, what are we going to do?* [Takes one step back. Hand gesture pointing opening arms and head slightly moving side to side giving a "no" expression.]
niña/pillo #2: *Ni yo tampoco.* [Toma un paso hacia atrás. Gesto de manos abiertas y la cabeza se mueve en un leve gesto de un lado a otro diciendo que "no."]	girl/robber #2: *I don't have either.* [Takes one step back. Hand gesture pointing opening arms and head slightly moves side to side doing a "no" expression.]
niña/pillo #1: *¡Tenemos que robar!* [Manos abiertas. Gesto con mano señalándose a ella misma y luego a la otra pillo.] *porque tu sabes como yo soy. Yo no quiero ser pobre.* [Ambas chocan las manos.] *¡Vamos!*	girl/robber #1: *We have to rob someone!* [Hands open. Hand gesture pointing first to self and then to other robber.] *because you know how I am. I don't want to be poor.* [Claps hands together. Hand expression getting rid of "dirt" from hands.] [Both girls/robbers high five] *Let's go!*
[niña/pillo #2 camina hacia un lado del pasillo para ejecutar el robo. No se actúa el robo como tal sino que esta implícito. Ella se vira y empuja una silla que representa un camión y regresa a donde pillo #1 luego del robo.]	[girl/robber #2 walks over to one side of the hallway to conduct the robbery. The actual robbery is not acted out but instead it is implied. She then turns around and pulls a chair across the hallway, which represents a truck, and comes back to girl/robber #1 after the robbing takes place.]
niña/pillo #1: *¿Dejaste unos chavos?* [Ella se mueve hacia atrás y sube las manos en expresión de frustración y luego apunta hacia donde se llevo a cabo el robo.]	girl/robber #1: *Did you leave some money behind?* [She moves back, raises hands in a gesture of frustration and then points to the area where the "robbery" took place.]
niña/pillo #2: *No se.*	girl/robber #2: *I don't know*

[Girl/robber #1 walks toward the other corner of the hallway where there is a boy in the role of a man. The man is lying on the floor supposedly in his house sleeping. The man wakes up. Girl/robber #1 kicks him and both wrestle for a moment. She points her hand to the man imitating a gun.]

man robbed: *Don't kill me.* [Covering his body with his hands] girl/robber #1: *Yes I am going to kill you. Pum!* [The girl/robber's hand moves up as she shoots the gun and her body moves backs from the speed and weight of the bullet coming from the gun. The robbed man curves his body as he receives the impact from the gun and falls to the floor.]

[Girl/robber #1 walks away from the crime scene and meets girl/robber #2, then two boys/policemen followed her. A girl/bystander, talking on a cell phone, crosses the street in front of girl/robber #1 and #2. Girls/robbers #1 and #2 hide behind the bystander/girl crossing the street and two shooters shoot the bystander/girl. The girl/bystander falls on the floor.]

boys/men with guns: *Let's go, let's go.* [All except the girl/bystander run away and hide behind walls.]

[All characters come out of role, walk to the center, high five each other, embrace each other, bow to salute the "audience."]

All at the same time: *Don't use weapons.*

[[La niña/pillo #1 camina hacia la otra esquina del pasillo en donde se encuentra a un niño en el rol de un hombre. El hombre esta acostado en el piso supuestamente durmiendo en su casa. El hombre se levanta. La niña/pillo #1 lo patea y forcejean por un momento. Ella apunta con la mano imitando una pistola.]

hombre robado: *No me mates.* [Cubriendo su cuerpo con sus manos] niña/pillo #1: *Si te voy a matar. Pum!* [La mano de la niña/pillo se mueve hacia arriba y su cuerpo se mueve hacía atrás como resultado del peso y velocidad de la bala cuando se dispara. El hombre robado encorva su cuerpo recibiendo el impacto de la bala y cae al piso.]

[La niña/pillo #1 camina hacia fuera de la escena del crimen y se encuentra con niña/pillo #2, cuando dos niños/hombres con pistolas la persiguen. Una niña/peatona hablando en su teléfono celular, cruza la calle y pasa frente a las niñas/pillos #1 y 2. Las niñas/pillos #1 & 2 se esconden detrás de la niña/peatona a la vez que los dos niños/hombres con pistolas le disparan. La niña/peatona cae al suelo.]

niños/hombres con pistolas: *Vámonos, vámonos.* [Todos excepto la niña/peatona corren y se esconden detrás de una pared.]

[Todos los personajes regresan al centro, chocan sus manos, se abrazan, se inclinan y saludan a la "audiencia."]

Todos a coro: *No usar armas.*

TABLE 8.3 Key analytical questions and data

1. Textual representations (see Q. 1)	2. Cultural norms, histories, knowledges (see Q. 2)	3. Interrelations (see Q. 3)	4. What is occurring? (see Q. 4)
Naming/absence of naming of characters in performance.	Objectification and subjectivities of self and other.	The relationship between individual names and power. The relationship between a lack of name/a categorized person and a lack of autonomy. Marking in relation to naming.	A generic and essentialized version of behavior and motivations of violence.
Narrative of media report on the local violent act that prompted the students' inquiry .	Landscape of local media relating to violence.	Relationship between media representations of violence, day-to-day occurrences of violence, researchers' perceptions of violence, and students' representations of violence.	One violent act supports an already established media narrative of violence that permeates day-to-day media.
School uniforms; enthusiastic verbal engagement with teacher; students all in close proximity to each other and the teacher .	Understanding of school culture, expectations, conventions of activity, and communication in that setting.	School culture of obeying rules (laws), performing versions of "good behavior" in relation to the activity of performing illegal and "bad" behavior.	Through an invitation to "play," students are engaging in imagined roles and worlds that are otherwise unacceptable in the school space.
The spoken dialogue and physicalized action in the performance.	Knowledges of language use, motivations, attitudes, and physical movement of people engaged in violent and illegal activity.	The active, vehement, and driven attitudes performed by students playing violence in relation to the passive, disengaged, and un-enthused attitudes of those playing the innocent characters.	Our (researchers') common associations with positive/good and negative/bad behavior are troubled by the performances of the students.

worlds, relationships, and identities that are performed. The first significant social inscriptions that emerge in this performance can be seen in the actions of economic material consumption in relation to dependence and a desire for social mobility. In the beginning of the scene in question, *niña/pillo* #1 (girl/robber #1) inscribes the notion of money, or lack thereof, as a fundamental and existential aspect of her life "porque tu sabes como yo soy. Yo no quiero ser pobre" (because you know how I am. I don't want to be poor) [moving head in a negative gesture] that serves as a justification to engage in the activity of robbery and murder. We, the spectators (teacher/researchers/peers/future imagined audience) are presented with the idea that violence and murder are not randomly enacted activities, but actions situated within the performance of consumption and material acquisition. In this way, in the improvisational space of the performance that has the specific objective of "addressing violence," we can see a subjective stance proposed by the *niña/pillo* #1 (girl/robber #1) that serves to justify or contextualize the violence in the context and performance of everyday lives.

In the relational space of the improvisation, the proposed justification and contextualization for violence is picked up by *niña/pillo* #2 (girl/robber #2) who establishes an identification with the larger ideology of social and economic mobility and material acquisition, "yo tampoco [puedo estar sin chavos]" ("I can't either [be without money]") to establish a complicit relationship for the robbery. This perspective on what emerges as subjective ways of knowing within an improvisation is significant to note in the analysis of dramatic inquiry, allowing us to pay attention to the specific ways in which rules and ways of knowing and being emerge, are improvised, and negotiated through each actor subjectivities. These ways of knowing emerge in relation to larger identity objectifications of poverty, economic status, and violence. These subjective objectifications are visible in numerous ways, for example, in the lack of character names in the scene—characters don't ever refer to one another by a name. Following on from the students' lead, instead of using pseudonyms in the improvisation transcript, we have named the characters by larger social identity markers such as "girl," "robber," "bystander. We as researchers analyzing this performative event consider the robbers in this case, as *any* robbers the children "know"; and in the same way the places—the street, the house—are any places they know. The children in the creation of cultural spaces in this performance recreate norms, histories, and identity markers in interactions with violence.

Playing Violence

Violence as socially performed is inscribed through the murder of innocent people and a mastery of robbery. The robbers and the robbed demonstrate their knowledge of violence and death through enacted death threats, guns, and the detailed embodied performance of death. Death is performed by a hand positioned to imitate a gun, followed by very calculated shooting gestures and verbal statements such as "no me mates por favor" (please don't kill me), and "si te voy a matar" (yes I'm going to kill you). A very precise and coordinated, yet improvised, sequence of gestures portrays the impact of a bullet in a body and then the action of falling to the floor.

> La mano de la niña/pillo se mueve hacia arriba y su cuerpo se mueve hacía atrás como resultado del peso y velocidad de la bala cuando se dispara. El hombre robado encorva su cuerpo recibiendo el impacto de la bala y cae al piso.
>
> (The girl/robber's hand moves up as she shoots the gun and her body moves back from the speed and weight of the bullet coming from the gun. The robbed man curves his body as he receives the impact from the gun and falls to the floor.)

In this improvisation, we can see the fluidity and ease of this enactment by the students; the inevitability of events initiated by the hand made into a gun. An interesting aspect to notice in the performing of death is how the students' (robber and robbed) movements establish an embodied relationship among people, space, artifacts, and sounds that can be seen as ritualistic. This enactment was more than a representative portrayal of violent action; rather it was an embodied, affective performance of the students' relationship to violence that brought our own visceral and sensational relationship to violence to the fore. Both in witnessing and in re-watching this scene, powerful semiotic as well as affective registers resonate in analysis. Embodied, cultural, and social histories of performers and spectators interweave and contribute to this youth performance of violence.

Troubling the Good and the Bad of Violence and Schools

The inquiry presented through this analysis occurred in the context of a model media campaign. This process afforded the space for students to play with stereotypes or grim realities of violence in the safe space of school and imagined worlds. Both the "realities" of violence and the "safety" of school are constructions entangled in the broader historical, cultural, and social landscapes of Puerto Rico. Put another way, violence by many is known through sensational media, and school is understood by most as an ideological and controlled space based on ethical and sanctioned values. Students in the case of this inquiry were "succeeding" at their school task by engaging in a performance of violence. The short scene then was a platform to put this type of violence in a negative light, to illustrate or remind ourselves of the fatal consequences. In this endeavor, the youth drew on their own impressions, experiences, and understandings of violence, of violent/criminal people, as well as of innocent people. These perspectives come from media, from home, from their immediate and virtual worlds, and these understandings of violence and innocence emerge in a number of ways. In the space of school, where ideology sanctions the "good" citizen as someone who succeeds, upholds the law, etc., the students endeavor to conform and support that ideology and they can be seen to be creating a scene representing violence as a negative ill. Nevertheless at the same time this scene disrupted in a complex way what was accepted in the "safe" school setting by even using bodies to represent guns and violence in this way. The normative discourse of non-violence in schools gets subverted within the improvisational space, creating new boundaries and rules for a new way for doing schooling that is traditionally silenced in schools. Therefore, in the process of developing this scene, drawing from recent media stories as well as their own exposures to and awareness of violence, this project reveals complicated relationships between "good" and "bad" and the how, where, and who does "good" and "bad." Furthermore, as researchers, our associations with good behavior include active, engaged, and aware citizens. These assumptions are ruptured by the way in which violence and non-violence is performed by the students. The violent characters are performed as active, engaged collaborators: They move quickly, interact with each other, speak persuasively, and demonstrate emotion. Innocent people are represented as either asleep or wandering, seemingly oblivious to everything around them except a mobile phone. These characters do not have voices (except "please don't hurt me") and do not seem alert to events unfolding around them; they appear passive, disengaged, and isolated.

These engagements, that bring personal perspective into imagined performance, do not directly shed light on the nature or demeanor of violent offenders in Puerto Rico, neither do they accurately demonstrate the youths' attitude to violence; rather, they create and re-create narratives of possibility in their individual and shared realities in the negotiation of multiple social geographies. The performance itself does not reflect reality any more than the media does, but it does reflect relations between media and student, between good and passive behavior, between safe and violent spaces.

Looking Forward

The analysis process that we have laid out in this chapter represents a negotiation of theories, analytic structures, and personal subjectivities. It engages with the complex and multiple spaces of student bodies/minds/selves in performance-based inquiries. We are aware that this process is contingent upon two key elements: first, the subjectivities of the researchers and authors of this chapter, and, second, the context and content of the data in question. With this in mind, we propose this work, not as a template for replication, but rather as a guide and a demonstration of work that we hope can support various and evolving questions and possibilities for research in this field.

Although this work offers new possibilities and challenges to our field, it builds off some notable work already completed. First, "In search of the glocal through process drama" (2007) by Gus Weltsek and Carmen Medina demonstrates an analysis grounded in social and cultural theory. "Theatre as a place of learning: The forces and affects of devised theatre in education" (2010) by Mia Perry is a dissertation project situated in the poststructural project of Deleuze and guided by an analysis of affect. The authors of this chapter first began to explore the affordances of marrying paradigms in "Embodiment and performance in pedagogy: Investigating the possibility of the body in curriculum experience" (2011). Certainly our work continues to explore the theoretical and philosophical possibilities in embodiment studies, cultural performance, and theories of affect, and with that exploration comes new ways to question and think about experience. In similar ways, new data brings new connections to these theoretical understandings, and in turn new questions to be asked. This chapter represents an articulation of our ongoing project, a methodological inquiry, "Methodologies of embodiment: Inscribing bodies in qualitative research" (Perry & Medina, forthcoming) that allow us to dedicate substantial space to a conversation on embodiment in research methods from various perspectives and disciplines.

As we move forward in our work we have become aware of the challenges and limitations of doing this kind of analysis. The most significant is the process of how translating an analysis of the body from embodied action to paper generates big problems and limits what we can represent. Although we have become aware and see much potential in the multiple methodologies on embodiment and performance that are available, translating our analysis to paper is a limitation that we share across approaches. We also have become aware of the limitations of grounding the analysis within polarized paradigms such as sociocultural or affective-relational. Working through the tensions of working across the cultural-political and the affective-relational provides us with a bigger picture of how learning emerges from a holistic perspective in dramatic and performative practices.

References

Boundas, C. V. (2005). Intensity. In A. Parr (Ed.), *The Deleuze dictionary* (pp. 131–132). New York: Columbia University Press.
Braidotti, R. (1993). Embodiment, sexual difference, and the Nomadic subject. *Hypatia, 8*(1), 1–13.
Butler, J. (1990). *Gender trouble*. New York: Routledge.
Butler, J. (2005). *Giving an account of oneself*. New York: Fordham University Press.
Butler, J., Laclau, E., & Zizek, S. (2000). *Contingency, hegemony and universality: Contemporary dialogues on the left*. London: Verso.
Clough, P. (2010). The affective turn: Political economy, biomedia, and bodies. In M. Gregg & G. J. Seigworth (Eds.), *The affect theory reader* (pp. 206–228). Durham, NC: Duke University Press.

Conquergood, D. (2002). Performance studies: Interventions and radical research. *Drama Review, 46*, 145–156.

Cruz, C. (2001). Towards an epistemology of the brown body. *Qualitative Studies in Education, 14*(5), 657–669.

Deleuze, G. & Guattari, F. (1987). *A thousand plateaus: Capitalism and schizophrenia* (B. Massumi, Trans.). Minneapolis, MN: University of Minnesota Press.

Diamond, E. (Ed.). (1996). *Performance and cultural politics.* New York: Routledge.

Dolan, J. (1993). Geographies of learning: Theatre studies, performance and the "performative." *Theatre Journal, 45*(4), 417–441.

Ellsworth, E. (2005). *Places of learning: Media architecture pedagogy.* New York: Routledge Falmer.

Ford, N. & Brown, D. (2005). *Surfing and social theory: Experience, embodiment and narrative of the dream glide.* New York: Routledge.

Franks, A. (2004). Teoría del aprendizaje y educación dramática: una perspectiva vygots-kiana, histórico-cultural y semiótica (Learning theory and drama education: A Vygots-kian, historical cultural and semiotic approach). *Cultura y Educación, 16*(1/2), 77–91.

Grosz, E. (1994). *Volatile bodies: Toward a corporeal feminism.* Bloomington, IN: Indiana University Press.

Grumet, M. & McCoy, K. (2000). Feminism and education. In B. Moon, M. Ben-Peretz, & S. A. Brown (Eds.), *Routledge international companion to education* (pp. 426–440). New York: Routledge.

Leander, K. M. & Rowe, D. W. (2006). Mapping literacy spaces in motion: A rhizomatic analysis of a classroom literacy performance. *Reading Research Quarterly, 41*(4), 428–460.

Leder, D. (1990). *The absent body.* Chicago: University of Chicago Press.

Ling, X. (2009). Thinking like grass, with Deleuze in education. *Journal of the Canadian Association for Curriculum Studies, 7*(2), 30–47.

Mason, M. (2008). *Complexity theory and the philosophy of education.* Sussex, UK: Wiley-Blackwell.

Medina, C. (2004a). Drama wor(l)ds: Explorations of Latina/o realistic fiction through drama. *Language Arts, 81*(4), 272–282.

Medina, C. (2004b). The construction of drama worlds as literary interpretation of Latina feminist literature. *Research in Drama Education, 9*(2), 145–160.

Medina, C. (2006). Critical performative literacies: Intersections among identities, social imaginations and discourses. *National Reading Conference Yearbook, 55*, 182–194.

Merleau-Ponty, M. (1962). *Phenomenology of perception.* Evanston, IL: Northwestern University Press.

Ngai, S. (2002). A foul lump started making promises in my voice: Race, affect, and the animated subject. *American Literature, 74*(3), 571–601.

Ngai, S. (2005). *Ugly feelings.* Cambridge, MA: Harvard University Press.

Perry, M. (2010). *Theatre as a place of learning: The forces and affects of devised theatre processes in education.* Unpublished PhD thesis, University of British Columbia, Vancouver, BC.

Perry, M. (2011). *Theatre as a place of learning: The forces and affects of devised theatre processes in education.* Unpublished dissertation, University of British Columbia, Vancouver, BC.

Perry, M. & Medina, C. (2011). Embodiment and performance in pedagogy research: Investigating the possibility of the body in curriculum experience. *Journal of Curriculum Studies, 27*(3), 62–75.

Pineau, E. L. (2005). Teaching is performance: Reconceptualizing a problematic metaphor. In B. K. Alexander, G. L. Anderson, & B. P. Gallegos (Eds.), *Performance theories in education* (pp. 15–39). Mahwah, NJ: Lawrence Erlbaum.

Pugh, A. (2009). *Longing and belonging: Parents, children and consumer culture.* Berkeley, CA: University of California Press.

Quick, A. (1994). Searching for redemption with cardboard wings: Force entertainment and the sublime. *Contemporary Theatre Review, 2*(2), 25–35.

Shilling, C. (2003). *The body and social theory* (2nd ed.). Thousand Oaks, CA: Sage.

Shilling, C. (2012). *The body and social theory.* London: Sage Publications Inc.

Sontag, S. (1999). Art and consiousness. In B. D. Marranca & G. Dasgupta (Eds.), *Conversations on art and performance* (pp. 2–9). Baltimore, MD: Johns Hopkins University Press.

St. Pierre, E. A. (1997). Methodology in the fold and the irruption of transgressive data. *International Journal of Qualitative Studies in Education, 10*(2), 175–189.

St. Pierre, E. A. & Pillow, W. S. (2000). *Working the ruins: Feminist poststructural theory and methods in education.* New York: Routledge.

Sumara, D. I. (2000). Critical issues: Researching complexity. *Journal of Literacy Research, 32*(2), 267–281.

van Manen, M. (1997). *Researching lived experience: Human science for an action sensitive pedagogy* (2nd ed.). London, ON: Althouse Press.

Weltsek, G. & Medina, C. (2007). In search of the glocal through process drama. In M. V. Blackburn & C. Clark (Eds.), *Literacy research for political action and social change* (pp. 255–275). New York: Peter Lang Publishers.

9

POETIC INQUIRY

Lorri Neilsen Glenn

Patches of thyme grow
on the side of a Crete mountain overlooking
the Aegean. Smoke from the taverna drifts
across the street. Men sit in the shade
from early morning to last call, their glasses
filling from below. Occasionally, a child comes
with a message, or to collect money. The women,
like an aquifer, remain unseen.

Over the last fifteen to twenty years, we have seen a promising shift in research in the field of literacy, not only in how we approach our research, but how we communicate to other educators, to communities and the public. Arts-based and arts-informed research practices – in particular, ethnographic poetry – are significant illustrations of this shift.

Ethnographic Poetry: The Wherefore and the Why

No single moment or published work marks the introduction of ethnographic poetry into the field of literacy research. It is more accurate to suggest an evolution of sorts: a narrative turn in anthropological texts, the kind we see in Clifford Geertz's (1973) account of a Balinese cockfight, may have been one of many early studies that paved the way for a more widespread use of narration as method both for data gathering and reporting in several branches of anthropology. By the end of the last century, narrative inquiry was firmly established as a qualitative methodology in anthropology as well as in the social sciences, including education and health care research.

Story – from case studies to critical incident descriptions to classroom narratives – began to appear in literacy research by the 1980s, particularly with the
rise of the whole language and writing process movements. Teacher narratives
became a methodology in and of themselves, a means to explore meaning in the
small, telling classroom moment. By the late 1980s, doctoral programs such as
those in New Hampshire were open to alternative approaches to researching
and writing dissertations; my doctoral research, which appeared in print as *Literacy and Living*, an ethnography of literacy in a small Nova Scotia seaside community, included story and ethnographic poetry (Neilsen, 1989). Literacy
journals such as *Language Arts* and *Reading Teacher*, among others, became places
where well-crafted story, and the occasional poem, brought inquiry insights to a
larger audience.

Narrative (Latin: *narrativus* – telling a story) is a primary means by which
humans make sense of the world; story undergirds our discourses and our histories in many disciplines as well as in daily life. For millennia, the art of telling a
story, either prosaically or lyrically, has drawn people around a fire, connected
communities, and, for good or ill, been the bedrock on which civilizations have
come to know and to perpetuate themselves. The oral and written works that
form the basis of world literary canons share a heightened attention to distilled
and artful language, a reaching for aesthetic expression that draws on shared
symbol and cultural experience to create works that transform, move and
inspire. For this reason, we often see lines blur; literary works described as
"poetic" are marked by qualities – perhaps word choice, rhythm and tone, or
condensed and allusive language – that defy boundaries. It is not much of a leap
from poetic narrative to poetry itself (sometimes the bridge is prose poetry);
neither is it a leap from inquiry-based narrative writing to ethnographic poetry.
We may see narrative explicitly in ethnographic poetry, writing that communicates a story; but we may also see non-narrative lyric expression, a writer
exploring a phenomenon, an emotion, a perception, sharpened into image-
evoking, compelling language.

An ethnographic poem is both the catalyst and the result of the same processes researchers and literary writers employ: close observation, careful attention to words and immersion in and understanding of cultural and symbolic
resonances. When I was asked to compose a documentary, historically based
poem for our University President's induction, for example, I drew on my
and others' knowledge of the University, on local histories, as well as contextual understandings earned over twenty years of being part of a community.
Composing a prose poem about my mother, I returned to letters and artifacts
from her life to reassure myself I had my facts straight (and my memories
clear). In Crete recently to lead a writing workshop, I was awash with new
sounds, sights, language and experiences, and such sensory immersion – along
with my wish to make sense of things – prompted my putting pen to paper. I
was fully engaged, and I documented what struck me or moved me in some

way. The opening epigraph to this chapter is one small ethnographic note, or memo, to myself.

Ethnographic Poetry and Research Literacy

When I began to study ethnography at Harvard in 1985, I read "Deep Play: Notes on the Balinese Cockfight" for the first time. I was transfixed. Having undertaken statistical studies in my first graduate degree, I found Geertz's (1973) "thick description" new and startling, both embodied and engaging. Later, I pored the shelves of every bookstore in Cambridge looking for Whyte's (1943) *Street Corner Society*. On the bus back to New Hampshire, immersed in the lives of the corner boys, I almost missed my stop in Durham. This – *this?* – is research?

Now, almost thirty years later, educators and scholars new to research creation approaches are asking the same question when they find a thesis written as a novel or a script, performed or showcased as an art installation, or created as a multi-genre bricolage of textual possibilities. Graduate students are often both skeptical and cautiously hopeful when they come across a poem, for example, in a scholarly work. You mean you can do this, they ask?

My response has always been that, yes, you can do this. More importantly, as researchers and language users in the field of literacy, we should do this. If we can urge teachers in schools to expand students' linguistic and rhetorical repertoire by creating environments where all language forms, genres, registers and functions can be developed – where we can support everyone's full communicative capacities – can we not expect the same of ourselves as researchers and scholars? Will we all become fiction writers, playwrights or crafters of fine haiku? No. But, just as we exercise our bodies to ensure all muscles are used, it's important that we are aware of, to appreciate and to cultivate experience in writing and reading all forms of our native language, including the aesthetic and literary.

Language theorists and linguists have long argued that human linguistic and intellectual development hinges on participation in a range of linguistic forms and functions. Following on the seminal work of Roman Jakobson, theorists such as James Britton and Janet Emig, among others, argued for the use of all modes of writing in education: expository (telling), argumentative (arguing), transactional (doing) modes, expressive and the poetic (imaginative, personal, reflective). In Louise Rosenblatt's reader response theory (1976), reading is a transaction, in which the "poem" or literary work is not realized without the reader's engagement with the text (1978). In Rosenblatt's conception (1978), readers engage with texts along a continuum: an "efferent" reading is largely for content and information; an "aesthetic" reading is an engagement with text for its effect on the reader. An aesthetic response can be at once emotional, psychological and physical (that click of recognition, goosebumps, a sigh). Her celebrated article (1980), "What facts does this poem teach you?" is an ironic comment on our tendency in schools to evaluate everything; many, like Rosenblatt, believe our reading repertoire ought to include the pleasures of an aesthetic response for its value alone, without having to do something with the text. Were she alive, Rosenblatt would have agreed with Billy Collins (2002), whose poem "Introduction to Poetry" includes the lines

> but all they want to do
> is tie a poem to a chair with rope
> and torture a confession of it.
> They begin beating it with a hose
> to find out what it really means.

As we develop over the life span as language users, we expand our repertoire and flex our linguistic muscles as both writers and readers in myriad contexts. We meet texts as composers and readers, and bring to those texts our unique local, social, personal and cultural backgrounds, as well as our intentions and agenda. The key components of message, audience and purpose – a reductive but useful characterization of the communicative act, one I have used with writers in all walks of life – adhere both in our considerations of our writing and reading processes.

The processes of inquiry (a roomier, more fluent word than "research"), I argue, are no different. As educational researchers, most of us have studied and are reasonably literate in a range of approaches to inquiry, from experimental design to action research. We have developed our own "research literacies" in order to be more effective in our professional work. When the focus of the research is literate behaviors and practices, when we layer literacy upon literacy, we "read" any given culture along many dimensions, both horizontally and vertically. We may undertake research in ways that mirror Rosenblatt's notions of efferent and aesthetic: we travel a loose, varied and changing continuum along which we might search for facts or content – knowledge or information – at one end; at the other, our immersion in the culture may open us to "read" and experience the ineffable, those transcendent moments of awareness in community, akin to Rosenblatt's idea of the aesthetic response.

When we sit down to write – or when we write through the inquiry process – we do the same: we draw on – and extend, and challenge – our linguistic resources to communicate meaning to local, community and larger circles of readers and interested parties in diverse ways. My idea of an ideal inquiry project is one in which all participants are challenged to be fully and deeply engaged: in "reading" a culture in all its complexity and gaps, in the inquiry practices we use to work inside and along with participants, and in the "writing" of connections and fissures, finding the means to express what we and participants believe is important to express and communicate.

Ethnographic poetry is an expansive and powerful medium through which we can begin, as researchers and as readers and writers of cultures, to advance innovative, responsive and enlarged notions of literacy – and literacies – and the settings that teach us about reading and writing the world. Many, including poet Lyn Hejinian (2000), philosopher Martha Nussbaum (2001) and writer Morris Berman (1990), argue that such full and expanded engagement and awareness cultivate empathy and compassion, and can be the basis for social and political change.

Ethical Considerations in Ethnographic Poetry

> You were told to make the strange familiar. Take your notebook and recorder to unknown places, be participant observer, just like Margaret, though this pale and angular woman wrapped awkwardly in the embrace of a bright sarong heard from gleeful village girls only what they knew she wanted them to say. All invention – all once upon a time, these tales of the field. You learned the sixth sense of the observed sent signals from above the tree line to below the Amazon. That when you gazed upon informants gazing back at you, another text was being written: write what you wish, white jester. Later you will dance in our stories wearing that odd hat, those clumsy shoes. Burnt nose twitching over your tight mouth. Your blind blue eyes. You were certain where civilization began and ended. A pen, a bible, table linen, a queen, the precision of a motor, a queue line at the station. Where was the ethnographer recording you, documenting your appetite to consume whatever's in your wanton path, because all the world is your dominion, because it's there, because all of it is food?
>
> (adapted from "Strange Familiar," Neilsen Glenn, 2010)

The ethical considerations I have as a poet and essayist are often different from those I consider in my practice of ethnography. As a poet, I simply write – my concerns are primarily for the truth and authenticity of the work and for what is necessary, in terms of craft and linguistic resources, to produce a poem whose aesthetic quality I feel comfortable with in order to take it out into the world.

In the example of the poem for our University President's induction (reprinted below, in the last section of this chapter), my concerns were for historical accuracy and aesthetic quality and for rhythm and rhetorical impact, in large part because the poem was to be performed. In the poem above ("Strange Familiar") I knew I was responding to a First Nation's friend's oft-repeated joke about an anthropologist being a member of her Northern family, and my concerns were to express succinctly the role, now changing, of the ethnographer in a community. In a poem about my mother, I am aiming to capture a resonant truth about her as a woman, and to do this with lyrical power. When she was alive, I often read my work to her, to ensure she was fine with the portrayal or to confirm details about family life; I do this regularly when a person I know appears in my work. This checking is not considered necessary in most literary communities where weaving the voices and stories of others in a work, while sometimes contentious, is rarely considered appropriating at all. My research training makes me aware – both in my literary and scholarly work – of who's writing whose story. In a poem about a small town in Crete, I consider the work documentary and – in this case – given that the scenes described are public, I have little hesitation about recording my impressions. I am not backed by an institution in this case, nor do I have a review committee to be accountable to as I document, ask a question or two of people on the street, jot down a snippet of a conversation, take in an impression of someone doing his or her work. The ethical standards I adhere to in writing poetry are those we must all attend to as human beings: to be humble, to understand the limits of our role, to do no harm and to accord the same degree of respect and dignity to others as we would have accorded to ourselves.

Writing ethnographic poetry in the context of educational inquiry, however, requires me to put the ethical dimensions of the work front and center. Am I writing this in collaboration with the participants in the study? Is there a power imbalance here? Have I ensured, at the very least, that I have arranged for member-checking in the process of crafting the work? Have I ensured that everyone in that community has an opportunity to read (if not write, or help write) the work, add or delete material, edit the work for tone, approach, accuracy and effect? While aesthetic considerations are important in creating ethnographic poetry, we must remember the work belongs as much to the community whose culture it is documenting as it does to the researcher. The researcher-poet (I have called these "scholartists"; Neilsen, Cole & Knowles, 2001) has a role different from that of a poet outside the academy; we are not only the instrument and medium through which the research is largely organized and facilitated (a fact which should make us feel more responsible and accountable than we might otherwise), but when we sit down to write, we are also a clearing house of sorts, where people, language, stories, interpretations, impressions, gaps, dislocations, anomalies, among other cultural factors and practices converge, mix and are negotiated and renegotiated.

While I do not wish to oversimplify, we have both the privilege and the responsibility to support literacy communities well through our work as poet-ethnographers; therefore, our ethical and professional obligations are to those communities and the meanings they shape (or we shape with them) in our collective practices. Shaping those meanings eloquently and memorably is testament to the importance of this relationship. As a researcher, I see my role less as a singular artist, and more as midwife to what communities create together. As poet-ethnographers, we have an opportunity to blur boundaries between the academic world and the literary world and to inform and re-energize both.

Language, Poetry and Knowing

The American poet Lyn Hejinian (2000) claims that the language of poetry is a language of inquiry, not of a genre. Poetry, she says, "takes as its premise that language is a medium for experiencing experience" (p. 2). Poetry is a social and political practice, and its power lies in it teaching us the fact of otherness – not naming or claiming or categorizing what's out there but, rather, witnessing it, acknowledging it. As Hejinian says, poetry (like life) is transitional and transitory, calling "aboutness" of poetry (and life itself) into question. It is enough, from this perspective, to see even briefly what the philosopher Levinas calls the face of the other. Such seeing is the root of ethical behavior and of compassion.

As we train our perception, as we recognize and embrace the transitional and the transitory through poetry, we learn to acknowledge *what is* and acknowledge its importance and value in its own right. Poet and philosopher Jan Zwicky (2003) writes of this phenomenon as well. Ontological awareness, or, learning *what is*, the *thisness* of what we see and experience, is a habit of mind important to cultivate. As Zwicky says, it is a response to particularity and to presence. "It is the antithesis of the attitude that regards things as 'resources,' mere means to human ends" (L52). This is where notions of what counts as knowing and knowledge become complicated. An ontological bias toward foundational knowledge is not always compatible with an ontological perspective that embraces ambiguity, the spaces between, intuitive leaps, ineffability and places of liminality (Neilsen Glenn, 2011).

I have written elsewhere (Neilsen, 2002a; 2002b) that what we understand to be knowledge is provisional, contextual, on its way to becoming. It is liminal; it never arrives. Further, it is shot through with our agenda, with political and social forces that shake our foundational claims – and should. At some fundamental level, the findings in our literacy studies, just as the thoughts and words in a poem, belong only to that particular context and time; change, new perspectives, new eyes and ears make what we assume to be knowledge problematic. That's a radical claim – "radical" meaning *to the root* – but, as researchers, we all understand this.

The pursuit of the hypostatic – an underlying substance or reality – is an important pursuit; however, the pursuit of the ineffable is equally necessary. We can look to ethnographic poetry to document, to report, to lay down tracks about an experience; but we can also look to it as a means of opening up, of questioning, of disrupting the given. Of leaving mystery and the inexplicable hanging, unresolved. There are political implications in this opening up, in accepting the liminal; this space is a space for change.

Simply engaging with our realities as we see and experience them is what the documentary theorist Nichols (1991) calls "epistephilia." The benefits and pleasures of the here and now – an emphasis on the experiencing rather than finding an outcome or creating a product – often mark poetry and ethnographic work. For this, and other reasons, the term "poetic analysis" can be problematic; something in the word analysis suggests planning. Yet the flashes of insight and leaps of imagination we experience in the field (and in writing) are not as systematically understood or auditable as we would like them to be. In ethnographic research, while we hope to see themes and patterns as well as disruptions and anomalies, we may find there are more blurred areas than we knew. We may realize that no static, reliable account can be given; research, like life, is always moving, stances and perspectives always shifting. Engaging in writing ethnographic poetry – whether it is to document our own or others' processes, behaviors or impressions – is a means, as Hejinian (2000) has written, to "experience experience." It is not merely a tidy gathering of data bits that can be outlined, organized, sorted, snapped into place and offered up as a "finding."

In a poem about the tensions between living an academic life in which propositional language and control are in a tug of war with the creative stance of letting go, common in writing poetry, I wrote: "They say reason alone/will thwart wild children, daydreaming and reckless/expression. Cognition will line them all up in rows, snap/his phone shut, grab his briefcase, chuck chins/on the way out the door" (Neilsen Glenn, 2010, p. 75).

Aesthetic Considerations in Ethnographic Poetry

The Demands of Ethnographic Poetry

As researchers and writers, we understand that language *is* inquiry, and we understand the difficulties of using the written word. Poet-academics struggle as much or more with expressing ourselves than most reasonably proficient language users: we are always learning what language cannot do. We take language out to what poet Don McKay (2001) calls the wilderness, the far reaches between phenomena and the unsayable or unspeakable.

With that assumption a given, however, we nonetheless have the opportunity to create work along many dimensions and in many forms. Ethnographic poetry may be largely documentary ("just the facts, ma'am"), or it may be impressionistic, lyrical, allusive, having taken its author down a conceptual or associative path she hadn't expected. The poem may be crafted directly from participants' spoken or written language; in that way, it is closest to what we know as "found poetry" (Butler-Kisber, 2002). The poem could appear as free verse, or it might appear in a traditional form such as a sonnet, villanelle or ghazal. There are no restrictions; the opportunities and constraints are inherent in the material itself and the writer's engagement with it. Some material – because of tone or content – lends itself more to prose; other, to more distilled, condensed language. A transcribed interview with an embedded story may invite a prose poem; a series of reflections in a life history may call for a more economical, aphoristic treatment. There are no "right" approaches, at least not until we realize through the writing we may have found them. Sometimes we find the approach in surprising and serendipitous ways; other times, we must experiment with several approaches before finding one that successfully conveys, elevates or transforms experience into words. At all times, however, we aim to honor both the material and participants' words and experiences.

For this reason, we owe it to the inquiry, the participants and to ourselves, as scholars and writers, to immerse ourselves in learning the art and craft of writing poetry. As I have written elsewhere, selections of phrases from transcribed data, centered on the page with white space around them, will not necessarily constitute a poem. A researcher's raw emotional output phrased in abstract language, however heartfelt, will rarely succeed as a piece of writing, let alone as poetry. With Maynard and Cahnmann-Taylor (2010), I believe not only that ethnographic poetry should meet the same high standards as poetry in the wider community, but also that no one is served in the enterprise by us writing inferior verse. In fact, as poet-researchers, we diminish ourselves and arts-based ethnography at large by not attending to the demands of artful expression.

Learning to do ethnographic work involves education, training and immersion in the culture of researchers: we learn about the roots of the discipline, its many forms and approaches, and how to use its tools and participate in its practices. We learn what works and what doesn't, and why. Learning to write poetry is no different. Maynard and Cahnmann-Taylor (2010) outline several activities and experiences poet-ethnographers might engage in, from attending poetry seminars, workshops and retreats, to studying craft, reading widely and working with other poets. As they say, "one must become an active participant-observer" (p. 13) in the culture of poetry.

Poets work long and hard on their craft, but that fact is not generally understood. A contradictory misconception persists in and out of the academy: anyone can write poetry (it's just rhyming verse after all), or a poet is born with the gift. An apocryphal story in Canadian literature puts the celebrated novelist Margaret Laurence at a dinner party where a surgeon, after learning she is a writer, says, "Ah yes, that's something I should take up after I retire. How hard can it be?" Poetry, for the most part, is celebrated in the early years, housed in English class in the middle grades and brought out for dissection in high school. Thereafter, unless a student reads and writes poetry in their college years, their only experience of it as adults is at funerals or commencement ceremonies. Who doesn't love Dr. Seuss, after all?

Learning to Live Inside Lyric Inquiry

Aside from participating in the culture of poetry and poets to prepare ourselves for writing ethnographic poetry, we must bring certain habits of mind to the enterprise. Some of these habits and skills we will have already cultivated as researchers: an acute attention to detail; an ability to listen beyond the surface of what's said and to see beyond the surface of what's given; the capacity and willingness to wait, a long patience that reaps insight and understanding; and the compassionate, reflexive muscle that allows us to see from others' perspectives, among other skills. Cultivating an embodied stance to phenomena is critical: Abram (1996), Ackerman (1990) and McGilchrist (2009) remind us that the mind *is* the body; it is not located in a separate place. Further, McGilchrist, in his superb discussion of language, reminds us that language evolved from music and, as such, "its foundations lie in the body and the world of experience" (p. 125).

The Canadian poet Dennis Lee (1998) calls lyricism a singing self, empathetic, embodied. Aside from its other meanings (words of a song, among them), the word "lyric" refers to a poem expressing the mood, feeling, or meditative thoughts of the poet. But lyric, as a singing of the self, is much more than a category of poem. As I have written extensively elsewhere, we can think of it as a marriage of expressive language with research. When we embrace the rich possibilities of what we once pejoratively called "the subjective," and as we accept the idea that, at some level, our engagement with the world is always and only through our own flawed lenses, we abandon notions of objectivity and look at other considerations: opening ourselves to cultural practices, our relationships with participants, alternative conceptions of validity and reliability, the possibilities in the liminal space between what we know as realities and our means of expression.

Lyric inquiry is a methodology that acknowledges the processes and demands, as well as the tropes, conventions, semiotic and sensory interplay involved in the creation of an aesthetic work. To engage in this inquiry is to engage in all manner of non-academic writing – narrative (including fiction and creative non-fiction), journal writing, memoir, poetry, dialogue and monologue (among other forms usually thought of as written artistic expression) to explore and communicate with and to others an issue, dilemma or phenomenon.

In my work with women writers, in workshop and in university settings, I provide ample opportunity for lyric expression in a range of forms, for several reasons, not least of which is the human need to understand our own perspectives before we can begin to understand or inquire into others'. But the responses to this opportunity – and my research findings – have taught me other, equally legitimate reasons for supporting the shift in our habits of mind from point-driven, propositional and agonistic discourse, the coin of the academic realm, to lyrical and expressive language. One reason is that many women writers, in particular, find much academic discourse off-putting and, in some cases, outright hostile to their way of speaking and writing. Lyric expression is not, nor should be, a solipsistic enterprise, but it does demand that the writer begin to understand herself in relation to the world around her; this fosters voice and agency. Further, lyric expression advances a writer's own craft and art, asking that the writer not be a ventriloquist for the current academic language *du jour*, but that she develop her own style and means of articulating ideas. Finally – and this will be no surprise – I have seen writers work harder, invest more deeply in their art and craft, and push each other more to succeed when the material and forms of expression are their own. Donald Murray taught this to graduate students in New Hampshire in the 1980s; while other students in other courses learned to parrot, we were learning how to think and write for ourselves. A strong background in lyric expression is critical to good writing in the academy and beyond; it is a rich platform from which to begin writing ethnographic poetry.

To those skills and habits of mind we can characterize as a lyric stance on the world, we will want to add others, ones we recognize in poets and other literary writers. These include a willingness to let go and see where the material takes us, both its content and its form and style; a heightened awareness of musicality, tone, as well as other aesthetic qualities of literary language often difficult to describe except in their absence; an ear for the aural potential of the work – poetic work may be more likely to be read aloud to an audience than most academic work is (and can amplify its power: the current growth of performance and spoken word poetry is testament to this); and an attunement to the echoes and resonances of language, the depth charges that we may not invite in discursive prose, but which add dimension and verticality (sometimes intentionally, and sometimes not) to ethnographic verse.

Practical Considerations in Writing Ethnographic Poetry

The more time and attention we invest in writing poetry, particularly if writing poetry is new to us, the greater the opportunity to come to understandings not available to us before. Two of those are worth mentioning here; and interestingly, each speaks not only to writing poetry, but to teaching and to inquiry as well.

Poetry and inquiry ask us to listen deeply. We must put ourselves in the context, to feel, taste, hear what someone is saying. We must learn to listen under the words, to hear what's not being said, and to recognize the depth charges of certain statements. We must be empathetic, aware and not hasty or judgmental. We must avoid the short-circuiting impulse to put things in words too soon. We may see a literature circle (to which we bring all our associations); but we have to see it as *this* literature circle.

Language is always inadequate. We dance with impossibility each time we put words on the page. Far better to be at a loss for words than to jump in with easy cliché, borrowed language. As the philosopher Simone Weil (1970) has said, "the mind is enslaved when it accepts connections it has not itself established" (p. 24). Honoring the circumstances and the individuals by careful, hard-won description is, fundamentally, an ethical choice we make each time we approach the page.

1. There are rhythms to the inquiry process just as there are rhythms in writing poetry and in the poem itself. (I refer here to rhythms – rhyming is another issue entirely.) Just as a good interview is not forced, but evolves, led by the rhythm of the participants' voices and flow of ideas, the dance of relationship, a poem evolves to become a creation with its own rush or sway or meditative motion. Listening – ontological attention – helps us to work inside and with the process.
2. Less is more. Always. Poems comprising raw data, for example, are not merely transcriptions placed on the page in small phrases with random line breaks – the work must be spare, economical, rich and resonant. An elixir. Potent. Less also means saying something once, and well, rather than nibbling around its edges with flabby or gassy language. A strong poem is a strong poem, regardless of its provenance. Each line break matters. Each space matters.
3. Raw, vague, self-involved language rarely leaves room for the reader. Essayist Nancy Mairs (1994) says that "my text is flawed when it leaves no room for stories of your own" (p. 74). Even in ethnographic poetry, where the poet/researcher is communicating her experience of and understanding of a literacy learning environment, the reader looks for evocative, specific, concrete and spare language that shows restraint and communicative skill.
4. The complex and the difficult are necessary: none of us benefit from easy description, or tidy summing-up when they are not warranted. Our training as teachers and researchers feeds our impulse to wrap up a plan or an idea, put a heading on it or a string around it; as poets we learn to accept letting go, insolubility, inscrutability. Sometimes there just isn't an answer or a result.
5. Our apprenticeship never ends.

Exemplars of Ethnographic Poetry

Two Examples

Following are two drafts of ethnographic poetry and notes about their genesis. One is the poem I referred to earlier, read at a University ceremony and subsequently published as a broadside. The second is written by a colleague,

Kathy Kaulbach, now studying the composing processes of visual inquiry. In that study, she explores her own history of reading.

Example 1.
To Begin
Here. Gondwana, and Pangea, and the drift of continents and seas that creates river bed and basin, drumlin fields, potter's ground, boonamoog-waddy, Mi'kmaq land of waters that breathe salmon and tomcod, of the sagamore Glooscap. Above, fish-hawk and corvid that swirl, turn, glide – From here, we set out with ax, adz, spear, arrow. Set out with basket, sled, canoe. Commencons ici, Dix-sept cent cinquante-cinq. A protestant colony with no room it seems for Les Acadiens. George's Island: une prison. Le Grand Dérangement. La douleur des enfants.

Set out again. Wade into water, this water, as those from troubled colonies to the south have, choosing allegiance to the Crown in 1783 in return for land – sojourners herded off ships of bitter passage, then them-selves marooned, souls entwined like wicker, leaking hope, while below the sea gathers bodies of scuttled ships, lost cargo, broken remains of boats and hearts. Sedimented story.

How she calls us, the deep, briny, drink, holds us hand over hand in her hollows, mother to father to son to daughter, carries us on the backs of the years at the caprice of the gods, all of us – human, slate, gull wing, iris, bayberry, quartzite, rock rose, lichen, spikerush, osprey, white-tailed deer – as we rise and fall, spring and neap, like the birthing, the ebb, the wreathing of tides—

And once more. Nineteenth century: An underground path from Long Island to the North. Swing low, and Steal away … Set out door to door by night, travel word of mouth with the aid of conductors like Harriet, the woman who never lost a passenger, the reach of Quakers depot to depot. Assemble at the old riverbed we now call Bedford, Birch Cove, Wrights, and Fairview – build new lives with timber and meager fire, strong heart and a song for the song of Africville – 1849, and young Eliz-abeth O'Neill rushes to the pier to greet sisters of God, pioneers of a foundation. Twenty years on, she is Mother Superior and the acres to the west of Africville are the property of the Sisters, a haven for orphans, for the sick, the Motherhouse a beacon on the hill for the abc's of faith, caritas, human spirit.

Here – this basin, base, bassinet, basket, cupped hands in the landscape – where storms can tear the flesh of the earth – a destination for British home children in 1912, burial place for souls lost during the maiden voyage of a New York-bound liner, site of collision in 1917 of the Imo and the Mont Blanc. Not until January 2006, between Seaview Park and the Motherhouse, do we mark a grave, finally, for nine-year-old Annie

Perry Campbell, found in the fresh snow covered with the ash of explosion. Here, too, resting places for men and women of World War II, Afghanistan, those we lost to the Spanish flu, war brides of the Forties.

And still we come, as immigrants of the 1970s, 80s, 90s have come – carrying elpida, esperanza, hoffnung, tumaini, hy vong. L'espoir. Amal. Hope: vessels of it toward the skywashed light of this shore. It arrives by rail, on barges, in containers, has shone through the window of the chapel in Evaristus, on the mute statues in the trees, makes music of ideas and communion among us on this hill, calls us, as crows at sunset call, to assemble, prepare for la nua, un Nuevo dia – for a moment that the simple gift of spirit and a compass called truth have brought us to, here, this place from which we rise, and rise again, offer ready hands and hearts to the world.

It is from here we set out. We begin.

How was this poem written? First, I began to undertake extensive research on the history of the Halifax Harbour, the Bedford Basin and the Sisters of Charity, founders of Mount Saint Vincent University, as well as on the expulsion of the Acadians and the story of Africville. I had some knowledge of the material beforehand, but it was necessary to review it thoroughly, ensure that I was accurate, and to consult a number of local sources.

I knew it would be a conceptual challenge: that is, my aim was to represent communities populating the region, to open the story (as I began to see it) from the long view of geological time to the current moment in which a campus, with its own history, sits on a hill in a city that now welcomes new Canadians.

The aesthetic challenge was greater: it is necessary, I find, when composing ethnographic poetry to ensure that the work is tight, the language is image-evoking and spare, that there is rhythm, torque and music. The work must lift itself out of words in order to become a kind of musical composition. The communicative challenge was to write the piece, which was historical after all, in a manner that is suited to oral reading and performance.

Example 2.
Blend and bend, fold up tight.
Tuck away, tuck away, tuck out of sight.
She sang the song and became an architect, a specialist of sorts in fort making. Blankets draped over bed and dresser, pillows stacked underneath. The blue dog with a pajama pocket as guest. Under the basement steps between the studs she erected a shelf for her books and created loan cards which she glued to the inside back pages so as to write her name when borrowed. A library with a single patron. But, I am mistaken, there was the dog. Then there was her favourite, at night, behind a closed door while other kids still shouted outside in the dusk, she tucked tight up

against the window and read using the flush from the still humming streetlight. Reading became a hiding place. And then she built her final tightest structure, a box surrounding and enclosing herself and the only I that remained. This she carried always.

Blend and bend, fold up tight.

Tuck away, tuck away, tuck out of sight.

(Kathy Kaulbach, 2012, unpublished)

Kathy describes how this prose poem was written. First, as she describes in her notes to me afterward, she undertook extensive research into strong memories of solitary moments and the artifacts that appeared. Her conceptual challenge was to portray a life history of internalization by showing external actions. This was written, she says, more to understand than portray; a reflexive – in process – activity. Her aesthetic challenge was to keep the piece short, visual and give it rhythm and flow. She decided to use the second person to avoid a stance of self-absorption. Her emotional challenge was to verbalize deeply internalized thoughts. Her communicative challenge: to show internal emotions by showing familiar external actions, to show self-discovery.

The end result was that, through the writing, Kathy realized the internal act of reading as a child was her way to hide or avoid the exterior world. Reading, she wrote, is a safe, peaceful place, allowing her to ask questions without being judged, and to explore freely.

Where the Poems are

Researchers and poets can now find rich and abundant ethnographic poetry – and lyric material – in literacy journals and educational publications. Not only do we find the work itself, but poet-researchers in increasing numbers are writing about poetic inquiry as a methodology and finding ways to create community around the enterprise.

Prendergast (2009) and Maynard and Cahnmann-Taylor (2010) offer helpful and thorough characterizations of the kinds and purposes of poetic inquiry and ethnographic poetry, along with descriptions of several examples. Online journals such as *Educational Insights* out of the University of British Columbia offer new possibilities for publishing poetic inquiry, including ethnographic poems. An international multi-disciplinary symposium in poetic inquiry is now preparing for its third international conference in six years. Several campuses across Canada, Australia and the United States now host an organization or a department that focuses on research creation or arts-based inquiry in education and the social or medical sciences. In all these forums, we see poets and poet-ethnographers creating rigorous and inspiring work that gives voice to often under-represented communities and challenges our assumptions of what research can be and can do.

Ethnographic poetry provides us an opportunity to achieve resonance, the first step to creating a form for understanding that neither appropriates nor simplifies. A poem can be a palimpsest, a bricolage; it can be lightning and mystery, a shiver or an elevator drop. A good poem can linger in the body long after we have forgotten a report. Poems resonate. In the words of poet and philosopher Jan Zwicky: "analysis is a laser, lyric is a bell" (2003). Writing to create resonance offers an ecology of presence in the abundant world.

The author wishes to thank Kathy Kaulbach for conversations about her writing process.

References

Abram, D. (1996). *The spell of the sensuous*. New York: Vintage Books.

Ackerman, D. (1990). *A natural history of the senses*. New York: Vintage Books.

Berman, M. (1990). *Coming to our senses*. New York: Bantam.

Butler-Kisber, L. (2002). Artful portrayals in qualitative inquiry: The road to found poetry and beyond. *Alberta Journal of Educational Research, 48*(3), 229–239.

Collins, B. (2002). *Poetry 180*. New York: Random House.

Geertz, C. (1973). Deep play: Notes on the Balinese cockfight. In C. Geertz (Ed.), *The interpretation of cultures* (pp. 412–453). New York: Basic Books.

Hejinian, L. (2000). *The language of inquiry*. Los Angeles: University of California Press.

Kaulbach, K. (2012). Personal communication.

Lee, D. (1998). *Body music*. Toronto, ON: Anansi Press.

Mairs, N. (1994). *Voice lessons: On becoming a (woman) writer*. Boston: Beacon Press.

Maynard, K. & Cahnmann-Taylor, M. (2010). Anthropology at the edge of words: Where poetry and ethnography meet. *Anthropology and Humanism, 35*(1), 2–19.

McGilchrist, I. (2009). *The master and his emissary: The divided brain and the making of the modern world*. New Haven, CT: Yale University Press.

McKay, D. (2001). *Vis a vis: Fieldnotes on poetry and wilderness*. Wolfville, NS: Gaspereau Press.

Neilsen, L. (1989) *Literacy and living: The literate lives of three adults*. Portsmouth, NH: Heinemann Educational Books.

Neilsen, L. (2002a). Learning from the liminal: Fiction as knowledge. *Alberta Journal of Educational Research, 48*(3), 206–214.

Neilsen, L. (2002b). Lyric inquiry: Line breaks and liminal spaces. Invited address at the University of Alberta.

Neilsen, L. (2004). Learning to listen: Data as poetry, poetry as data. *Journal of Critical Inquiry into Curriculum and Instruction, 5*(2), 40–42.

Neilsen, L., Cole, A.L. & Knowles, J.G. (Eds.). (2001). *The art of writing inquiry*. Halifax, NS: Backalong Books.

Neilsen Glenn, L. (2010). *Lost gospels*. London, ON: Brick Books.

Neilsen Glenn, L. (2011). *Threading light: Explorations in poetry and loss*. Regina, SK: Hagios Press.

Nichols, B. (1991). *Representing reality: Issues and concepts in documentary*. Bloomington, IN: Indiana University Press, p. 178.

Nussbaum, M. (2001). *Upheavals of thought*. New York: Cambridge University Press.

Prendergast, M. (2009). Introduction: The phenomena of poetry in research. In

M. Prendergast, C. Leggo & P. Sameshima (Eds.), *Poetic inquiry: Vibrant voices in the social sciences* (pp. xix–xlii). Rotterdam: Sense Publishers.

Rosenblatt, L. (1976). *Literature as exploration* (3rd ed.). New York: Noble and Noble Publishers.

Rosenblatt, L. (1978). *The reader, the text, the poem: The transactional theory of the literary work*. Carbondale, IL: Southern Illinois University Press.

Rosenblatt, L. (1980). What facts does this poem teach you? *Language Arts, 57*(4), 386–394.

Weil, S. (1970). *First and last notebooks*. Oxford: Oxford University Press.

Whyte, W.F. (1943). *Street corner society: The social structure of an Italian slum*. Chicago: University of Chicago Press.

Zwicky, J. (2003). *Wisdom and metaphor*. Kentville, NS. Gaspereau Press.

10

A/R/TOGRAPHY

Always in Process

Carl Leggo and Rita L. Irwin

The Emergence of A/r/tography

In the past few decades arts-based research in education has developed in diverse and even dazzling ways (Barone & Eisner, 2012). Arts-based researchers in education promote the significant value of the creative arts for inquiring about experiences as well as presenting and representing the themes and understandings that emerge from the research. In turn, the arts are valuable for opening up theories and perspectives for guiding practice and policy-making. Like all arts-based research in the social sciences, a/r/tography is committed to incorporating the arts in all aspects of the research process. So, a/r/tographers lean on their arts experiences and practices and understandings to conceive innovative research questions and possibilities, as well as to conduct research in ways that will open up emerging and provocative and engaging insights. Moreover, a/r/tographers are committed to seeking artful ways to mobilize knowledge for wide audiences. A/r/tographers are always engaging in inquiry as a process, as a verb, and they are open and flexible, ready to embrace new questions, and revisit their research plans, and pursue other directions with a creative disposition that fires their research as well as their art-making and teaching. We are enthused about a/r/tography as a methodology because it recognizes how our art-making and research and teaching are all best understood as life-long and living commitments to practice. We are always in process. Even when we produce poems and art and essays, we know these products are not final and complete. There is always room for revisiting and revising all our work. Literacy researchers might find it useful to compare a/r/tography to the kind of best practices that emerge in the writing classroom where the process of composition is promoted as a pedagogical journey that includes ongoing inquiry.

Out of that process, we will produce texts for sharing with wide-ranging audiences, but the researching and writing are always in process.

A/r/tography has emerged, particularly at the University of British Columbia, out of a scholarly commitment to arts-based educational research, where research explorations are undertaken among groups of faculty and graduate students. Out of these explorations, a/r/tography has emerged (Irwin & de Cosson, 2004; Kind, de Cosson, Irwin, & Grauer, 2007; Prendergast, Gouzouasis, Leggo, & Irwin, 2009; Prendergast et al., 2008; Springgay, Irwin, Leggo, & Gouzouasis, 2008; Wiebe et al., 2007). From the beginning, a/r/tographers focused on the interconnections between the artist *and* researcher *and* teacher, and acknowledged a keen satisfaction in a hybrid identity where the experiences, practices, and perspectives linked to each specific identity informed all the others. A/r/tography has now been enthusing and guiding scholars for more than a decade (Sinner, Leggo, Irwin, Gouzouasis, & Grauer, 2007).

A/r/tography is a hybrid form of practice-based research that attends to the complex identities and practices of artists *and* researchers *and* teachers as integrally engaged in living inquiry. In naming a/r/tography as a hybrid form, we recognize that a/r/tography is connected to the theories, traditions, and practices of many qualitative research methodologies, including arts-based research, teacher research, action research, poetic inquiry, and narrative inquiry, but the distinctive focus of a/r/tography is on the intersections of the identities of the artist, the researcher, and the teacher as integrally and contiguously connected. As a/r/tographers, we do not wear different hats to represent our identities as artists, researchers, and teachers. In all our creative pursuits and research projects and teaching and graduate supervision, we acknowledge the holistic nature of our identities as vigorously and vibrantly connected. We pursue creative and pedagogical possibilities in all our research, and all our research shapes and invigorates our teaching. Like the creative arts, a/r/tography is focused on process. A/r/tographers are always asking questions as they inquire and engage in art-making and consider how pedagogy is connected to ways of knowing and becoming. For literacy researchers, a/r/tography is an especially promising research methodology because *graphy* (*graphein*, to write) is at the heart of a/r/tographic inquiry.

So, a/r/tography invites a dynamic dialogue among all the arts as a way of inquiring about teaching and teaching about researching. By weaving the arts and inquiry and teaching in contiguous relationships of living inquiry, creative possibilities for questioning and understanding emerge. Living inquiry is the intentional and unintentional engagement pursued through embodied questioning, interpretation, and analysis. Individual and collective creative possibilities flourish within living inquiry. While a/r/tography is significantly connected to autobiography, the understanding of self-study that a/r/tographers promote is inextricably connected to social, cultural, historical, and ideological contexts. A/r/tographers often collaborate in communities of practice where they encourage and interrogate one another, where they bring distinct expertise to braiding a more complex research agenda with diverse perspectives and practices. In turn, they nurture more and more complex research questions, and mobilize and disseminate knowledge in creative and engaging ways that honor the ways that the arts characteristically evoke and provoke insightful understandings.

The Disposition of A/r/tography

While a/r/tography initially emerged from the thinking and practice of visual art educators, educators with expertise in diverse creative arts, including creative writing, music, drama, theatre, dance, and performance have quickly embraced it (see Carter, Beare, Belliveau & Irwin, 2011; Prendergast et al., 2009). A/r/tography is an emerging research methodology. Like all artists, a/r/tographers are committed to creativity, imagination, curiosity, risk-taking, especially as integral to an organic process of engaging in a research process that is full of surprises and twists. A/r/tography is not a method that can be used like a road map or GPS.

Hargreaves (2003) contends that educators need to address with clear courage and creativity "how we should live our lives, and for what kind of life we should be educating young people" (p. 48). After thoughtfully ruminating on teacher qualities and dispositions such as flexibility, problem-solving, risk-taking, continuous improvement, cosmopolitan identity, and personal and professional maturity (p. 29; pp. 65–66), Hargreaves proposes that "engaging with the knowledge society and its human consequences calls on us to make teaching into a social mission and a creative, passionate profession" (p. 203). Resonant with Hargreaves' hope, the primary goal of a/r/tographic research is to promote teaching and learning as transformative, creative, and passionate.

In a recent research study we conducted known as "Becoming Pedagogical," we directed our attention to teacher candidates in language and literacy education.[1] Instead of focusing on teacher candidates as people who are *learning to teach*, we promoted the understanding of teacher candidates as people who are *learning to learn*. We focused on the concept of "becoming pedagogical" in order to recognize how teachers are always in a process of living inquiry that includes asking many questions and reflecting on experiences and imagining possibilities (e.g., Irwin & O'Donoghue, 2012). This is the disposition of the a/r/tographer. From September to December, 2009, a class of teacher candidates at the University of British Columbia completed a Bachelor of Education course entitled "English language arts: Secondary curriculum and instruction". As the instructor, Carl introduced himself as an a/r/tographer and invited teacher candidates to consider their possible identities as a/r/tographers who are engaged in a creative process of learning and becoming. In presenting the concept of *becoming pedagogical*, Carl invited the students to interrogate how *becoming pedagogical* is a complex process that includes personal, professional, and political perspectives, contexts, experiences, and identities.

Over a decade ago, Berman (1999) wrote the article entitled "Teacher as poet" where she discussed five qualities that she claims are "pertinent to the poet and poetry," and that she believes "may characterize the teacher and teaching" (p. 18). According to Berman, "these qualities include: (a) giving voice to the unspoken, (b) befriending mystery, (c) connecting heart/mind conversations, (d) bearing witness, and (e) delighting in surprise" (p. 18). As a/r/tographers, we ask how the image of the "teacher as poet" or the "teacher as artist" might inform our practices, research, and policies. In our *becoming pedagogical* study, Berman's qualities resonated with the dispositions of our teacher candidates. As the teacher candidates wrote credos about their emerging identities as artists, researchers, and teachers, they exemplified the qualities that Berman outlined: (a) giving voice to the unspoken by bringing one's passion for life to teaching, (b) befriending mystery by sharing creative gifts between teachers and students, (c) connecting heart/mind conversations by thinking creatively and critically, (d) bearing witness by creating classroom experiences that exemplify care, cooperation and community, and (e) delighting in surprise by creating a vibrant learning environment with patience, passion, and empathy.

The disposition of the a/r/tographer is fired by a commitment to curiosity, and embracing questions as necessary for any living quest, and never assuming that we know all there is to know. The a/r/tographer is abundantly agnostic, always sure there are more questions, more insights, more possibilities to pursue. As a/r/tographers we address questions like the following: How might a/r/tography promote practices and policies of pedagogy as transformative, integral, holistic, ecological, spiritual, radical, and critical? What are the dispositions of artists and teachers and researchers? What is good art? What is art good for? What is effective teaching? Why is research important? Can teacher education programs foster imagination in learning and living and becoming? What kinds of teachers are needed for contemporary schools? What kind of teacher education is needed in order to help nurture the kind of teachers that are needed? Can a/r/tography contribute to nurturing the kind of teachers and learners that are needed?

Rogers (2011) argues that while teacher education programs ought to make "available a highly valued repertoire of practical skills," they "should also communicate an accessible set of personal values and vision in learning and teaching which help to inform and shape the professional identities of new teachers" (p. 250). A/r/tographers promote and support the development of "values and vision" for both teacher candidates and teacher educators. A/r/tographers seek to promote a vibrant and vital teacher education experience that invites both creative and critical attention to remembering the past, attending to the present, and imagining the future. A/r/tographers are committed to embracing complexity and transformation. This kind of creative process cannot be formulaic or predictable. A/r/tography does not offer a toolbox of skills and strategies for creativity or teaching or researching. A/r/tographers are always engaged in processes of becoming. All teachers (beginning and experienced) need to embrace the same values, predispositions, approaches, and commitments that artists and researchers bring to the critical and creative work of pedagogy. There are no simple answers or strategies for either teaching or teaching teachers.

The Practice of A/r/tography

It is not really possible to spell out how a researcher uses a/r/tography as a method to analyze data because each research project is approached as unique and idiosyncratic, much like a poet's approach to writing a new poem. Nevertheless, a recent essay describes using a/r/tography in a language arts class (Leggo et al., 2011) and provides a demonstration of how a team of researchers emerged in their confidence regarding the value of a/r/tography as an approach that helped to inquire about the experiences in a language arts classroom. As members of that research team, we initially planned to use a version of ethnography in order to research the ongoing experiences of a class of students who were invited to participate in process-oriented approaches to reading and writing. This research project proved to be pivotal in our emerging understanding of the value of a/r/tography for inquiring about experiences in elementary classrooms. We had initially invited the teacher, Kathy Pantaleo, to think about herself as an a/r/tographer, and to consider how this identity might inform her teaching practice. What emerged in the course of a year's research is that the students and Carl Leggo, as the lead researcher, also began to understand how a/r/tography could shape all aspects of the complex experiences of teaching, learning, and researching in the classroom. As the research unfolded in the Grade 6/7 class, the students and their teacher engaged in an exploration of community action that involved research, writing, and communicating with local politicians. What began as an ethnographic research study evolved into an exemplar of a/r/tography in action, a living inquiry that was always transforming our pedagogical and research practices in the creative pursuit of teaching and learning experiences that were critical, transformative, holistic, and collaborative.

The following passage from Leggo's research journal (see Leggo et al., 2011, pp. 11–12) exemplifies the emergent and process-focused approach of the a/r/tographer:

> I think the challenge I faced in the Richmond project is that I wanted to understand how the arts inform teaching and learning, especially how creative approaches to teaching writing can foster classroom environments where young people know themselves as writers. I began my research with an ethnographic approach, but quickly became frustrated with the

realization that I was not sufficiently present in the classroom in order to discern the complex dynamics of the learning and teaching experiences. In other words, I was a visitor who caught glimpses of the classroom experiences. The project began as an attempt to understand how the integration of the arts in classrooms contributes to teaching and learning. From my visits to Kathy's classroom, I can readily claim that the arts contribute to learning. But what I have found most disconcerting is the sense of disjuncture between my goal and the method I was using to achieve the goal. Above all, I was concerned about how little I could experience, and hence lay claim to understanding, in the context of my limited research visits.

I have reflected on the experiences of the writing class, and I have interpreted some of the experiences, but I am no closer to understanding the experiences than I was when I was in the experience. In fact, whatever understanding is available to me about the experience in Kathy's class is a tentative and malleable understanding. I don't know what to make of the experience. So, in the end the most I can do is write and read and speak my story, over and over, like the Ancient Mariner, and in the writing and reading and speaking perhaps find some revelation, possibilities for revelation and understanding, especially in the gaps and silences that lie hidden in the written and read and spoken texts, always quest/ion/ing the ways that words are written and read and spoken, in order to see other ways of writing, reading, and speaking the words.

Subsequently, at this place and time in my re/search I still have more questions than answers, but I am discovering in the questions fecund places for dwelling. As I seek to write the narratives of my experiences in the writing class, and as I seek to interpret the narratives I write, and as I seek to make sense of the narratives written by the students in the course, I am constantly reminded how complicated this whole business of research is that focuses on narrative. My desire to write lines of connection between searching literacy and re/searching literacy is then a quest/ion/ing that opens up many possibilities concerning issues of narrative and lived experience and identity, representation, and discourse.

Out of the experience of this research project, we learned many significant lessons. First, we better understood how in our research experience as a/r/tographers we were negotiating the messiness of field research through living inquiry, and how this messiness is characteristic of the many challenges that teachers live daily in their classrooms. As researchers and educators, we grew more confident that by embracing a/r/tography as a methodology of living inquiry we could investigate ways to support teachers and learners in innovative pedagogic practices. In the course of a year's research in the Grade 6/7 class, we began to understand how our research goals and plans changed as we engaged a/r/tographically with the teacher and students. As artists, researchers, and teachers we learned to linger in the liminal or in-between spaces of knowing and not knowing, of questioning and transforming practice, as each of us inquired into our own practices in a community of living inquiry that attended to the creative possibilities of language and literacy for knowing, understanding, and communicating. Lingering in these in-between liminal spaces allowed us to question, reflect, and question again, as we became ever more committed to learning to learn.

The Performance of A/r/tography

Borko, Liston, and Whitcomb (2006) recommend that: "alternative views of teacher education and alternative methodological approaches for studying teacher education need to be disseminated and discussed" (p. 202). In our research informed by a/r/tography, we actively seek an alternative approach to how we engage in teacher education and how we research teacher education. In the research study *Becoming pedagogical*, teacher candidates wrote three statements or credos in which they reflected on what they believed about teaching in general, and English teaching in particular. They wrote a brief credo at the beginning of the course, followed by longer credos in the middle of the course and at the end of the course. The teacher candidates were invited to expand on their initial credos, and to continue revising their credos so they could incorporate their responses to the curricular and pedagogical experiences they had encountered in the course.

Like Cooper and White (2004) recommend, the purpose of the credo assignment was to focus "on understanding how teachers' personal lives influence and inform their professional lives" (p. xii). Cooper and White propose that teacher candidates need to begin with their "own lived experiences" (p. xii) in order to "reconnect teachers' personal and professional lives through a process of critical inquiry" (p. xxii) that motivates teacher candidates to consider cosmopolitan contexts that extend far beyond any one person's limited experience. At the beginning of the course, Carl explained to the teacher candidates that the word *credo* means *I believe*, but that it also more accurately signifies *what I have given my heart to*. He explained that every educator, both beginning and experienced, needs to ask: "What have I given my heart to?"

In order to invite teacher candidates in the course to ruminate on the experiences and hopes that fired their credos as beginning teachers, Carl shared narrative and poetic accounts of his own beginning as a teacher in order to engage teacher candidates in personal memory and reflection. He explained how he was a teacher in process, a teacher-researcher, searching again and again through his poetic and pedagogical practices and experiences in order to grow in confidence, skill, and imagination. He has been engaged in a long process of becoming pedagogical. He invited teachers to engage with action research, teacher inquiry, narrative inquiry, poetic inquiry, arts-based inquiry, and a/r/tography. He explained how he wants teachers to know themselves as artists or poets. Like poets or artists, teachers improvise, explore, experiment, and practice. Above all, they live their vocation.

Five teacher candidates in the course agreed to join the research project. As an exemplar of a/r/tographic inquiry, we next focus on the writing of Cynthia, one of the teacher candidates.

Cynthia's Credo

At the beginning of the semester Cynthia took up Carl's invitation to consider herself an a/r/tographer. She wrote:

> I am looking forward to learning all that I can in order to be a great teacher. My hope is that I can learn the tools to encourage students to think creatively and critically. I love this idea of being an a/r/tographer. I know I am an artist in the sense of my work in the theatre, but I also love to take photos, paint just about anything, and I have even written a few poems. As a researcher, I am a continual learner and a Googler. The path that led me here actually came through my research in directed theatre studies which involved drama as education and drama as therapy. I am here to develop my skills as a teacher and this includes a better understanding of how to be an a/r/tographer.

Following her two-week teaching practicum, Cynthia wrote about the process of becoming pedagogical by focusing on the pedagogical relationship between the educator and the learner. She is especially concerned about "the structure of school," including the dilemma of time in the classroom:

> A creative process in any sense takes time, more time than is possible in the present system. I struggle because I am unable to give students enough of my time, enough time and space to develop skills to write, to act, and to create. Maybe what makes this so difficult is because I know there needs to be changes made, but what is the next step? What can I do? How is change possible?

A cornerstone of Cynthia's credo is that "each student comes with a different life story and is looking to be a part of a community in some way." In order to foster a sense of community, Cynthia advocates the value of preparation:

> For now what I can bring as a teacher to the classroom is to be prepared. In thinking of ways that I can be prepared, there is a motto that I created for myself that has been helpful. I try to keep the following in mind; to be

positive, proactive and personable. I affectionately call these the 3 Ps. I find that if I can keep these concepts a priority, I am prepared for my day and better able to be an encouragement or a help to another.

In addition to promoting preparation as important for nurturing community in the classroom, Cynthia hopes to "create a positive environment" for her students by developing "a safe and comfortable atmosphere" where "trust and respect" are enjoyed by everyone, and where everyone is encouraged "to ask questions." Above all, Cynthia hopes to create opportunities for students to "grow, create, and discover what is in their hearts."

Meijer, de Graaf, and Meirink (2011) observed that most of the teacher candidates with whom they worked perceived "their own development not as a steadily ascending line referring to the improvement of teaching practice, but as a path with highs and lows, and with transformative moments or periods" (p. 127). In a similar way, it is clear in our study the teacher candidates understand the process of becoming pedagogical as if journeying on a Möbius strip where there is no binary opposition between the inside and the outside, no division between the past and the present, no separation of the personal and the professional. Credos proved to be one strategy to explore how teaching is a creative profession. The Möbius strip metaphor illustrates the living inquiry desired in a/r/tography. Teacher candidate credos not only illustrate their beliefs and desires toward their practice, they also guide us as teacher educators as we create programs attentive to teacher candidate interests. Teacher candidates genuinely want to have an impact on students. By concentrating on sustaining their hearts as teacher candidates, we are leading the way to sustaining their hearts as they enter the profession. Perhaps more importantly, they are engaging in learning to learn through a/r/tographic living inquiry in and through time. Sustaining our hearts by becoming pedagogical, we live our lives on a Möbius strip where our identities and stories and hopes all circulate in the ways of the heart's rhythms—integral, connected, and vital.

The Usefulness of A/r/tography

A/r/tography is not a formulaic method that can be simply adopted and used by other researchers. Instead, researchers who wish to approach their inquiries with a/r/tography need to engage creatively with their research in the same ways that artists engage with their art making. It is unlikely that any a/r/tographic research project will look or sound or feel like any other. Like art, a/r/tography is always seeking to be innovative and imaginative. This does not mean that a/r/tography is not connected to the many long traditions of scholarly and artistic practice. A/r/tographers are always informed by other researchers, including other a/r/tographers, past and present, but there is no template or checklist for guiding a new a/r/tographic research venture. A/r/tography does not seek to be derivative. Instead, a/r/tography is committed to being dynamic. The a/r/tographer is always attentive and responsive in the process of art-making and researching and teaching, seeking always new possibilities, even transformation.

In a further research study focused on teacher education,[2] we explore the trope of *irony* in order to invite teachers and teacher candidates and teacher educators to ask questions that can startle, surprise, and arrest our perspectives and views so we can begin to imagine new possibilities. Like Aoki (2005a) we are "drawn into the fold of a discursive imaginary that can entertain 'both this and that,' 'neither this nor that'—a space of paradox, ambiguity and ambivalence" (p. 317). When irony is invited into our discursive practices, we find "the tensioned space of both 'and/not-and' is a space of conjoining and disrupting, indeed a generative space of possibilities, a space wherein in tensioned ambiguity newness emerges" (p. 318). And out of these in-between spaces, we hear "the voice of play in the midst of things—a playful singing in the midst of life" (Aoki, 2005b, p. 282).

Barakett and Cleghorn (2008) ask: "What kind of education would teachers need to have in order to integrate critical thinking into the curriculum?" (p. 7). We think that irony is integral to critical and creative thinking. In our research as a/r/tographers we frequently address themes of identity, representation, meaning, and agency. One of the biggest challenges we face in teacher education is that we want to invite new teacher candidates to interrogate the ways that their images of teachers and teaching have been constructed, and to acknowledge that these images have been constructed through a complex concatenation of cultural experiences that include many years spent in school and university classrooms, as well as TV, film, and fiction. But the teacher candidates often want to be trained or prepared, inducted or indoctrinated.

So, in a course that focuses on teaching English language and literacy, Carl introduced teacher candidates to the trope of irony as a potentially valuable way to challenge the ways that they have been interpellated or hailed according to cultural experiences and views. Irony is the trope of juxtaposition. Irony juxtaposes appearance and reality. What happens is the opposite of what is expected. Or, what is said is not what is meant. With irony, there is always an incongruity or discordance between surface meaning and underlying meaning. With teacher candidates, we have begun to generate a list of questions that we recommend asking frequently and ironically about teacher education. The list currently comprises more than 120 questions. Here is a sample of 15 to whet the imagination:

1. Who teaches teachers?
2. Who taught the teacher educators how to teach educators?
3. Why do teachers teach?
4. How do teachers teach?
5. How do teachers learn how to teach?

6. How do teachers teach how to learn?
7. Are teachers always teaching?
8. What do teachers know?
9. What do teachers not know?
10. What do teachers need to know?
11. What do teachers not need to know?
12. How do teachers sustain their spirits, their inner lives?
13. Are teachers artists?
14. Are teachers researchers?
15. How might irony haunt a teacher education program?

These questions and many others were used to keep teacher candidates engaged in their own independent inquiries while contributing to the inquiries of their peers. The process inspires the desire for continuously engaging with ideas, often uncomfortable ideas, thus probing ever more deeply into a phenomenon of interest. It is the process of living inquiry, of engaging with questions, and more questions, that invites understanding teaching and learning in nuanced and creative ways. In this way, a/r/tography is always in process.

Conclusion

A/r/tographers are always engaging in their art and research and teaching with an abiding and heartful commitment to intuition, inquiry, investigation, and interrogation that is creative, emergent, risk-taking, interdisciplinary, reflexive, organic, and even ironic. Andrews (2006) recommends approaching life with wonder, "to never feel that we have the final answer, but to keep searching" and "never close yourself off to a new form of wisdom or aliveness" (p. 152). And in a similar way Bloch (2006) refers to "the terror of the desire to know" (p. 167). He thinks we need to promote more wonder: "Almost no one kept up his questioning wonder past the first answer" (p. 170). A/r/tography promotes questioning and wonder. A/r/tographers are always committed to creativity and inquiry and teaching as transformative and hopeful. In the spirit of a/r/tography we end with one of Carl's poems.

> Verb
> Oh, to be a verb
>   a creative word
>   makes statements
>   gives commands
>   asks questions
> too long I have been
> written a noun only,
> a name for a person

animal place thing
quality idea action
Oh, to be a verb
an efficacious word
declares authors
interrogates with
alphabetic delight
always becoming
endlessly mutable
subject in process
naming without end

Notes

1. We wish to thank the Social Sciences and Humanities Research Council of Canada for funding our research program entitled: "Becoming Pedagogical through A/r/tography in Teacher Education." This article examines a study within this larger project entitled "Becoming Pedagogical: Sustaining Hearts through Living Credos." We also wish to thank our co-investigators in the "Becoming Pedagogical" study for their commitment to creative and critical a/r/tographical inquiry: Peter Gouzouasis, Kit Grauer, Donal O'Donoghue, and Stephanie Springgay.
2. Another study within the "Becoming Pedagogical" study is a smaller study entitled: "Who am I? Questioning teacher education with irony." Manuscripts detailing this smaller study are in preparation.

References

Andrews, C. (2006). *Slow is beautiful: New visions of community, leisure and joie de vivre.* Gabriola Island, BC: New Society Publishers.

Aoki, T. (2005a). Imaginaries of "East" and "West": Slippery curricular signifiers in education. In W. F. Pinar & R. L. Irwin (Eds.). *Curriculum in a new key: The collected works of Ted T. Aoki* (pp. 313–319). Mahwah, NJ: Lawrence Erlbaum.

Aoki, T. (2005b). The child-centered curriculum: Where is the social in pedocentricism? In W. F. Pinar & R. L. Irwin (Eds.). *Curriculum in a new key: The collected works of Ted T. Aoki* (pp. 279–289). Mahwah, NJ: Lawrence Erlbaum.

Barakett, J., & Cleghorn, A. (2008). *Sociology of education: An introductory view from Canada* (2nd ed.). Toronto, ON: Pearson Education Canada.

Barone, T., & Eisner, E. W. (2012). *Arts based research.* Thousand Oaks, CA: Sage.

Berman, L. M. (1999). Teacher as poet. *Theory into Practice, 38,* 18–23.

Bloch, E. (2006). *Traces* (A. A. Nassar, Trans.). Stanford, CA: Stanford University Press.

Borko, H., Liston, D., & Whitcomb, D. A. (2006). A conversation of many voices: Critiques and visions of teacher education. *Journal of Teacher Education, 57,* 199–204.

Carter, M., Beare, D., Belliveau, G., & Irwin, R. L. (2011). A/r/tography as pedagogy: A promise without guarantee. *Canadian Review of Art Education, 38,* 17–32.

Cooper, K., & White, R. E. (2004). *Burning issues: Foundations of education.* Lanham, MD: Scarecrow Education.

Hargreaves, A. (2003). *Teaching in the knowledge society: Education in the age of insecurity.* New York: Teachers College Press.

Irwin, R. L., & de Cosson, A. (Eds.). (2004). *A/r/tography: Rendering self through arts-based living inquiry*. Vancouver, BC: Pacific Educational Press.

Irwin, R. L., & O'Donoghue, D. (2012). Encountering pedagogy through relational art practices. *International Journal of Art and Design Education, 31*, 221–236.

Kind, S., de Cosson, A., Irwin, R. L., & Grauer, K. (2007). Artist–teacher partnerships in learning: The in/between spaces of artist–teacher professional development. *Canadian Journal of Education, 30*, 839–864.

Leggo, C., & Irwin, R. L. (in preparation). *Who am I? Questioning teacher education with irony*. Unpublished manuscript, University of British Columbia, Vancouver.

Leggo, C., Sinner, A., Irwin, R. L., Pantaleo, K., Gouzouasis, P., & Grauer, K. (2011). Liminal spaces: A/r/tography as living inquiry in a language arts class. *International Journal of Qualitative Studies in Education, 24*, 239–256.

Meijer, P. C., de Graaf, G., & Meirink, J. (2011). Key experiences in student teachers' development. *Teachers and Teaching, 17*, 115–129.

Prendergast, M., Gouzouasis, P., Leggo, C., & Irwin, R. L. (2009). A Haiku suite: The importance of music making in the lives of secondary students. *Music Education Research, 11*, 303–317.

Prendergast, M., Lymburner, J., Grauer, K., Irwin, R. L., Leggo, C., & Gouzouasis, P. (2008). Pedagogy of trace: Poetic representations of teaching resiliance/resistance in arts education. *Vitae Scholasticae: The Journal of Educational Biography, 25*, 58–76.

Rogers, G. (2011). Learning-to-learn and learning-to-teach: The impact of disciplinary subject study on student-teachers' professional identity. *Journal of Curriculum Studies, 43*, 249–268.

Sinner, A., Leggo, C., Irwin, R., Gouzouasis, P., & Grauer, K. (2007). Arts-based educational research dissertations: Reviewing the practices of new scholars. *Canadian Journal of Education, 29*, 1223–1270.

Springgay, S., Irwin, R., Leggo, C., & Gouzouasis, P. (Eds.). (2008). *Being with a/r/tography*. Rotterdam, Netherlands: Sense Publishers.

Wiebe, S., Sameshima, P., Irwin, R. L., Leggo, C., Gouzouasis, P., & Grauer, K. (2007). Re-imagining arts integration: Rhizomatic relations of the every day. *Journal of Educational Thought, 31*, 263–280.

11

ARTIFACTUAL LITERACIES

Kate Pahl and Jennifer Rowsell

In this chapter, we argue that artifactual literacies as a lens, opens up new worlds for educators; as teachers grapple with the complexities of their students' social worlds we offer the artifactual as an attuned and powerful listening methodology for use in the classroom and beyond (Back, 2007). By making sense of children's material worlds, this process can open up cultural spaces that are rich in opportunities to exchange home 'funds of knowledge' with students in ways that are equitable and respectful (Moll, Amanti, Neff, & Gonzalez, 1992).

An artifactual literacies approach values the epistemological complexity of diversity in classrooms. A number of scholars have argued for the need to value the complex cultures young people bring to classrooms (Compton-Lilly, Rogers, & Lewis, 2012; Gonzalez, Moll, & Amanti, 2005; Lee, 2008; Rogers, Mosley, Kramer, & Literacy for Social Justice Teacher Research Group, 2009). Teachers can listen to their students through their linguistic repertoires (Hornberger, 2000), through their literacy practices (Street, 1993), and multimodal literacies (Flewitt, 2008), as well as by way of their oral storytelling (Heath, 1983), language varieties (Coupland, 2010), and interactional genres (Lefstein, 2008). However, by seeing the world as materially, as well as culturally situated, and applying this insight to meaning making, students can bring in a broader range of discourses and practices to this process (Gee, 1999; Miller, 2008). By drawing on an approach that values the situated, everyday, and ordinary world from which our students make meaning, we can provide educators with a theory of meaning making that is grounded and respectful (Williams, 1961).

Below we outline the roots of our theory making and offer some thinking we have developed since the writing of our book, *Artifactual Literacies* (Pahl & Rowsell, 2010). We do this through the fieldwork we have carried out in Canada and the UK, in situated domains of practice (Barton & Hamilton,

1998). We then provide educators with an account, drawn from our lived and practical experience of working with teachers in the classroom, of how they can develop this approach in the classroom. We provide some case studies of artifactual literacies in practice and consider new directions for this field. We conclude by offering some insights from recent research and practice.

Why Artifactual Literacies?

We came together with a shared appreciation of the work of Brian Street (1984, 1993, 2008) in recognizing the situated nature of literacies. Street's insight that there are different literacies connected to different domains of life enabled us to privilege the ethnographic lens that saw everyday literacy practices as important and valuable. We were able to translate that knowledge into our research. We were also able to document the strategies teachers used to harness these out of school literacies and ways of knowing and draw on them in their classroom (Pahl & Rowsell, 2012). We are interested in researching the permeable nature of the boundaries between home and school and how these boundaries can be crossed as literacies travel across and between these borders (Dyson, 1993; Pahl & Rowsell, 2006). We have conducted our research in shopping malls, libraries, health centers, schools, homes, parks, after school clubs, youth centers, and on the streets of many different locations across the UK and Canada. As part of our ethnographic lens, we look for the extraordinary in the everyday, and this involves an attention to the signs and patterns we see around us (Scollon & Scollon, 2003).

Literacy is embedded in 'things,' that is, objects, artifacts, the 'stuff' of life. These might include, for example, digital objects such as a mobile phone, or material objects such as a piece of embroidery, and these things matter to the way literacy is presented and understood. The materiality of each object in which literacy is found or embedded matters to us as researchers. Each material object has specific qualities or values. While a keyboard might present a particular surface, a wipe clean whiteboard is a different surface, a tablet something else, a chalk stick different again; and the sweep of a finger on a surface of a dusty car is another. We are interested to follow the lines and traces (Ingold, 2007) of these temporary embodiments of writing and oral language. We see writing and oral language as entwined and often mixed closely together, drawing on our observations of everyday literacy and language practices (Finnegan, 2007).

This quest has led us to the world of material cultural studies. We began by reading Miller's (2008) book, *The Comfort of Things*, in which he interviewed all the residents of a street in South London and found that things were very much the anchor for people's experience, values, and emotional lives. We drew on Hurdley's (2006) insight that people tell different stories about objects found in the home but that these stories are key identity markers, and these objects also matter to people as traces of identity. We found the work of Csikszentmihalyi and Rochberg-Halton (1981) in *The Meaning of Things* – a study of Chicago residents' attachment to objects – very helpful in alerting us to the alive connections between people and their objects, a process they called 'flow.' We learned from Raymond Williams (1961) that culture is 'ordinary' and recognized, from Hoggart (1957) that culture is present in small embodiments, which locate the local with specific forms of cultural experience (Willis, 2000). We value the small and sometimes ephemeral-seeming objects and artifacts that signal the cultures that the students we encounter value and live within (Pahl, 2002).

Within this landscape strewn with material objects, found, made, inherited, lost, and often layered and littering homes, communities, schools, and other spaces of learning, we found children and young people making meaning (Lawn & Grosvenor, 2005). These meaning making spaces might include a bedroom strewn with small play objects or cardboard constructions (Ring, 2006). We combined our understanding from New Literacy Studies of the concept of literacy practices with a recognition of the way in which these practices were themselves multimodal (Kress, 1997; Pahl, 1999). We began to work with multimodality as a theory that accounted for the way children and young people put together assemblages of meaning that drew on modal choices in order to express the 'best fit' of these assemblages. By seeing meaning making as being about the choice of affordance of different modes to create representations, the scope of literacy could be widened.

We have both found in conducting ethnographic work in homes, community hubs, and schools, that meaning makers have tacit understandings of the best fit for a mode. Sometimes they draw on visual texts as the best way to complete an assignment or transmit a message, and, at other times, they will opt for words. Working with young children and their families, Kate has found that children can construct storied worlds out of objects, materials, and chalk (Pahl & Rowsell, 2010). So too, in Jennifer's work with teenagers, she has noted how young people have definite views on what music should accompany a moving-image text and how gaze can play a powerful role in visually based texts. Modal learning, as we call it, has become more prominent in our work together. That is, learning through the modes of expression and representation that meaning makers draw on when they produce or consume texts across contexts.

Within this set of ideas, of multimodal meaning making, of the materiality of cultural worlds, of the way in which small embodiments and social practice, constructed literacy, we realized we were looking at a conjoined set of ideas which we have labeled 'artifactual literacies' (Pahl & Rowsell, 2010).

A Theory of Artifactual Literacy

My favourite object is probably a tiny little babygro, this big.
When I had my little girl, she was only two pounds

so her babygro fit her Barbie doll now, (ohh)
despite the fact she is now fourteen
and I can't believe she ever was that small
but it reminds me of her
(a class teacher describing her special object on the first day of the My Family My
Story *project, from Pahl & Rowsell, 2010)*

We begin with the idea of the found object as a cultural artifact. When we have asked educators to work with students to describe or narrate their favorite object, we have discovered that this methodology is a powerful mechanism for creating equity in the classroom. We consider digital storytelling as a methodology, by which students create stories about their valued objects combining words and images, a helpful way of listening to students' stories of their favorite objects (Pahl & Rowsell, 2010; Pahl, 2011). We realize that the collage created by an object image and a voice-over can powerfully leverage different voices into the classroom (Hull and Nelson, 2009). We believe that stories about objects can create equitable learning spaces for students. This insight was also corroborated by the work of Scanlan (2010) and others who asked students to fill shoeboxes with objects and develop learning opportunities from that initial activity.

This mode of thinking about valued artifacts reverses some of the ways objects are presented in contemporary societies. The ways people value everyday objects are not necessarily reflected in their monetary value; in fact, often this monetary value is immaterial to the importance of the object to the person. This idea is expressed in a reflection from a parent when she was considering the impact of a digital storytelling project called 'My Family My Story' in a primary school in the North of England, UK, from a project that Kate conducted:

PARENT: I thought it was good that we were talking about the objects – what we held precious were such random things like an old tin of my nan's and it was the memories. Also, it's nice for them [the children] to know that such precious things, everyday objects, it's the meanings and the feelings that are with the objects, not necessarily expensive things from consumer culture, or material culture.

(audio recording, March 2008)

This kind of reversal can create spaces for children who may not be materially affluent to describe objects that are 'handmade' and valued in different ways to articulate their identities (Whitty, Rose, Baisley, Comeau, & Thompson, 2008). We have found this reversal of value particularly helpful in work with migrants where objects might be few in their homes, but these objects or memories of objects might serve as an important way of articulating identities that otherwise might not be heard in classrooms. This highlights the role of social memory (Connerton, 1989; Fentress & Wickham, 1992) in this process of appreciating students' life worlds.

We have drawn upon theories of everyday life to enable us to see these patterns and ways of being. Bourdieu's (1990) concept of habitus, that is, the governing structures within which we live that are handed on across generations, enabled us to think through ways in which intergenerational practices are key for young people's sense of identity and are drawn upon in meaning making (Rowsell & Pahl, 2007). These intergenerational schemas or dispositions could be found sedimented within texts that children made and, from this research (2007), we created a theoretical framework called 'sedimented identities in texts.' Distant meanings and ideas, from grandparents and, in many cases, far-off places, were recognizable within children's text making. Embedded within these drawings and assemblages were the objects the children's parents and grandparents carried with them. For example, Ruksana, below, describes a suitcase her father carried with him around the world and its importance to her in her life. When she looked for it, she found it had gone missing but its resonance was clear for her.

KATE: And you also talked about an old suitcase?
RUKSANA: Yes, mum's, I do believe she has still got it. I will ask her. I remember
        very vividly as a child this brown leather suitcase with all these labels on
        it. I assume they had labels at that time – they weren't the kind you could
        take off – and mum saying dad had used it for several years, and this is all
        the places he had gone to – I think she's got it somewhere.
        (interview, RK, Rotherham, South Yorkshire, UK, September 19, 2006)

We found that the cultural 'suitcases' or what Gonzalez et al. (2005) might call 'funds of knowledge' that children and young people carry with them into school are infused with their material, cultural, and intergenerational experiences.

Jennifer has worked with young people who carry objects and artifacts with them or on them as talismans of people they love or that represent parts of their identities. For example, Alisha talked about the handing-down of her bracelet that she wears all of the time. The bracelet passed down from her grandmother, then mother, and then to her, and she intends to pass it onto her own child. During our interview together, Alisha talked about the bracelet as carrying funds of knowledge:

JENNIFER: So … Alicia, tell me about your bracelet.
ALISHA: Well, um, this bracelet came from my great grandmother who gave it to
        my grandmother who gave it to my Mom, who gave it to me.
JENNIFER: Do you wear it all the time?

ALISHA: I wear it all the time because it makes me feel like I am carrying my family around, well like, I know they are always there for me.

This artifact has worked its way from one generation to the next and, in this way, Alisha feels like she is carrying part of her identity with her. Alisha's attachment to the object showed in her description of it and in her gestures with it: she touched the embossed flowers and pointed to small dents in them and how worn the bracelet had become with time.

Our sedimented identities theory combines an understanding of the cultural heritage children bring with them as being materially situated, with a recognition of what the telling of this heritage brings to children's articulation of their situated identities in the classroom (Gee, 1999). An artifactual literacies approach to research brings the materially situated nature of experience to the fore, and locates it within literacy and children's meaning making. However, it also sees literacy as in itself artifactual. In a research project Kate conducted she was able to observe how the creation of stories within a South Asian British home was informed by a number of artifactual properties, including textiles, glitter, craft, and gardening practices. Excavating this process of meaning making linked to materiality enabled a richer, more complex understanding of the meaning making of the children and young people in the study.

Artifactual Literacies in Action

Here we offer situated examples of how we have used an artifactual literacies approach to understand how literacies are connected to everyday objects and how this understanding aids in the recognition of meaning making processes. In the first example, the artifactual is manifested in the concept of garden as text. In the second, we present a contrasting, secondary perspective on artifactual literacies and on modal learning. The project is a multi-year study on multimodal approaches to the teaching of English, and is set in an urban high school in Canada, where Jennifer conducts her fieldwork. Both, however, unite a focus on the artifactual with leveraging the agency of meaning makers to listen more attentively to their habitus, their voices, and their lived experiences.

Garden as Text

Lucy and Tanya were 12 and eight, respectively. They were originally from a British Asian Pakistani heritage and lived in a Northern town in the UK. Their mother was born in the UK and their father was born in Pakistan. Their house included a forecourt with brightly colored flowers and a back garden, in which Tanya, who loved gardening, grew flowers from seeds. I (Kate) conducted an ethnographic study of the family's home writing practices, over a period of one year (funded by the Arts and Humanities Research Council, UK) (Pahl 2012).

The study involved visiting on a regular basis and asking the children to collect images, writing and descriptions of the nature of their home writing practices over time. One day, I was invited into the garden where Lucy and Tanya described to me their gardening practices:

LUCY: Tanya also had her very own little green house and tubs where she had planted seeds. Daffodils and all them kinds of flowers.

(audio recording July 11, 2011)

I was struck by the beauty and vibrancy of the colors of the plants in the family's garden. I asked the girls' aunt about this,

AUNT: The vibrancy of the colour is definitely seen in the courtyard. Because he [the girls' father] worked as a builder in Pakistan, the houses, that's where he got it from, the houses.

(recorded discussion September 5, 2011)

At the same time I was observing the writing of stories by the eldest child, Lucy, who told them to her youngest sister, Saima, as a bedtime story.

Once upon a time in a land far away there lived a princess called Saima. She was so pretty. Everybody loved her. One summers' day she was picking flowers for her bigger sister Queen Lucy [pseudonym]. 'Oh Thank you Saima. They are pretty just like you. But remember not to pick any more as the villagers will get angry.' 'We hate you Saima' The villagers said. Saima began crying. Lucy began crying. Everyone started crying. 'I know I'll go to the magic shop to buy some seeds' Saima said.

(excerpt from the story written by Lucy)

When I came into the home about two months after this story was written, Saima, the youngest child, who was three, was excited about telling me her story. Their mother encouraged her to tell it to me:

SAIMA: Once upon a time, there lived a princess called Saima, once again there lived far away a princess called Saima who everybody loved her. One day she was picking flowers for Queen Lucy when the villagers cried

LUCY (older sister aged 12): Why did they cry?

SAIMA: Wa Wa!

LUCY: You took all the flowers didn't you?

What did you do you went to the/

SAIMA: /Shop to buy some seeds.

(audio September 2011)

Within an artifactual approach, the researcher can see how echoes of the seed planting experienced by Tanya is then transformed into a written story by Lucy and, subsequently, into an oral story by Saima who then re-tells the story her elder sister tells her every night. The seeds are materially experienced and turned into a story; they are the family's lived experience, the 'habitus' from Pakistan, as their aunt describes, translated into lived experience in the UK. The implication of this story and its re-telling, with the link to family experiences, is the artifactual mediation of the story through seed planting.

Artifactual Literacies in the Digital Age

We are at a moment when we have started to use the theory of artifactual literacies to develop new ideas and create new challenges in our work. One challenge is the customary divide between the online and offline worlds. Rather than seeing the two as separated by the screen, we are beginning to watch the flow across from sitting on a couch to moving to a screen, as being a shift that can appear minute. We can then develop this idea of the online/offline interface through an artifactual literacies approach.

We offer another example of a digital artifactual world, one that is more fully realized in relation to material artifacts. This is the artifactual world of Club Penguin, which is a popular children's website, www.clubpenguin.com. Club Penguin has a main street that looks much like contemporary town life with a coffee shop, a dance club, and a store, and within each hub of activity there are repertoires of practice that children can engage in. Within a short walk from main street, a child can find a snow-capped outdoor play area where penguins can meet up and chat over a bonfire or even surf. The main concept of the site is to have users take on the identity of animated penguins, who interact, play together, and share in the activities and events in the Club Penguin community, *but* in a safe environment. Club Penguin was designed as a safe social networking site for six- to 14-year-olds to hang out and play games. From an artifactual literacy perspective, the site appeals to children's desire to play at adulthood by designing their own home (in this case an igloo) and by choosing different outfits for their penguin avatars. As such, the website offers a material, artifactual perspective into how children creatively improvise with materials and modes to play with identity mediation.

When Jennifer spoke to a marketing manager at Club Penguin, Cassandra Mathers (pseudonym), it became clear that a source of popularity for the website was its artifactual qualities. Mathers focused on material dimensions of the Club Penguin world such as purchasing clothes, choosing decorations and suitable objects for their igloo homes so that children can experiment with identities in a safe, interactive environment. Mathers spoke at length about the 'expansive world of Club Penguin' that allows children to move around into different areas. She also talked about fostering a safe and nurturing environment. Safety and security within the Club Penguin world is a priority for the company. An additional priority is developing a sense of community and charity. To encourage a sense of community within Club Penguin, the website endorses community projects and initiatives such as preserving and reconstructing historic sites; an example of such civic engagement comes from this portion of the interview:

> we have had different activities that have allowed users to give their coins to help improve club penguin … in the early days the 'lighthouse' was not complete, it was derelict, and there was a whole campaign, much like you would have in a community to restore a heritage building, to restore the lighthouse to its former glory and to get it up and running again to you know help wayward sea farers help find their way to club penguin … so kids could donate their coins to help with the refurbishing of the lighthouse, so this was one of the first community improvement programs that happened in the world – last Christmas they had one where you could purchase ornaments for the community Christmas tree that was in the town square, so we've had quite a few things like that, that are designed to help students understand their role in community … and um take that sort of notion of giving and social responsibility to the next level … and for some kids that was amazing.
>
> *(audio recorded interview, October 2007)*

In the interview excerpt, Mathers speaks of two instances when the artifactual, material qualities of Club Penguin played a key role in making meaning from the site. Refurbishing a lighthouse or buying ornaments for Christmas trees fostered the notion of social responsibility, belonging, and, again, reinforced that notion of children existing and orienting to figured worlds (Holland, Lachicotte, Skinner, & Cain, 1998). In the next section, we illustrate how a ten-year-old makes meaning within the Club Penguin world.

Amy and Club Penguin

In 2007, Jennifer and a graduate student conducted a small-scale study of Club Penguin with a ten-year-old girl from central New Jersey. Marika Autrand and Jennifer conducted two interviews with Amy (pseudonym) about her use and enjoyment of Club Penguin. During one interview, Marika observed Amy playing games and interacting with other penguins while on the Club Penguin website. When not occupied with flute or her other extra-curricular activities, Amy colors, listens to music on her iPod, and plays her favorite videogame, Club Penguin.

The interview with Amy took place in her home situated in a New Jersey town outside New York City. Marika prefaced the interview by telling Amy that she wanted her to log into the Club Penguin website, go about her usual activities on the site, answer questions, and talk through some of her activities on the site. Amy immediately understood the expectations and she began the interview by talking Marika through some of the basics about the site. Through-out, she simultaneously concentrated on talking through an activity and per-forming that activity. Amy navigated the site and gave a grand tour with full confidence and little effort. At various points in the interview, Amy talked about her penguin, dressing her penguin, getting a pet (a puffle) for her penguin, and so on. Here is an excerpt from the interview:

MARIKA: Okay ... So, what makes you want to re-dress your penguin?

AMY: Well, if you have a certain job you can re-dress your penguin. So, if you have a job as a pizza person, you can make them have pizza. Or, you can be a tourist [tour guide] and give people tours. Or, and, I'm also a secret agent and I can go to the HQ [pulls up Head Quarters screen], which is the secret hide-out, and you go around places and see if anybody is doing stuff against the rules, and if you [they] are you report them, and they may get kicked off of Club Penguin for a little while. So, you need to follow all of the rules of Club Penguin or else that might not be so well.

MARIKA: So, with the HQ, is it just kids who monitor the site, or are there adults too who monitor?

AMY: That I don't know, but there can be adults who run Club Penguin there are like these two adults who are like the two big penguins. Like, in the newspaper [pulls up newspaper screen] there's Ask Aunt Arctic, where you can ask questions, so there's probably an adult answering those questions.

(audio interview July, 2007)

What was most insightful for Jennifer and Marika was how Amy's simulated recall while navigating through the Club Penguin website threw her interest in material worlds and artifacts into relief. All of the different identities and locales on the website relied on materials and artifacts to fulfill practices and aspects of identity. From an artifactual dimension, Amy's navigation relied on descriptions of things such as pizza and secret hide-outs for the Head Quarters. What was significant to our method of data collection and analysis was interpreting the role of artifacts and how they connect with deeper understandings of characters and settings.

Some New Directions for Artifactual Literacies

In this section we provide some insights from the field that we have made since the publication of our book entitled *Artifactual Literacies: Every Object Tells a Story* (Pahl & Rowsell, 2010). We begin by considering the impact of place-based education on our work. Since the publication of Soja's work (2010) on seeking spatial justice, we are now interested in the way the material and the artifactual are a neighborhood construction, and make us think about the affordances of different kinds of material artifacts in some neighborhoods over others.

In the UK, I (Kate) worked with a group of children to look at the literacy affordances in a neighborhood of socio-economic deprivation and developed a way of recognizing and valuing the literacies in the neighborhood. In this work, we logged everyday literacies in a series of walk arounds with film cameras and audio recordings to document the experiences. Literacies were in the form of signs, graffiti, and inscribed upon fences, slides, and out of the sides or sometimes walls of houses. The children were concerned about the level of obscene and offensive graffiti around them and decided to do something about it. They were able to make a film in which the children described the artifactual literacies in their neighborhood, and as a result, the neighborhood police officer responded to their complaints about the obscene graffiti they encountered and took measures to erase it from the play space.

In Canada, Jennifer continues to work with teenagers on the nuances of modal learning. Building on a large corpus of interviews with professionals who have expertise in design and multimodality (Rowsell, 2012), Jennifer applies what such professionals as architects, clothes designers, animators, videogame developers, and documentary film-makers, have to say about thinking and practicing multimodality in the work that she does with high school teachers and their students. This kind of research is about materials and mapping emotions into the manipulating, improvising, and composing of modes during meaning making. The work is also quite centrally concerned with thinking about agency, local needs, and properties with global needs and properties, and it is about creating artifacts that express ideas and embodied senses.

This approach explores in depth the labyrinthine nature of meaning making today. One way into modern-day meaning making is through modal learning and through aesthetics. Approaching literacy from the artifactual and modal learning entails more of a guild or studio approach to teaching and learning. That is, providing an idea from which a composition can emerge. 'A competent rendering,' we put in quotation marks because competence is a part of schooling experiences and requires choosing the best mode possible to transmit the idea. It could be a garden or a sewn text or even an audio text. We feel that the examples offered in the chapter reveal a clustering of ideologies of the artifactual, which might better suit contemporary needs and dispositions in literacy education.

We offer this methodology to educators and researchers as an accessible portal into lived experience that is respectful and offers a listening space for students to occupy. We would like to also consider the ways in which an artifactual literacies approach situates meaning making differently. The things young people value and the everyday aesthetic (Saito, 2007) they bring to meaning making can be accessed through an attention to their material cultural practices. By making cultural materialism the focus of our study, we are creating new and inclusive meaning making spaces for the students of tomorrow.

References

Back, L. (2007). *The art of listening*. Oxford, UK: Berg.

Barton, D., & Hamilton, M. (1998). *Local literacies: Reading and writing in one community*. London: Routledge.

Bourdieu, P. (1990). *The logic of practice* (R. Nice, Trans.). Cambridge, UK: Polity Press.

Compton-Lilly, C., Rogers, R., & Lewis, T. Y. (2012). Analyzing epistemological considerations related to diversity: An integrative critical literature review of family literacy scholarship. *Reading Research Quarterly, 47*(1), 33–60.

Connerton, P. (1989). *How societies remember*. Cambridge, UK: Cambridge University Press.

Coupland, N. (2010). Accommodation theory. In J. Jaspers, J. Östman, & J. Verschueren (Eds.), *Society and language use* (pp. 21–27). Amsterdam: John Benjamins.

Csikszentmihalyi, M., & Rochberg-Halton, E. (1981). *The meaning of things: Domestic objects and the self*. Cambridge, UK: Cambridge University Press.

Dyson, A. H. (1993). *Social worlds of children learning to write in an urban primary school*. New York: Teachers College Press.

Fentress, J., & Wickham, C. (1992). *Social memory: New perspectives on the past*. Oxford, UK: Blackwell.

Finnegan, R. (2007). *The oral and beyond: Doing things with words in Africa*, Chicago: University of Chicago Press.

Flewitt, R. (2008). Multimodal literacies. In J. Marsh & E. Hallet (Eds.), *Desirable literacies: Approaches to language and literacy in the early years* (2nd ed., pp. 122–139). London: Sage.

Gee, J. P. (1999). *An introduction to discourse analysis: Theory and method*. London: Routledge.

Gonzalez, N., Moll, L., & Amanti, C. (Eds.). (2005). *Funds of knowledge: Theorizing practices in households, communities and classrooms*. Mahwah, NJ: Lawrence Erlbaum.

Heath, S. B. (1983). *Ways with words: Language, life and work in communities and classrooms*. Cambridge, UK: Cambridge University Press.

Hoggart, R. (1957). *The uses of literacy*. London: Penguin.

Holland, D., Lachicotte, W., Skinner, D., & Cain, C. (1998). *Identity and agency in cultural worlds*. Cambridge, MA: Harvard University Press.

Hornberger, N. (2000). Multilingual literacies, literacy practices, and the continua of biliteracy. In M. Martin-Jones and K. E. Jones (Eds.), *Multilingual literacies: Reading and writing different worlds* (pp. 353–369). Amsterdam: John Benjamins Ltd.

Hull, G., & Nelson, M. E. (2009). Literacy, media, and morality: Making the case for an aesthetic turn. In M. Baynham & M. Prinsloo (Eds.), *The future of literacy studies* (pp. 199–228). Basingstoke, UK: Palgrave Macmillan.

Hurdley, R. (2006). Dismantling mantelpieces: Narrating identities and materializing culture in the home. *Sociology, 40*(4), 717–733.

Ingold, T. (2007). *Lines: A brief history*. London: Routledge.

Kress, G. (1997). *Before writing: Rethinking the paths to literacy.* London: Routledge.

Lawn, M., & Grosvenor, I. (Eds.). (2005). *Comparative histories of education: Materialities of schooling: Design-technology-objects-routines.* Oxford, UK: Symposium Books.

Lee, C. D. (2008). The centrality of culture to the scientific study of learning and development: How an ecological framework in education research facilitates civic responsibility. *Educational Researcher, 37*(5), 270–279.

Lefstein, A. (2008). Changing classroom practice through the English national literacy strategy: A micro-interactional perspective. *American Educational Research Journal, 45*(3), 701–737.

Miller, D. (2008) *The comfort of things.* Cambridge, MA: Polity Press.

Moll, L., Amanti, C., Neff, D., & Gonzalez, N. (1992). Funds of knowledge for teaching: Using a qualitative approach to connect homes and classrooms. *Theory Into Practice, 31*(1), 132–141.

Pahl, K. (1999) *Transformations: Meaning making in nursery education.* Stoke on Trent, UK: Trentham Books.

Pahl, K. (2002). Ephemera, mess and miscellaneous piles: Texts and practices in families. *Journal of Early Childhood Literacy, 2*(2), 145–165.

Pahl, K. (2011). My family, my story: Representing identities in time and space through digital storytelling. In S. Schamroth-Abrams & J. Rowsell (Eds.), *Rethinking identity and literacy education in the 21st century: National society for the study of education yearbook* 110(1), (pp. 17–40). New York: Teachers College, Columbia University.

Pahl, K. (2012). 'A Reason to Write': Exploring writing epistemologies in two contexts. *Pedagogies: An International Journal, 7*(3), 209–228.

Pahl, K., & Rowsell, J. (Eds.). (2006). *Travel notes from the new literacy studies: Instances of practice.* Clevedon, UK: Multilingual Matters Ltd.

Pahl, K., & Rowsell, J. (2010). *Artifactual literacies: Every object tells a story.* New York: Teachers College Press.

Pahl, K., & Rowsell, J. (2012). *Literacy and education: The new literacy studies in the classroom* (2nd Ed.). London: Sage.

Ring, K. (2006). What mothers do: Everyday routines and rituals and their impact upon young children's use of drawing for meaning making. *International Journal of Early Years Education, 14*(1), 63–84.

Rogers, R., Mosley, M., Kramer, M. A., & the Literacy for Social Justice Teacher Research Group. (2009). *Designing socially just learning communities.* London: Routledge.

Rowsell, J. (2012). *Doing multimodality: The new literacies.* London: Routledge.

Rowsell, J., & Pahl, K. (2007). Sedimented identities in texts: Instances of practice. *Reading Research Quarterly, 42*(3), 388–401.

Saito, Y. (2007). *Everyday aesthetics.* Oxford, UK: Oxford University Press.

Scanlan, M. (2010). Opening the box: Literacy, artefacts and identity. *Literacy, 44*(1), 28–36.

Soja, E. (2010). *Seeking spatial justice.* Minneapolis, MN: University of Minnesota Press.

Scollon, R., & Scollon, S. (2003). *Discourses in place: Language in the material world.* London: Routledge.

Street, B. V. (1984). *Literacy in theory and practice.* Cambridge, UK: Cambridge University Press.

Street, B. V. (Ed.). (1993). *Cross-cultural approaches to literacy.* Cambridge, UK: Cambridge University Press.

Street, B. V. (2008). New literacies, new times: Developments in literacy studies. In B. V. Street & N. H. Hornberger (Eds.), *Encyclopedia of language and education* (Vol. 2: Literacy; pp. 3–14). New York: Springer Science.

Whitty, P., Rose, S., with Baisley, D., Comeau, L., & Thompson, A. (2008). Honouring educators' co-construction of picture books. *Child Study, 33*(2), 21–23.

Williams, R. (1961). *The long revolution.* London: Penguin.

Willis, P. (2000). *The ethnographic imagination.* Cambridge, UK: Polity Press.

12

GEOSEMIOTICS

Sue Nichols

Introduction: Spatially Sensitive Literacy Research

The term 'geosemiotics' combines the elements of *geography*, the study of places, with *semiotics*, the study of sign systems. The term was created by Ron and Suzi Scollon to describe their approach to studying 'discourses in place' (Scollon & Scollon, 2003, p. 1). This approach recognizes that the physical, material and symbolic aspects of places are resources in producing meanings for the signs and practices that are found in them. What has been in the background demands to be included in explanations of what is happening. The Scollons were interested in how people navigate through complex urban spaces, especially those that are sign-saturated and which host multiple kinds of activity, such as shopping malls.

Literacy researchers in the sociocultural tradition have long drawn attention to the importance of attending to social context as helping to determine how reading, writing and multimodal text production are practiced (Graff, 1991; Street, 1995). At times, sociocultural studies have highlighted place as an element of context. One of the most influential studies in this tradition, Heath's (1983) ethnographic analysis of family literacy, clearly situated each of the three contrastive neighborhoods geographically as well as socially.

However, place has been more often in the background of literacy studies which are carried out in classrooms, homes or laboratories. The focus has often been on the immediate participants in literacy practices with qualities of their material environments assumed knowledge or, if described, left behind when it comes to the researcher's analysis.

The move to spatially sensitive literacy research methods reflects a more general movement in educational research. This 'spatial turn' owes much to the conceptual work of Lefebvre (1991) who argued that space is socially produced.

In other words, there is no such thing as a purely physical space divorced from social practice. Spaces are built, experienced and represented by people and their social institutions. The social production of physical space is easiest to understand in relation to the architectural environment, such as a school building, which is clearly designed by humans in order to encompass human activity. Lefebvre argued that even what is believed to be pure nature is, in contemporary conditions, socially produced, for example by an agreement not to exploit the natural resources in a wilderness.

As a critical social theorist, Lefebvre was interested in power and in the ways that social space can be shaped to control social subjects. His comments on spatial practice are particularly resonant in relation to the role of space in systems of schooling:

> Spatial practice … embraces production and reproduction, and the particular locations and spatial sets characteristic of each social formation. Spatial practice ensures continuity and some degree of coherence … this cohesion implies a guaranteed level of competence and a specific level of performance.
>
> *(p. 33)*

Thus spaces can contribute to producing performances such as the performance of the student subject in the material and social space of a classroom.

The spatial turn in education has been associated with concerns about the status of local knowledge and practice in relation to the generalizing force of standardized curriculum and assessment. This move has encouraged educators and researchers to attend to the neighborhoods, regions and natural environments within which schools and their students are located. These places are invested with pedagogical potential as a means of countering the hegemonizing power of the 'placeless institution of schooling' (Grunewald, 2003, p. 620): 'Becoming aware of social places as cultural products requires that we bring them into our awareness for conscious reflection and unpack their particular cultural meanings. Such is the educative potential of place-conscious education' (Grunewald, 2003, pp. 626–627). In relation to literacy, this raises questions about the pedagogic role of spaces in shaping literacy practices.

What is Happening Here?

Studies from a geosemiotic perspective begin with the question: What is happening here? What distinguishes such studies from many ethnographic or anthropological studies of literacy practice is in where one looks for the answer. The meaning of a literacy practice is understood to be produced in the interaction between participants and their world, where the world is understood to be social, cultural and material. Geosemiotics takes a social semiotic perspective, and extends this to the non-human, non-linguistic dimensions of meaning-making (Halliday, 1978). The Scollons illustrate this point by asking the reader to consider a stop sign in the same light as they would consider a person who has spoken:

> We need to ask of the stop sign the same four questions we would ask of a person: Who has 'uttered' this (that is, is it a legitimate stop sign of the municipal authority)? Who is the viewer (it means one thing for a pedestrian and another for the driver of a car)? What is the social situation (is the sign 'in place' or being installed or worked on)? Is that part of the material world relevant to such a sign (for example, is it a corner of the intersection of roads)?
>
> *(Scollon & Scollon, 2003, p. 3)*

The second point to make about the question 'What is happening here?' is that it refers to the totality of activities, signs, environments and their interaction. That is, geosemiotics is a holistic method which is less about deconstruction than it is about layering of meanings. For literacy researchers, it enables an appreciation of the ways in which dimensions of practice are impacting on each other.

Finally, 'What is happening here?' recognizes that 'here' is linked to many 'theres' because people, signs and activities are mobile. Here, the concept of networked space, drawn from social geographer Doreen Massey (2000), is a useful adjunct to a geosemiotic approach. Massey defines the 'activity space' as 'the spatial network of links and activities, of spatial connections and of locations, within which a particular agent operates' (p. 54). This raises questions about what is moving, where it has come from and where it is going to.

Research Design Elements

While geosemiotics is an emerging methodology and not a formula, there are two elements that recur in descriptions of geosemiotic analysis. First, data must be collected in a manner that captures the physical and material elements of the spaces in which literacy practices take place, as well as the social and linguistic characteristics of these practices. Second, just as with the social and linguistic dimensions, aspects of place must be analyzed in terms of the meanings and modes of participation that they make available. Places are described not simply to form a background to the activities of participants but are analyzed as participants in their own right.

In calling for spatially sensitive research, Gieryn (2000) challenged social researchers to work in a 'visual key': 'Sociologists could become more adept with maps, floor plans, photographic images, bricks and mortar, landscapes and cityscapes, so that interpreting a street or forest becomes as routine and as informative as computing a chi-square' (pp. 483–484). Beyond the visual, geo-semiotics requires a fuller sensory repertoire for capturing and representing data because place semiotics encompasses elements, such as texture and temperature, that impact on the embodied experience of participants. Language can still be one of the most sensitive instruments for representing these dimensions, making field notes an important tool in the geosemiotic kit bag.

The Language of Spatial Description in Field Notes

Taking detailed field notes is a familiar discipline for ethnographic researchers. From a geosemiotic perspective, the researcher's attention as a participant in the field is oriented to spatial and material elements and the ways in which partici-pants interact with these, as well as to texts and talk. This sensitized attention manifests in the language of description.

The example below is taken from previously unpublished materials relating to a project which has been reported elsewhere (Nichols, Rowsell, Nixon & Rainbird, 2012). These notes were handwritten by me during a visit to a library branch. Although a laptop computer would have saved transcription time, I find a flip top notebook less obtrusive and more portable when on the move. These days, I might use an electronic tablet which would facilitate integration of photographic and written notes.

The notes describe my interaction with the space. They include references to the *perceptual space* of the participant in terms of what she senses while moving through the space ('I can see …,' 'I don't notice initially'). The researcher notes that the library desks in the foyer 'don't look to be "in" the library.' Feelings of being in or out of particular areas, responding to the arrangement of furniture and openings are also an aspect of the interaction order. An aesthetic response, for instance to color ('attractive'), is also an aspect of interaction.

Activities in space are also an aspect of the interaction order. Although this excerpt does not describe participants other than the researcher, they clearly indicate how the arrangement of spaces, signs and objects is designed in relation to particular kinds of activity. For instance, alcove signage points to the activ-ities that might be expected to take place in these sub-spaces (e.g., reading and learning). The contents of alcoves hint at how these activities should be carried out (e.g., by searching a library catalog or browsing community information in the 'reading' alcove). The description of this alcove as 'easy to miss' and 'very tidy' allows for the inference that it may not actually be the scene of much activity.

Visual Documentation

Photographic and other means of capturing visual traces of a site are, unsurpris-ingly, important in geosemiotic studies. It has this in common with visual

TABLE 12.1 Handwritten notes by Nichols during a visit to a library branch

I can see all the main part of the library from here including sets of shelving on the inner side (furthest from windows looking out on to the street), sets of armchairs, sets of tables and two more banks of computers set on high desks with bar-type stools. There is no clutter.

On the long inner-most wall are pillars each a different color. On each is a vertically oriented metal plate with a word on it. These words are:

L	C	G	L	R
I	R	R	E	E
V	E	O	A	A
I	A	W	R	D
N	T	I	N	I
G	I	N	I	N
	N	G	N	G
	G	G	G	

[I can't see from here but later discover that each pillar signals an alcove containing resources.]

I've walked through the main space and am in the spacious well-lit foyer. It's a walkway from one side of the building to the other and takes you past the university areas. The library desks are on the opposite side and in a way don't look to be 'in' the library. There is a single small display module in the centre of this large space. On one side are art and craft books and on the other are fiction books and information about the One Book One Community festival. Bookmarks promoting this event are fanned out neatly. One other bookmark is also displayed promoting Thomson and Gale's Health and Wellness database. I think it's there because of its attractive colors. This is a very color coordinated space.

Walking back into the library I can now see an alcove. It's the Reading alcove but I don't notice the label initially. In here is a Community Information display of the kind more usually seen in foyers. There are also two displays of newspapers and magazines and a PC for library catalog searching only. This space is tucked away and easy to miss. It's very tidy.

sociology which makes Pauwels' (2010) discussion of visual methods pertinent. Pauwels distinguishes between photographic documentary and researcher-produced imagery. The former is characterized by a high level of 'resemblance' while the latter, which includes drawings, diagrams and personal maps, opens up an interpretive or abstracted level of representation. An image may begin in the documentary category but through processes of transformation can take on expressive qualities. This transformational work may assist researchers to apprehend some of the semiotic qualities of places such as textures, movements and light.

Mannion and colleagues (2007) used a creative repertoire of documentation practices to investigate literacy practices in a college of education. The team set out to contextualize these practices in terms of their social and institutional settings; in other words, they considered the college not as a single place but as a set of spaces in which different kinds of literacies might be practiced. They were particularly interested in texts as elements in spaces (such as the exam timetable on a noticeboard in a corridor) and on the textual practices which occurred within these spaces (such as copying out another student's notes in the cafeteria). They took photographs and compiled these into visual narratives, made floor plans and maps and used sticky notes to annotate these documents.

Considerable preparation may be required before visual documentation even begins. Permissions may have to be sought, routines understood, sites visited and shots planned to include as many views as will enable later reconstruction. Pauwels (2010) advises that 'significant contextual information should, whenever possible, be part of the visual record or product itself' (p. 564). This may mean including place markers such as signs and doorways. It is also useful to have a consistent code for naming images and to take the time to give files names rather than rely on the number codes that are automatically generated.

Researchers may also take advantage of existing documentation such as are offered through open access digital services. Digital images of city streets, offered through Google search engine's *Street View* service formed the primary data set for Yamada-Rice's (2010) exploration of environmental print (referred to above). This service provides video footage of selected places, which can be navigated by arrow button, enabling the viewer to 'look' left and right, up and down. In order to gather these images for later analysis, this researcher explains how he used the 'print screen' function on his computer keyboard to transfer them into an image viewing program (such as 'Paint') and then save to hard disc.

A limitation of this method is that not all places available through *Street View* have been subjected to the same degree of photographic documentation. By choosing major world cities (London and Tokyo) for his comparative study, Yamada-Rice was able to access a relatively complete view. Also snapshots of places have not all been taken at the same time so they may be more or less up to date.

Collaborating with participants can offer not only assistance with the work of documentation but insights into how places are experienced. Early childhood researcher Britt (2009) wanted to understand how children related to the various spaces of kindergarten settings as well as to engage them in multi-modal text production. She invited them to help her understand their place through mapping, drawing and recorded talk. Comber and colleagues (2009) worked with Architecture students and school children both to understand and to intervene into child residents' experience of urban renewal in a poor neighborhood. The children were equipped with the 'vocabularies, and visual and conceptual resources that architects deploy' which enabled them to attend to and communicate about local and less familiar places (Comber, Nixon, Ashmore, Loo & Cook, 2009, p. 232). However the researchers acknowledge the need to develop ways of analyzing these visual texts, as distinct from writing about the process of producing them. This reflects the emergent status of spatially sensitive approaches in literacy research.

Probing for Space, Place and Mobility in Interviews

Interviews can be a very useful resource for geosemiotic analysis but they may require an adjustment of orientation on the part of researcher and interviewee to be effective. Literacy researchers are often interested in *what* the informant has been doing in relation to literacy. In early literacy research, for instance, researchers often ask parents about the kinds of reading, writing and language practices that children participate in at home. From a geosemiotic perspective the focus is also on *where* these practices have taken place, the *material* and *social* qualities of these spaces and the mode of *access* to these places. These are not details that researchers often ask or informants ordinarily volunteer, probably because no one wants to get 'bogged down' in what are assumed to be minor details.

In the example below, researcher Helen Nixon shows polite persistence in maintaining a focus on spatiality during an interview (Nichols et al., 2012). The informant is the chief librarian of a municipal library which has a single branch serving a large diverse community. The librarian at first states she is unable to recall which of the surrounding suburbs most of the library's clients come from. Note Nixon's questioning keeps the focus on where the library's clients come from, how they get there and the implications for equitable service provision.

RESEARCHER: So do you know, can you name suburbs or suburbs that you do reach and maybe that you don't reach, you know, middle [class] or … because Midborough Council district is quite large, isn't it?

LIBRARIAN: Mm, it is. In terms of…?

RESEARCHER: Or you're privy to that sort of information?

LIBRARIAN: No, I do have that information, I just don't remember it. I can get that information for you.

RESEARCHER: OK, you might be able to get … that would be good.

LIBRARIAN: And that's my problem. I know, yeah, it's interesting, I've looked at specific … I was looking at the statistics the other day in terms of the specific wards, like the local government ward boundaries and which wards had a high membership rate, as opposed to other wards, which was interesting, but I can get that information for you.

RESEARCHER: Yeah, that would be good. We looked up the wards, you know, how the [district] … how it's divided into wards. I mean just generally we're thinking about, you would imagine that there were fewer people say from the sort of Falcon Rise area compared with Midborough or…

LIBRARIAN: Yes, there is a lot fewer. Yeah, there's places where there is a low socio-economic area, they're probably not as high users of library service, and we're quite aware of that. It's something that we're trying to, well one of our goals that we're trying to improve upon is we want to work with the Community Services Department and Council a lot more, and actually put more of our service within the community centres, where the community is at. So they don't have to come to the one location. We do recognise that that is an impediment for lots of people who want to use the library but can't get here.

RESEARCHER: It's quite particularly isolated in many ways, even though…

LIBRARIAN: Because we've got the big great road in between with the shopping centre.

Eventually, the librarian names a significant concrete spatial feature of the library's relationships to its surroundings, the 'big great road' which those clients without car transport have to cross in order to reach the service.

Analysis and Interpretation

In building up a geosemiotic analysis, the Scollons (2003) identify three layers of meaning which should be considered. The *semiotics of place* refers to the meanings produced through the built and natural environment. This includes how the environment is organized as a collection of zones such as seating areas, margins and passageways, each with its own particular qualities. The placement and mobility of objects (such as wheeled furniture) and their material qualities (such as glossy, metallic or rough textures) are also considered in relation to their potential impact on social practices and meanings. From this perspective, *texts* come into view as *material objects in space*. This means rather than just attending to the linguistic content of, say, a poster on a classroom wall, the analyst also attends to where it is placed (e.g., in a high traffic area or a hidden corner) and its material qualities (e.g., glossy and new or dog-eared and torn).

An example of literacy research which attends to the semiotics of place is the article on 'book nooks' by Rainbird and Rowsell (2011). They present four case studies of early childhood literacy in middle-class homes based on home visits, parent interviews and floor plans. They considered how parents used particular domestic spaces and arrangements of objects to differentiate activities such as book reading, media use and homework. They also noted how 'borders between designated learning spaces and family spaces become blurred' (p. 220) as parents attempted to simultaneously manage different tasks of family life.

The second layer of meaning is *visual semiotics*. Here, the Scollons draw on Kress and van Leeuwen's (1996) framework of visual grammar which provides categories for the analysis of the composition of images as a means of interrogating their meaning effects. The application of visual analysis in semiotics attends particularly to the relationship between visual elements and their place context. This is particularly relevant to considering the contribution of signage, displays, media presence (such as live video screens) and can also include visual aspects of participants such as the color block of sports fans in team gear at a stadium. It is important to note that print language is considered within visual semiotics in terms of its orthography or visual composition.

An example of literacy research which attends to visual semiotics in place is Yamada-Rice's (2010) aforementioned comparison of the textual environments of city neighborhoods in the UK and Japan. Underpinning this analysis is an appreciation of the different spatial and visual characteristics of the two writing systems; while English text has left-to-right orientation, Japanese is multi-directional with 'space being orientated from a central point of each kanji' (p. 33). He shows how this extends to the three-dimensional city landscape with signs extending from ground level up the walls of buildings, and signs projecting out at 90% angles to be seen from street level. Overall, he notes the 'density of images' in the Japanese landscape which almost 'overpowers' the sense of a built environment, compared to the 'scattering' of images in the London scene (p. 35). He considers implications of the impact of these visual semiotic orders on the prior to school literacy knowledge of preschool children in each context.

The third layer is the *interaction order*, or the patterns of social interaction that are formed by participants' activities in a space. Units of activity are identified such as 'selecting a book' or 'circle sharing time.' The analyst considers how these actions are able to be performed by participants including considering how resources such as physical capacities, language and other representational resources, objects and the knowledge of how to use them, social identities and relationships and time, support these performances.

An example of literacy research which interrogates the interaction order is Leander and Rowe's (2006) *Talking Spaces Project* which focuses on student participation in oral presentations in urban high school classrooms. Drawing on Deleuze and Guatarri's (1987) concept of rhizo-analysis, the researchers ask: What dynamic relationships of bodies, texts, objects and spaces are being formed as the performance unfolds? (p. 435). Exemplifying this approach is their case study of three African American boys' presentation on the subject of corruption in the meat packing industry for the subject American Studies. This presentation is treated by the researchers as an assemblage in which the elements include the poster the students have produced, their talk referencing this poster, their gestures and gaze in relation to the poster, and each other and their audience. Through this multilayered analysis of an embodied performance the researchers consider how, and in what ways, the students simultaneously perform traditional and subversive student identities.

These three layers, each composed of several elements, are brought together to produce a complete geosemiotic account of the event space that the researcher is interested in. In fact, I have introduced the layers in a different sequence from that taken by the Scollons (who start their explanation with the interaction order) to stress that this is a multi-faceted, not a linear, methodology. The outcome is a rich account in which each element of what is happening is considered in relation to all the other dimensions.

How to describe the relationship between dimensions in an event space is one of the challenges for researchers using a geosemiotic approach. This is a somewhat similar challenge to that facing literacy researchers looking at multimodality, where the relationships between the modes in a text or literacy practice are of central importance. The Scollons (2003) warn against attempting to resolve the analysis into a single narrative. This is because the different elements 'work as interactions among small or sub-systems, not as grand, overarching semiotic systems. These sub-systems operate quite independently of each other in a dialectical and negotiated way' (p. 160). Discourse operates as a connecting concept for systems of meaning which can be discerned through geosemiotic analysis. This allows for a consideration of 'any particular place as an aggregate of discourses' which 'give it a particular "feel"' (pp. 193, 195). At the same time relationships between different places (and between physical and virtual spaces) can be considered in terms of the 'discourses which flow into, through, and out of' them (p. 193).

A Geosemiotic Exemplar Study in Literacy

A three year study focused on parents' access to resources for supporting preschool children's learning and development utilized geosemiotics as one of its major approaches, along with discourse and network analysis (Nichols, Nixon & Rowsell, 2009; Nichols et al., 2012; Nichols & Rainbird, 2013; Nixon 2011; Rainbird & Rowsell, 2011). This multi-sited study investigated the location, accessibility, mobility, content and participation structures of relevant services, resources and activities in each of three regional sites.

For the purpose of discussing the application of geosemiotics to literacy research, this chapter will focus on part of this project which has been reported separately – the comparative case studies of libraries (Nichols, 2011). Four libraries were compared:

- Gumtree Library in a large suburban service hub;
- Paraton Library in a disadvantaged outer suburb;
- Deepwater Library in a small rural town;
- Greystone Library in a prestigious university town.

The first aspect to note is that the literature on libraries is reviewed through a geosemiotic lens. That is, Nichols pays attention to what prior historical and social research about libraries may have to say about spatial and material qualities and their impact on modes of participation. She notes historian Manguel's (2007) definition of the library as 'a paradox, a building set aside for an essentially private craft (reading) which now was to take place communally' (p. 31). She traces this theme of the relationship between private and public uses through the work of Viseu, Clement, Aspinall and Kennedy (2006) regarding internet use in home and community spaces. In that study the library is described as a hybrid 'private-in-public' space (p. 648) in which patrons carry out both personal and communal activities. Nichols notes that this hybrid quality raises questions for the participation of young children and their caregivers in relation to the private and public aspects of their library use and how spaces within libraries cater to these.

We have already encountered some of the data collection strategies employed in this study in the examples from the field notes and librarian interview above. Digital photographs, map making, artifact collection and inventorying were also employed to document libraries in relation to their external physical environments, their internal spaces and specific features such as furniture and signage. Finally, participant observation was employed to explore interaction patterns in activities for young children and carers.

Information from all these sources is woven into case portrayals for each library site. Taking one of these cases as an example, we will see that portrayals foreground issues of spatiality, materiality, mobility and access. From the portrayal of Greystone:

> At the opposite end of the social spectrum is the North American university town of Greystone with an imposing new library building located right in the town's centre. The small size of the commercial zone means that the residential areas are in close proximity to the centre and many Greystone residents can walk to their library. However, non-residents, as they do not contribute to the local tax base, have no borrowing rights.
>
> Despite this, the library has become a 'destination,' in the words of the children's librarian, ever since the new building has been opened. Despite

being unable to take books away, people come in from housing estates and other towns, one mother telling us that it was 'worth it to me to drive twice as long and pay for parking to go to the Greystone (library).' Though Caren had borrowed books from her 'little, tiny' local library, she associated the Greystone library with high cultural capital:

> *It's a bit akin to a one-room schoolhouse versus a multi-level vast new school that's been built. [. . .] Maybe if there was nothing else around but to have that little, tiny place next to this incredible, nationally recognized library and it just seems to me that it's one of the best things about Greystone. [. . .]*

The architectural presence, size, reputation and resources of this library speak of modernity, prestige and power.

(Nichols, 2011, pp. 173–174)

Libraries are described in terms of their different social and geographic locations impacting on local practices of use and perceptions of their relevance and status.

A geosemiotic approach can operate at different scales. From a consideration of the library as a local institution in a regional context, the researcher zooms in to examine the characteristics of a sub-space within each library, the 'children's activity space.' Based on analysis of the spatial and material qualities of these spaces, she draws conclusions about the social meanings associated with these design features:

> Children's spaces ... were characterised by design elements of curved shapes and bright colours. Paraton's Family Reading Centre was marked by a green circular carpet and distinctive circular lighting and contained low circular chairs and tables. Greystone's story reading room had a curved exterior wall of glass covered by long gauzy curtains.... Recalling Manguel's (op. cit.) point about the 'library of straight lines' representing a 'compartmentalised and hierarchical universe,' the design of children's areas seems a deliberate attempt to counter this bounded system with a sense of flow and connectedness.

(Nichols, 2011, p. 178)

Signage within libraries is analyzed in terms of what it communicates about the kinds of interactions and movements that are and are not encouraged for children and caregivers. The visual semiotics of these signs are considered as elements in the overall message system. So, for instance, the sign found in Gumtree library is selected for comment (Figure 12.1).

Nichols comments on its 'curvilinear cloud form' and how this can be read as an attempt to ameliorate the 'authoritarian tone' of its message regarding the library's requirement that parents control their children's behavior (p. 179).

FIGURE 12.1 Paraton Family Reading Centre (source withheld to preserve site anonymity)

When it comes to the participation of children and caregivers in literacy activities, the focus is again inclusive of the material, embodied and spatial dimensions of these interactions as well as the linguistic dimensions. So, for instance, Nichols notes the 'dance produced by negotiations between children's independent movements and adults' regulation of children's bodies' during early literacy sessions facilitated by librarians (p. 182). In this description it is possible to see that dispositions to literacy and learning are formed through embodied practices in relation to other bodies, text and space. As also noted by Rowe (2008) in her description of the 'boundary contract' limiting marks to the surface of a page, young children often breach these contracts in the initial stages of being socialized into literacy practices.

In this study, the library is conceptualized as a 'semiotic aggregate' (Scollon & Scollon, 2003, p. 12) produced through the intersection of multiple discourses in place. An earlier study by Ward and Wason-Ellam (2005) had concluded that public libraries operate according to two discourses, the 'dominant/academic/hier-archical literacy model' and an alternative 'informal literacies [model] more closely allied to popular culture' (p. 206). Nichols adds early learning as a discourse that has entered libraries, along with other social institutions, and her analysis provides a description of how the early learning discourse operates within the overall land-scape of meaning, or semiotic aggregate, of the library.

While these discourses are understood as generally available to be taken up, analysis attends to how the particular qualities of sites contribute to particular localized semiotic aggregates. So, for instance, in the small rural town of Deep-water, the early learning discourse was not so fully materialized as at Gumtree and Greystone. In considering why this might be, social, spatial and institutional dimensions are layered into the researcher's interpretation: 'the physical con-straints of a space too small to easily accommodate mobile toddlers,' the 'librari-an's policing of children's behavior' and parents' expectation that children would be taught to read at school rather than inculcated into literacy prior to school are all considered as elements accounting for the relatively lower profile of early literacy in Deepwater library (Nichols et al., 2012, p. 155).

Potential of Geosemiotics for Advancing Literacy Research

In this chapter, I have introduced the geosemiotic approach as an orientation that combines semiotics and ethnography to investigate the meanings of spaces in relation to the practices that occur in those spaces. One of the reasons for literacy researchers to adopt this approach is that it can yield fresh insights into some of the most familiar and taken for granted subjects. Soja (2010) writes: 'this strategic foregrounding of the spatial flexes interpretive muscles that have not been well developed or widely applied in the past. This in turn raises new possibilities for discovering hidden insights, alternative theories and revised modes of understanding' (p. 17). What has been in the background now comes to be included in explanations of what is happening. The researcher's focus keeps shifting between layers of an event space. Thus geosemiotics both challenges and supports literacy researchers to look at familiar scenes in unfamiliar ways.

One of the most problematic issues in literacy education is the relationship between the institution of schooling and the other contexts within which children and teenagers encounter and acquire literacies. However, discussion on this relationship is still too often driven by assumptions about children's lives outside school, rather than knowledge produced through inquiry. At the same time, the classroom is naturalized as the site of privilege and referred to as 'the classroom' as if all classrooms were the same whether located in New York or New Delhi.

The classroom has been described as both a 'hard' and a 'soft' technology (Lawn, 1999). Geosemiotics recognizes both the 'hard', physical, materiality as well as the 'soft' sociality and ideological basis of event spaces such as classrooms. A geosemiotic approach views all sites as semiotic aggregates formed by discourses that network them to other spaces but which are also materialized in localized ways. There are globalized discourses of literacy that connect New York and New Delhi but whether and how these can be transformed into practices is impacted by the hard and soft technologies of the places within which people and literacies meet.

References

Britt, C. (2009). 'Did you see the picture of our hiding place?' Illuminating and exploring children's shared understandings of place through arts-informed methodologies. Paper presented at the Symposium 'Geographical Methods in Education Research,' Annual Conference of the Australian Association for Research in Education (AARE), Canberra, ACT, November 30 to December 3.

Comber, B., Nixon, H., Ashmore, L., Loo, S. & Cook, J. (2009). Urban renewal from the inside out: Spatial and critical literacies in a low socioeconomic school community. *Mind Culture and Activity, 13*(3) 228–246.

Deleuze, G. & Guattari, F. (1987). *A thousand plateaus: Capitalism and schizophrenia* (B. Massumi, Trans.). Minneapolis, MN: University of Minnesota Press.

Gieryn, T. (2000). A place for space in sociology. *Annual Review of Sociology, 26,* 463–496.

Graff, H. (1991). *The legacies of literacy: Continuities and contradictions in western culture.* Bloomington, IN: Indiana University Press.

Grunewald, D. (2003). Foundations of place: A multidisciplinary framework for place-conscious education. *American Educational Research Journal, 40*(3), 619–654.

Halliday, M. (1978). *Language as social semiotic: The social interpretation of language and meaning.* London: Edward Arnold.

Heath, S. B. (1983). *Ways with words.* Cambridge, MA: Cambridge University Press.

Lawn, M. (1999). Designing teaching: the classroom as a technology. In I. Grosvenor, M. Lawn & K. Rousmaniere (Eds.), *Silences and images: The social history of the classroom.* New York: Peter Lang.

Leander, K. M. & Rowe, D. W. (2006). Mapping literacy spaces in motion: A rhizomatic analysis of a classroom literacy performance. *Reading Research Quarterly, 41*(4), 428–460.

Lefebvre, H. (1991). *The production of space.* Oxford, UK: Basil Blackwell.

Kress, G. & van Leeuwen, T. (1996). *Reading images: The grammar of visual design.* London: Routledge.

Manguel, A. (2007). *The library at night.* Toronto, Canada: Vintage Canada.

Mannion, G., Ivanic, R. & LfFE Research Group. (2007). Mapping literacy practices: theory, methodology, methods. *International Journal of Qualitative Research in Education, 20*(1) 15–30.

Massey, D. (2000). The conceptualisation of place. In D. Massey & P. Jess (Eds.), *A place in the world? Places, cultures and globalisation* (pp. 45–85). New York: Oxford University Press.

Nichols, S. (2011). Young children's literacy in the activity space of the library: A geosemiotic investigation. *Journal of Early Childhood Literacy, 11*(2), 164–189.

Nichols, S., Nixon, H. & Rowsell, J. (2009). The 'good' parent in relation to early childhood literacy: Symbolic terrain and lived practice. *Literacy, 43*(2), 65–74.

Nichols, S. & Rainbird, S. (2013). The mall, the library and the church: Inquiring into the resourcing of early learning through new spaces and networks. *International Journal of Qualitative Studies in Education, 26*(2), 198–215.

Nichols, S., Rowsell, J., Nixon, H. & Rainbird, S. (2012) *Resourcing early learners: New networks new players.* New York: Routledge.

Nixon, H. (2011). 'From bricks to clicks': Hybrid commercial spaces in the landscape of early literacy and learning. *Journal of Early Childhood Literacy, 11*(2), 114–140.

Pauwels, L. (2010). Visual sociology reframed: An analytical synthesis and discussion of visual methods in social and cultural research. *Sociological Methods and Research, 38*(4), 545–581.

Rainbird, S. & Rowsell, J. (2011) 'Literacy nooks': Geosemiotics and domains of literacy in home spaces. *Journal of Early Childhood Literacy, 11*(2), 214–231.

Rowe, D. (2008). Social contracts for writing: Negotiating shared understandings about text in the preschool years. *Reading Research Quarterly, 43*(1), 66–95.

Scollon, R. & Scollon, S. (2003). *Discourses in place: Language in the material world.* London: Routledge.

Soja, E. (2010). *Seeking spatial justice.* Minneapolis, MN: University of Minnesota Press.

Street, B. V. (1995). *Social literacies: Critical approaches to literacy in development, ethnography and education.* London: Longman.

Viseu, A., Clement, A., Aspinall, J. & Kennedy, T. L. (2006). The interplay of public and private spaces in internet access. *Information, Communication and Society, 9*(5), 633–656.

Ward, A. & Wason-Ellam, L. (2005). Reading beyond school: Literacies in a neighbourhood library. *Canadian Journal of Education, 28*(1), 92–108.

Yamada-Rice, D. (2010). New media, evolving multimodal literacy practices and the potential impact of increased use of the visual mode in the urban environment on young children's learning. *Literacy, 45*(1), 32–43.

PART III

Methods of Analysis in Digital Technologies, Gaming, and Web-based Research

13

RESEARCHING YOUNG CHILDREN'S LITERACY PRACTICES IN ONLINE VIRTUAL WORLDS

Cyber-ethnography and Multi-method Approaches

Jackie Marsh

In this chapter, I explore methodological and analytical approaches that might be used when undertaking research on young children's literacy practices in online virtual worlds. This work is key to building an understanding of how literacy is changing in the digital age. Children's use of virtual worlds is a growing area of interest for researchers and this chapter, therefore, intends to raise a number of questions about how the literacy research community might develop further the methodological tools employed to study the phenomenon. First, however, I will attempt to address the question: 'Why is this area of research of interest to literacy researchers?'

Young Children's Use of Virtual Worlds

Children in contemporary society are increasingly using online spaces (Livingstone, 2009). In the UK, Ofcom (2011) reported that 91% of children aged five to 15 have access to the Internet at home. Children have access to a range of technologies from birth and develop a range of skills, knowledge and understanding as a result of this use (Blanchard and Moore, 2010; Marsh, Brooks, Hughes, Ritchie & Roberts, 2005). An example of this might be found in Monteney Primary School in Sheffield, a school in which I have been exploring children's use of online virtual worlds for approximately five years (see Marsh, 2010, 2011). In the most recent study conducted in the school, 180 children completed a survey of their media-related activities. A total of 173 children completed a question which asked them to report on the frequency with which they accessed the Internet. Figure 13.1 outlines the responses.

Children reported accessing a range of online sites, including websites related to media brands (e.g. Disney) and favourite television channels and programmes,

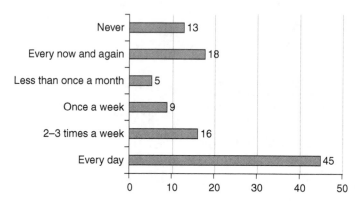

FIGURE 13.1 Percent frequency of Internet use (n = 173)

massively multiplayer online games (MMOGs), games and social networking sites and virtual worlds. The interest in virtual worlds has grown steadily over the past few years, with some reports that the fastest growing demographic of virtual world users is children between the ages of five and nine, a group that will see 27% growth in the use of these sites over the next five years (Gilbert, 2009). There are currently over 150 virtual worlds either operating or in development that are aimed at children and young people under 18 years of age, with approximately 355 million users aged five to ten of virtual worlds in 2012 (Kzero, 2012). The most popular virtual worlds for children share a number of features:

- They are password-protected sites that are often moderated to ensure cyber-safety.
- They enable users to create and maintain online identities in the form of an avatar.
- They provide avatars with a home base that can be decorated.
- Game play is central to the in-world activities and users can often earn virtual currency in the games to spend in the virtual world.
- Users can adopt virtual pets that they have to look after.
- Avatar-to-avatar communication is possible through chat facilities, the sending and receiving of notes/cards and so on.
- Some worlds offer opportunities for reading, e.g. virtual newspapers and catalogues.

These virtual spaces are of interest to literacy researchers in a number of ways. First, the virtual worlds themselves offer a range of opportunities for children to engage in reading and writing practices (Black, 2010; Burke & Marsh, in press; Marsh, 2011). Second, children engage in a wide range of online literacy practices related to virtual worlds outside of the games themselves, such as fan fiction, chat rooms and the creation of machinima, which are films created within computer games or virtual worlds, using screen capture software (Marsh, 2012a). Finally, given the way in which children's online and offline practices are becoming increasingly interrelated, it is important to ensure that we have a sound understanding of what children are doing in virtual worlds in order that we can understand the continuities and discontinuities in literacy in online and offline contexts. In the following section, I consider the methods that can be employed to study this popular phenomenon.

Researching Children's Virtual Worlds

One of the ways that children's engagement in virtual worlds may be studied is through extended ethnographic observation. Cyber-ethnography, or virtual ethnography (I will use both terms interchangeably, as both are used within the literature in this field), is a methodology that involves applying the principles of ethnography to online contexts. Cyber-ethnography is different in nature from digital ethnography (Murthy, 2011). The latter is a term used to refer to the way in which ethnography can now be mediated by digital technologies. For example, researchers can keep digital fieldnotes written in both online and offline contexts and research participants are able to make contributions to wikis or blogs. Digital means of storing data ensures that the data can be accessed by numerous individuals across research teams. In the case of cyber-ethnography, the focus is not on the processes by which the digital can facilitate ethnographic research but on researching virtual cultures.

Ethnography involves extended observation of cultures in order to gain understanding. In the case of virtual ethnography, the researcher is still focused on research that involves immersion within a culture, but this is a process undertaken in relation to an online culture. Hine (2004, pp. 1–2) outlines ten key principles which, she suggests, underpin virtual ethnography:

1. We can use ethnography to investigate the ways in which use of the Internet becomes socially meaningful.
2. Interactive media such as the Internet can be understood as both culture and cultural artefact.
3. The ethnography of mediated interaction often asks researchers to be mobile both virtually and physically.
4. Instead of going to particular field sites, virtual ethnography follows field connections.
5. Boundaries, especially between the 'virtual' and the 'real', are not to be taken-for-granted.
6. Virtual ethnography is a process of intermittent engagement, rather than long-term immersion.

7. Virtual ethnography is necessarily partial. Our accounts can be based on strategic relevance to particular research questions rather than faithful representations of objective realities.
8. Intensive engagement with mediated interaction adds an important reflexive dimension to ethnography.
9. This is ethnography *of*, *in* and *through* the virtual – we learn about the Internet by immersing ourselves in it and conducting our ethnography using it, as well as talking with people about it, watching them use it and seeing it manifest in other social settings.
10. Virtual ethnography is, ultimately, an adaptive ethnography which sets out to suit itself to the conditions in which it finds itself.

These principles point to the way in which ethnographies of online cultures may be more complex than offline ethnographies. Where does the offline/online boundary occur and is it the same for all contexts? How can the researcher address notions of authenticity and trust in situations in which he or she may never meet the participants? These and other questions become significant when considering extended observations of virtual communities.

The methodology emerged in the mid 1990s as Internet communities began to grow, primarily through the use of Multi-User Dungeons (MUDs). In a review of the history of cyber-ethnography, Robinson and Shultz (2011) suggest that the early years were characterised by the representation of cyberspace as offering opportunities for the creation of new identities, identities which were perceived to be very different from the real lives of Internet users. This view was superseded in the late 1990s by a recognition that there is overlap between online and offline life and personas (Kendall, 2002; Markham, 1998). Recent research in this area (Boellstorff, 2008; Nardi, 2010) has pointed to the complex interactions between online and offline identities and activities.

This shift to a more nuanced view of the territory was related to a concomitant development in ethical considerations. If there is overlap between online and offline identities, then researchers need to respect the rights of participants in online sites as much as they do in offline sites. So, for example, people should be given, or choose, pseudonyms for their avatars, thus enabling their online identities to be protected as far as possible. This does not guarantee anonymity, however, if text from online interactions is to be reported by researchers, as sometimes the text is publicly available and thus could be traced with the use of search engines. This might be the case, for example, if a researcher quotes text from a participant's Facebook page and that page does not utilise Facebook's privacy settings. There may be a case, therefore, for changing text in some instances, or deciding not to report it in order to protect the identities of research participants.

A further ethical challenge occurs when making decisions about what to observe in-world. It may be assumed that as participants in a virtual world are not recognisable in their human form, it would be acceptable to observe them covertly. This, however, assumes that online environments automatically operate as public spaces, when in fact many sites need passwords in order to enter them. In addition, normally a researcher would be observable to people in a public space as someone who was recording notes, or video recording, whereas this would not be the case in relation to a researcher who was represented by an avatar when examining online spaces, or who is merely present online in chat forums, without a virtual representation. There are ways in which this issue might be addressed in virtual fieldwork. For example, an avatar's identity card may contain details of the researcher's role and institution and the researcher could make it clear through text chat that he or she is observing a specific context. Gillen (2009) reports how, in a study of teenagers in *Teen Second Life*, she was able to have the tag 'Researcher' appear above her avatar's head when she was actively researching. This is not always possible in some of the environments that researchers may wish to observe in order to examine children's use of virtual worlds and in these cases, researchers will need to find other ways to identify themselves as ethnographers.

An additional ethical consideration in this context is the position of the researcher as an adult in a child-focused virtual environment, if the ethnography involves participant observation. Adults can, and do, undertake ethnographic research in child-focused environments in offline contexts, but they are physically identifiable as adults in those situations. This is not the case in virtual environments, in which both adults and children might be represented by the same set of avatars and, therefore, it would not be possible to distinguish differences in age. Again, this situation will need careful consideration by the adult researcher and ways of informing child users of his or her presence adopted.

Methods employed in virtual ethnography are the same as those in standard ethnography – primarily, observation and interviewing. Issues relating to authenticity and trust can be developed over time, as the researcher builds relationships with others through the online forums and sites. Virtual texts and artefacts can be analysed as part of the cultural practices of the online communities, in the same way that texts and artefacts in offline ethnographies offer significant information about the cultures under study. Indeed, analysis of virtual artefacts can offer valuable insights regarding what virtual communities consider to be of importance, as identified by Nardi (2010) in her study of *World of Warcraft* in which she identified how important 'modding' (the adaptation of virtual artefacts and game experiences) was to the users.

Ethnography in virtual worlds need not focus solely on texts. The principles of multimodal ethnography (Flewitt, 2011) can be applied in an online environment; that is, the ethnographer can focus not just on language, but on the visual, gestural or other modes. This is particularly salient in studies of online interactions which might involve a range of modes in communication, and where modes such as colour, for example, can be meaningful in terms of the presentation of online identities.

There are some disadvantages to undertaking ethnography in virtual spaces. First, the ethnographer may not view himself or herself as sufficiently immersed in the culture in order to understand it. Immersion is not always as easy to achieve in online spaces as offline spaces, given the potential distractions that one might face whilst attempting to become immersed, such as interruptions by family, friends or colleagues. Second, research participants may not feel as comfortable being virtually observed or interviewed as they do in offline contexts and, thus, may offer restricted viewpoints and observations. (Conversely, of course, some participants may feel more at ease in the virtual environment and, therefore, more able to open up to the interviewer.) Third, given that researchers cannot pick up on non-verbal cues online unless they are using video-conferencing, some nuances and further leads in the interview may be overlooked. Finally, given the skills required to navigate virtual worlds, researchers may be focused on technical issues rather than observing the events themselves. It is difficult to make notes about the research context, for example, when one's avatar is flying in the wrong direction! Despite these potential challenges, virtual ethnography has much to offer the study of literacy and literacy education in the digital era.

Cyber-ethnography in Practice

An example of a cyber-ethnography undertaken in a children's virtual world is outlined by Connelly (in press). Connelly describes how she undertook an analysis of the virtual world *Barbiegirls* through a cyber-ethnographic study in which she joined the virtual world as a member and adopted an avatar she named Goonengerry. As an ethnographer does in offline contexts, Connelly spent long periods of time immersed in the environment, observing and documenting events, texts and artefacts she encountered.

In one sense, Connelly's study could be seen as a cyber-autoethnography. Autoethnography is a form of ethnography that focuses on describing the experiences of the researcher and placing this autobiographical account in a wider social, cultural and historical context. Connelly adapts this approach for the virtual environment, so that she offers a critical analysis of her avatar's experiences in *Barbiegirls*. This enables her to provide a detailed critique of the process of creating a virtual identity and becoming enculturated in the commercial context of the Mattel-produced environment. Using a mixture of field-notes, visual and discourse analysis, Connelly highlights how the literacy opportunities in *Barbiegirls* are limited and constrained by issues relating to gender stereotyping and economic capital. For example, the virtual world had two levels of membership, one free and one that required payment – VIP membership. Connelly (in press) describes how being a non-VIP member restricted in-world activities:

In the *Games Room* Goonengerry was unable to answer many of the simple quiz questions (all based on the virtual world locations and the activities that go on inside them). In *Extreme DreamPark* she could not ride the Sparkle Coaster, nor visit *Twilight Woods*. In *Shop-a-Mallics* (the shopping mall) she could have lots of fun trying on clothes but even though she may have earned *B* Bucks she could not spend them on the fashions she liked. When attempting to take part in any restricted activities Goonengerry was constantly blocked via a pop-up screen that reminded her that *'This feature is available when you join Barbie Girls V.I.P.'*

This approach, which required Connelly to spend long periods of time as a cyber-ethnographer in the virtual world, enabled her to gain an emic perspective on *Barbiegirls* in ways that would not have been possible had she simply observed children using the space.

Multimethod Approaches

There are methodologies other than virtual ethnography by which children's and young people's use of virtual worlds might be studied by literacy researchers. A study conducted by Marsh (2012a) utilised multiple methods, including non-participant observations of children using virtual worlds. Children were filmed as they engaged in the use of the Disney-owned virtual world 'Club Penguin' and they were interviewed about this use whilst they were being filmed. These methods do require some considerations that would not apply if the researcher was filming offline interactions. For example, the focus of the camera is of significance. If the lens is focused solely on the screen, then key aspects of the research context, such as the child's gaze and expression, will be missed. One way to address this is to utilise specialist software that enables both screen capture *and* the filming of the user of the virtual world.

Terminology regarding the use of virtual worlds is also important – how does one refer to the virtual/ non-virtual when interviewing children about their actions and experiences, for example? In Marsh (2012a), I used the terms 'real' and 'virtual' as I felt that detailed explanations related to alternatives would not be appropriate for this age group, but this is problematic when one considers that everything occurring on the virtual plane originates in the offline world and thus all is 'real'. As Malpas (2009, p. 135) notes:

A basic starting point for any serious discussion of the virtual must be recognition of the *non-autonomy* of the virtual – a recognition of the fact that the virtual does not constitute an autonomous, independent, or 'closed' system, but is instead always dependent, in a variety of ways, on the everyday world within which it is embedded.

This points to the importance of not artificially separating online and offline domains, but instead paying attention to the boundaries between them and analysing children's literacy practices across this divide. This is particularly necessary given the way that virtual world franchises are now distributed across multimedia platforms. 'Club Penguin', for example, the site that featured in the Marsh (2012a) study, is instantiated across the texts and artefacts, outlined in Table 13.1

Carrington (in press) proposes, drawing from Deleuze (1991), to use the term 'assemblages' to account for the polycentricity and multi-layeredness of inter-connected media texts, as in Table 13.1. New media assemblages permeate the literacy practices of children and young people and, therefore, any study of children's virtual worlds needs to take account of the way in which they operate. Further, as already identified, one of the features of users' engagement in the use of virtual worlds is that the related literacy practices spill out from the confines of the virtual world and are distributed across online and offline spaces. Steinkuehler (2007) notes that the literacy practices related to the MMOG *World of Warcraft* include websites that contain fan forums, chat rooms and online magazines; she terms this a 'constellation' of literacy practices. This constellation offers opportunities for users to create a range of multimodal, multimedia texts related to their favourite virtual worlds, including machinima. The production and distribution of these texts could offer a further focus for research on children's use of virtual worlds, given their significance. The analysis of the texts themselves could be undertaken through the deployment of some of the methods discussed elsewhere in this book, such as discourse and visual analysis.

Other methods used to study virtual worlds include keeping records of online verbal interactions, such as chat logs (Gillen, 2009), asking participants to keep research diaries of their online activities and taking snapshots of the virtual world itself, equivalent to the use of still photography in offline contexts. Indeed, most means of capturing data in offline contexts can be utilised in the study of virtual worlds, although some of the aspects of sensory ethnography

TABLE 13.1 Texts and artefacts that link to the 'Club Penguin' virtual world

Online virtual world
DS Nintendo game
Wii game
Mobile app
Magazine
Books
Toys
Games
Clothing
Bedding

outlined by Pink (2009) cannot be employed – it would be impossible to identify and note smells in virtual contexts, obviously. In studying literacy practices in virtual environments, researchers need to identify what they want to find out and employ the most appropriate methods to do this.

The final method to be considered here is the analysis of user logs. Kafai, Quintero and Feldon (2010) had access to such data in their study of the virtual world *Whyvillle*. They tracked the log files of 595 players aged ten to 14, which included details of activities, locations and time spent there and chat content. They used this data to provide detailed accounts of user behaviour on the site, including their responses to an outbreak of 'Whypox', a virtual epidemic. Whilst this is a very rich source of data, it is not usually possible to obtain in many of the popular virtual worlds that children and young people use because of the commercial sensitivity of such data.

Analysing Children's Literacy Practices in Virtual Worlds

There are no specific approaches that are utilised in the analysis of children and young people's literacy practices in virtual worlds. Researchers may analyse the data in any way they see fit, according to their research questions. Approaches may include discourse analysis, visual analysis and multimodal analysis, as described in other chapters in this book. Approaches to analysis of data collected in virtual worlds are subject to the same considerations as data arising from offline studies. However, given that we are at a relatively early stage in developing an understanding of literacy in virtual environments, one of the ways in which such data may be considered is to contrast and compare with data collected in offline environments. This would enable conclusions to be drawn about the way in which literacy practices across online and offline domains might be the same or differ. This knowledge is important in building an understanding of the affordances of virtual worlds for literacy learning. In the following section of the chapter, I outline a study in which this process was undertaken.

An exemplar study which involves analysing literacy practices in a virtual world can be found in Marsh (2012a), mentioned previously. This paper reports on a study, conducted in Monteney Primary School, Sheffield, UK, in which a range of methods was employed to undertake research on children's use of the virtual world 'Club Penguin'. The first step was to conduct an online survey in which children's online activities were explored. Online surveys can offer a useful means of developing an overview of a specific topic, but they should also be used with caution with this age group. For example, one of the questions requested participants to note down the virtual worlds that they used. A minority of participants noted sites that could not be categorised as virtual worlds, suggesting that they would have benefited from further discussion concerning the definition of virtual worlds.

Children who stated in the survey that they used virtual worlds on a regular basis were invited to take part in the interviews during lessons in an Information Technology (IT) suite in the school. Twenty-six children across the year groups, 15 boys and 11 girls, took part in a series of group and individual semi-structured interviews over the course of two academic years. The interviews were undertaken in the school dining room and were digitally recorded, then transcribed. The interviews explored in depth children's activities when using virtual worlds outside of school. In addition, three 11-year-old children were filmed using the virtual world *Club Penguin* in their homes, Emily, John and Sally. The children were all white, monolingual and were from working-class families. Each child was filmed four times over the period of one month, from the time at which they logged on to *Club Penguin* to the time they logged off. If the children were already logged on to the virtual world when I arrived, I filmed them from the point of my arrival to the time they logged off. Emily was filmed in total for 2 hours, 38 minutes and 52 seconds, John for 3 hours, 19 minutes and 38 seconds and Sally for 2 hours, 50 minutes and 25 seconds. I asked the children questions occasionally as they used the virtual world and interviews were conducted with children and one of their parents after the final filming session in order to explore children's uses of and responses to the virtual world and parents' attitudes towards their children's use of *Club Penguin*. I have chosen to focus on this study because it exemplifies a means of analysing online interactions using an analytic framework developed in an offline context.

The data from the video observations were analysed in relation to the literacy events that were observed or reported. Following Barton and Hamilton (1998), 'literacy event' was defined as an activity in which children could be observed reading or writing in *Club Penguin*. An event began when children began to read or write a particular text and ended when they stopped reading or writing that specific text. If children returned to a text and began to read/write again, the event was deemed to be new. I then undertook a process of deductive coding in which literacy events were categorised using a priori codes consisting of the four purposes identified by Cairney and Ruge (1998, p. 38), which are:

- literacy for establishing and maintaining relationships;
- literacy for accessing or displaying information;
- literacy for pleasure and/or self-expression;
- literacy for skills development.

Further to these categories, I also analysed the data in the light of fifth purpose, identified in a previous study of young children's engagement with media and new technologies (Marsh, 2006), that of literacy for identity construction and performance.

An example of this process of deductive analysis is as follows. Emily, one of the three children who were filmed, wished to find out how her virtual flat television screen could display pictures. She entered an igloo in which three avatars were engaged in a game of imaginary football. They did not have a (virtual) ball to play with, but used the chat facility to outline their imaginary actions as they raced around the igloo:

> Emily entered an igloo to face three avatars that were running around. The users were using the chat facility to signal their footballing moves:

> Avatar 1: *Misses*
> Avatar 2: *U better*
> Avatar 1: *Takes shoot*
> Avatar 3: *Whacks round hed*
> Avatar 1: *Heart stops*
> Avatar 2: *Hands up*
> Avatar 3: *Good*

> Emily's avatar: How did you turn on your TV?

> Avatar 1: *Falls*
> Avatar 1: *Waaaaaaaaa*
> Avatar 2: *Catches*
> Avatar 3: *I weaving*

Eventually, Emily gave up her attempt to obtain information and left the igloo, moving on to another igloo to ask the same question.

This episode was categorised as 'literacy for accessing or displaying information' because Emily used the chat facility to try and find out how to turn her TV on. The example also offers insight into how literacy is used in virtual worlds for pleasure or self-expression, as the avatars enjoyed their virtual game of football through their written exchanges.

Once this deductive process was complete, I analysed the data inductively in order to identify any additional purposes for literacy which were not classified by Cairney and Ruge (1998) or Marsh (2006) and an additional purpose emerged from this analysis: literacy for establishing and maintaining social networks. This purpose could be seen, for example, when avatars clustered together in public spaces and engaged in ritualistic play, such as all doing the same activity, saying the same phrase or activating the same emoticon as other avatars. In this way, users could establish connections with multiple users at the same time, thus developing social networks.

Table 13.2 outlines examples from the data that were matched against all of the aforementioned purposes.

TABLE 13.2 Purposes for literacy in Club Penguin

Purposes for literacy	Examples from observational and interview data
Literacy for accessing or displaying information	• Reading the newspaper to find out about events/tips etc. • Reading catalogues • Using environmental print to navigate the virtual world, e.g. signs • Reading game instructions • Reading clues on quests
Literacy for constructing and maintaining relationships	• Communicating to other penguins via chat/safe chat • Using emoticons to express emotions to other penguins • Sending postcards to other penguins • Using *Club Penguin* to instant message others
Literacy for pleasure or self-expression	• Literacy integral to play – fantasy play, socio-dramatic play, role play • Reading poems, jokes and stories in the newspaper • Reading books in the library • Submitting jokes, poems and stories to the newspaper • Language play • Searching for *Club Penguin* machinima on YouTube
Literacy for identity construction and performance	• Choosing avatar's clothes and artefacts • Choosing emoticons and phrases to express identity
Literacy for establishing and maintaining social networks	• Communicating to two or more other penguins via chat/safe chat • Using chat in group ritual play

Source: from Marsh, 2012a.

This analytical process, therefore, enabled me to identify that there was much overlap between children's literacy practices in online and offline spaces and that virtual spaces facilitated a new practice that had not been identified in offline contexts, that of literacy for establishing and maintaining social networks.

Highlighting the analytic process in this way is not intended to convey the message that children's literacy activities in virtual worlds should always be compared with their offline literacy practices. This might signal that online activities only have validity when viewed side by side with offline experiences, which is clearly not the case. Virtual literacy activities offer a rich source of texts and practices that can be studied in their own right in a variety of ways, e.g. in terms of their linguistic and/or multimodal content and structure, the generic conventions used, the social practices surrounding virtual instances of literacy and so on. Rather, what this example illustrates is the potential for studies of virtual worlds to offer insights into the relationship between literacy practices in both online and offline domains.

Conclusion

As the use of virtual worlds becomes more prevalent in the years ahead, there are a number of areas that deserve focused attention from literacy researchers. Given the extent to which the use of such environments can be motivating for young children, there are numerous possibilities for using virtual worlds within the literacy curriculum. For example, pupils could interact with pupils from other classes and schools in virtual worlds that have been specifically created for that purpose, using open source software. Any such initiative should be informed by rigorous research in order to identify how far such pedagogical approaches are successful and whether or not the literacy skills and knowledge acquired in such activities are transferable to other contexts.

Further, children's out-of-school use of these environments deserves sustained attention. Studies in this field are emerging and serve to highlight the rich array of literacy practices children undertake in virtual worlds (Black, 2010; Burke & Marsh, in press; Gillen, 2009; Marsh, 2012a; Wohlwend, Vander Zanden, Husbye & Kuby, 2011). Nevertheless, there remain significant questions that have not yet been addressed. What, for example, is the impact of engagement in virtual worlds on young children's motivation for reading and writing offline? Disney has recently launched a *Club Penguin* magazine in the UK and it remains to be seen how far this initiative will inspire reluctant readers. Finally, given the extent to which children's use of virtual worlds promotes the creative production of multimedia, multimodal texts, such as fan fiction and machinima, there are potential avenues for further research in this area. How do children, for example, decide on the appropriate modes and media for their texts and what is their understanding of their audience? What processes are involved in the circulation of these texts?

These are some of the research questions that will be important to address in the years ahead. There is also a need to develop new and innovative methodologies for this work in order that children's voices can be placed at the centre of such research. Participatory methods have been utilised in previous studies of children's engagement with media (Marsh, 2012b) and these approaches could be adopted, and adapted, in the study of virtual worlds. Avatar-to-avatar interviews within virtual worlds might be an effective means of children finding out about other users' experiences, for example. Auto-cyber-ethnography is a further possibility in that virtual world users could investigate their own literacy histories in online environments over time. Auto-ethnography as a methodology (see Ellis & Holman Jones, 2012) has been underutilised in studies of literacy and there is much potential to develop this approach in cyberspace. These research directions offer exciting possibilities for the future and, in pursuing them, literacy researchers will be addressing key issues in the twenty-first century communication landscape.

References

Barton, D. & Hamilton, M. (1998). *Local literacies: Reading and writing in one community*. London: Routledge.

Black, R. W. (2010). The language of Webkinz: Early childhood literacy in an online virtual world. *Digital Culture and Education, 2*(1), 7–24.

Blanchard, J. & Moore, T. (2010). *The digital world of young children: Impact on emergent literacy*. Pearson Foundation White Paper. Retrieved from www.pearsonfoundation.org/downloads/EmergentLiteracy-WhitePaper.pdf.

Boellstorff, T. (2008). *Coming of age in second life: An anthropologist explores the virtually human*. Princeton, NJ: Princeton University Press.

Burke, A. & Marsh, J. (eds.) (in press). *Children's virtual play worlds: Culture, learning and participation*. New York: Peter Lang.

Cairney, T. H. & Ruge, J. (1998). *Community literacy practices and schooling: Towards effective support for students*. Canberra, Australia: DEET.

Carrington, V. (in press). An argument for assemblage theory: Integrated spaces, mobility and polycentricity. In A. Burke & J. Marsh (eds) *Children's virtual play worlds: Culture, learning and participation*. New York: Peter Lang.

Connelly, J. (in press). Virtual play or virtual clay? Barbiegirls.com as a space of constructive play or identity shaping. In A. Burke and J. Marsh (eds) *Children's virtual play worlds: Culture, learning and participation*. New York: Peter Lang.

Deleuze, G. (1991). *Empiricism and subjectivity*. New York: Columbia University Press.

Ellis, C. & Holman Jones, S. (eds) (2012). *Handbook of autoethnography*. Walnut Creek, CA: Left Coast Press.

Flewitt, R. S. (2011). Bringing ethnography to a multimodal investigation of early literacy in a digital age. *Qualitative Research, 11*(3), 293–310.

Gilbert, B. (2009). *Virtual worlds market forecast 2009–2015*. Strategyanalytics. Retrieved from www.strategyanalytics.com/default.aspx?mod=ReportAbstractViewer&a0=4779.

Gillen, J. (2009). Literacy practices in Schome Park: A virtual literacy ethnography. *Journal of Research in Reading, 32*(1), 57–74.

Hine, C. (2004). *Virtual ethnography revisited*. Paper presented at Research Methods Festival, Oxford, July 1, 2004.

Kafai, Y. B., Quintero, M. & Feldon, D. (2010) Investigating the 'Why' in Whypox casual and systematic explorations of a virtual epidemic. *Games and Culture, 5*(1), 116–135.

Kendall, L. (2002). *Hanging out in the virtual pub: Masculinities and relationships online*. Los Angeles: University of California Press.

Kzero (2012) *Kzero survey, 2012*. Retrieved from www.kzero.co.uk.com.

Livingstone, S. (2009). *Children and the internet*. Cambridge, UK: Polity.

Malpas, J. (2009). On the non-autonomy of the virtual. *Convergence: The International Journal of Research into New Media Technologies, 15*(2), 135–139.

Markham, A. N. (1998). *Life online: Researching real experiences in virtual space*. Walnut Creek, CA: Atlanta Press.

Marsh, J. (2006). Global, local/ public, private: Young children's engagement in digital literacy practices in the home. In J. Rowsell and K. Pahl (eds) *Travel notes from the new literacy studies: Case studies in practice* (pp. 19–38). Clevedon, UK: Multilingual Matters.

Marsh, J. (2010). Young children's play in online virtual worlds. *Journal of Early Childhood Research, 8*(1), 23–39.

Marsh, J. (2011). Young children's literacy practices in a virtual world: Establishing an online interaction order. *Reading Research Quarterly, 46*(2), 101–118.

Marsh, J. (2012a). Purposes for literacy in children's use of the online virtual world 'Club Penguin'. *Journal of Research in Reading*. Article first published online: 11 JUN 2012. DOI: 10.1111/j.1467-9817.2012.01530.x.

Marsh, J. (2012b). Children as knowledge brokers. *Childhood, 19*(4), 508–522.

Marsh, J., Brooks, G., Hughes, J., Ritchie, L. & Roberts, S. (2005). *Digital beginnings: Young children's use of popular culture, media and new technologies*. Sheffield, UK: University of Sheffield. Retrieved from www.digitalbeginnings.shef.ac.uk/.

Murthy, D. (2011). Emergent digital ethnographic methods for social research. In S. N. Hesse-Biber (ed.) *Handbook of emergent technologies in social research* (pp. 158–179). Oxford, UK: Oxford University Press.

Nardi, B. (2010). *My life as a night elf priest: An anthropological account of 'World of Warcraft'*. Ann Arbor, MI: University of Michigan Press.

Ofcom (2011). *Children and parents: Media use and attitudes report*. Retrieved from http:// stakeholders.ofcom.org.uk/binaries/research/media-literacy/oct2011/Children_and_ parents.pdf.

Pink, S. (2009). *Doing sensory ethnography*. London: Sage.

Robinson, L. & Schulz, J. (2011). New fieldsites, new methods: New ethnographic opportunities. In S. Hesse-Biber (ed.) *The handbook of emergent technologies in social research* (pp. 180–195). Oxford, UK: Oxford University Press.

Steinkuehler, C. (2007). Massively multiplayer online gaming as a constellation of literacy practices. *E-Learning, 4*, 297–318.

Wohlwend, K., Vander Zanden, S., Husbye, N. E. & Kuby, C. R. (2011). Navigating discourses in place in the world of Webkinz. *Journal of Early Childhood Literacy, 11*, 141–163.

14

VIDEO GAMES AND ELECTRONIC MEDIA

Catherine Beavis

Purpose, Origin and Description of the Method

Videogames and gameplay, and young people's engagement with them, are of considerable interest to literacy educators and researchers concerned with new forms of literacy (multiliteracies, digital literacies and the like), the place of videogames and digital culture in young people's lives, the literate and social practices that surround them, and the ways in which participation in game play provides an 'every day arena of action' for the exploration and performance of identity, values and community. Games and game play provide dynamic exemplars of contemporary communicative forms, and an important forum for the analysis of diverse semiotic systems, the interactions between these, and the 'reading' and 'writing' practices and understandings needed to play. They exemplify literacy constructed as design. Game play constitutes a powerful form of socially situated textual practice. What young players bring to play, what they know and learn, and how participation in play shapes their sense of self, identity and community are inextricably related, with important implications for how we understand contemporary literacy texts and practices, and the centrality of these in young people's lives. Such matters are very much the business of literacy educators and researchers.

However, challenges remain about how to understand and conceptualise videogames and game play, and what approaches to use that will capture their complexity while also doing justice to the hybrid nature of the form, the fluid, situated and dynamic nature of game play, the role of the player and what the player 'gains'. To do so requires bringing together analytic approaches from two fields – that of Literacy, where lenses such as those provided by the literature in New Literacies, Multiliteracies, Discourse and Design, foreground understandings of literacy as social practice, and connections between texts, participation and identity – and that of Games Studies, which provides a very different set of referents and emphases.

Games Studies Perspectives on Researching Games and Game Play

The emergence of videogames or digital games is a relatively recent phenomenon, with approaches to game study and analysis reflecting the newness of the field, and the diversity of epistemological frameworks and traditions different disciplines bring to bear. Games studies and literary/literacy perspectives and research methodologies have historically had some difficulty accommodating each other. As computer games developed, the use of existing frameworks to analyse games and games aesthetics, such as those used in the analysis of Literature, Film or Art provided useful starting points and points of connection; however, at the same time they were also not a direct 'fit' – and did not fully correspond to the ways in which games were constituted and played. The importation of methodological approaches developed in the context of quite different forms ran the risk of ignoring or distorting the very nature of games. Analytic methodologies need to reflect the complexity of games as both textual and non-textual forms; the situated nature of play; the player's role and that of the machine; the network of texts, practices and paratexts that surround the game; and the centrality of action to the making and progress of the game (Apperley 2010; Bogost 2007; Consalvo 2007; Galloway 2006; Stevens, Satwicz & McCarthy 2008; etc.).

Literacy Perspectives on Researching Games and Game Play

There is a strong and growing body of research studies and methodological frameworks within the fields of Literacy, New Literacies and Multimodality that addresses digital literacies and young people's participation in the online world (e.g. Alvermann 2010; Coiro, Knobel, Lankshear & Leu 2008; Merchant, Gillen, Marsh & Davies 2012). Amongst these, there are common understandings of literacy as socially situated, and as social practice; a recognition of the power of digital culture and new media in young people's lives, the importance of contexts, relationships and 'affinity groups' (Gee 2007), and of the mutually constitutive relationships between textually mediated forms of representation and engagement, and the construction and performance of self.

Core to research in this area is an understanding of literacy as composed not just of print or oral language, but, rather, as entailing many elements, so that literacy is synonymous with multiliteracies, conceptualised as multimodal and comprising different semiotic systems working together in patterns of 'design'. Design, as both verb and noun, is central to the ways in which meaning is made

(Kress 2003), in digital contexts as elsewhere, and to understanding and analysis of contemporary 'reading' and 'writing' practices. Design includes, but is not limited to, print-based forms of literacy, but extends also to include visual, gestural, audio and other forms of semiosis, working in combination to create the whole. In videogames, as elsewhere, Gee (2007) argues, 'Learning about and coming to appreciate interrelations within and across multiple sign systems (images, words, actions, symbols, artifacts, etc.) as a complex system is core to the learning experience' (p. 42).

A further thread running across literacy research and writing on digital literacies is a focus on the energy and commitment young people often bring to participation in digital culture and Web 2.0, the high levels of skill developed and displayed there, and evident agency. There is also increasing awareness of the ways in which literacy practices within these spaces are situated within multiple dynamics – 'intersecting trajectories of discourse and action' (Dressman, McCarthey & Prior 2012, p. 1). In the case of videogames and game play, games themselves, as well as players' engagement with them, must be understood in terms of both text and action (Apperley & Beavis 2011; Beavis & Apperley 2012; Beavis, O'Mara & McNeice 2012); the dynamic relationship between the two and the mutually informing elements of situation, action and design; the player, other players, and world and narrative of the game.

Methods for Analysing Video Games and Play

While the field is not yet settled, one of the most flexible and persuasive methodologies for analysing games and game play arises out of considerations that understand literacy and literacy practices as socially situated and purposeful, address relationships between context, discourse and identity, and construct literacy as design. There has been increasing interest in analysing games and game play, particularly massively multiplayer online role play games in ways that bring together dimensions such as these, and games studies and literacy approaches and methodologies. Amongst these, Gee's view of language, the role of 'big' and 'little' Discourse, and his conception of literacy as design have provided a powerful basis for the analysis of games and game play that bridge games studies and literacy epistemological perspectives effectively (Gee 2007, 2012). Steinkuehler's doctoral studies, undertaken with Gee, provided a sustained and extended analysis of *Lineage I* and *II*, the massively multiplayer online game (MMOG) with respect to discourse and cognition. Her accounts of this research, and papers detailing her approach and methodology (Steinkuehler 2006, 2007, 2008) provide the primary exemplars in discussing methodological approaches for analysing games in this chapter.

In this research, analysis focuses collectively on the game, the player and game play, consistent with Games Studies' emphasis on the active nature of play, and the intricate interrelationship between the player and the game, and with views of literacy and literacy practice as purposeful and socially situated. In this view, literacy – language-in-use – is seen as simultaneously serving a number of ends, including the development and maintenance of values, relationships and identity, the shaping of outcomes in the 'real' (or virtual) world as well as broadly or narrowly negotiations of meaning and 'communication'. This approach shares the view that 'all language-in-use functions not only as a vehicle for conveying information but also, and equally importantly, as part and parcel of *ongoing activities* and as a means for *enacting human relationships*' (Gee, cited in Steinkuehler 2008, p. 39).

Gee's discourse theory, with 'big' and 'little' D Discourse, provides a means of mapping and understanding the ways language and related symbol systems work to create particular ways of seeing things and understanding oneself and the world. Through participation in, or affiliation with, particular Discourses and Discourse communities, people align themselves with the values and outlook of those communities, which shape or confirm their sense of identity and the world. The purpose of analysis of games and game play in this tradition is to understand the complex interactions players are engaged in as they play, including the negotiation of meaning, values, relationships and the self, and the ways in which games such as these 'work as rich spaces for social interaction and enculturation, requiring complex cognitive and cultural knowledge and skills' (Steinkuehler 2008, p. 49). As such, the study of games like these provides insights into the kinds of literate, cognitive and social practices players are engaged in as they play; what is valued in MMOGs and the games world and how these values are communicated and enacted; and the nature of participation in virtual communities, clans or guilds in games, and how that is established through play.

The method itself entails the collection of a wide range of data over an extended period, facilitated through the researcher's own participation in the game, as both player and virtual ethnographer. In role, the researcher is able to experience first hand what it is to play, observe actions and relationships, participate in the creation and maintenance of action within the game, and through their virtual representations – their avatars – interact with others in the making and progress of the game. As researcher, she or he has access to a wide range of data both within the game and in contexts related to the game, and through her or his relationships with other players. Data is subject to fine-grained multimodal analysis, with a focus on the detailed analysis of small, selected incidents to illuminate processes entailed through the larger working of the game.

Dimensions and Tenets Guiding the Analysis of Games and Gaming

Finding a language for analysis and for identifying separate but related elements is an important part of any methodology. In the case of videogames, analysis of games is inseparable from analysis of game play, with the world created by the

TABLE 14.1 Views of the internet correlated with MMOG researcher vocabulary and views of research

View of internet	space ←——————————————→ place	
	How researchers talk about	
	Location	Medium	Community, culture, world
	Object of study	Publication, public, published	Players, avatars, residents
	Ethical rights	Author rights (copyright), researcher rights (public access)	Gamer/resident rights, community norms, gameworld conventions
View of research	text based ←——————————————→ person based	

Source: McKee & Porter, 2009, p. 117.

game and in which the game takes place, shaping the narrative and players' experience of the game, which in turn is also shaped by the knowledge, values and prior experiences players bring to play. In outlining a typology of game research, Aarseth (2003, p. 2) proposed three dimensions that characterise games and game play. These are

- gameplay (the players' actions, strategies and motives);
- game-structure (the rules of the game, including the simulation rules);
- game-world (fictional context, topology/level design, textures etc.).

This division provides a useful way of separating out interdependent elements, making them available for discussion individually while not obscuring their relatedness and the organic nature of play. It provides an explanatory backdrop for discussion, which assumes interrelatedness of on and offline worlds, and the complexity of identity, sociality and presence within each, without having continually to revisit these.

A number of the key tenets guiding researchers using Discourse-based methodologies to their studies have been referred to already above. They include:

1. The need to take account of both literacy and games studies traditions and perspectives, and to recognise the distinctive qualities and affordances of games and game play.
2. The need to recognise games and game play as dynamic, socially situated and constructed by the player(s) in interaction with the game algorithms and machine.
3. The need to see game play as purposeful social practice, and as a site for the representation and performance of self.
4. An understanding of literacy as multimodal and constructed as design.
5. An understanding of connections between Literacy, Discourse and Identity and between Discourse and cognition in online games.

Ethics issues in conducting internet research are complex. Much depends on whether the contexts for research, such as MMOGs, are conceived of as space or place. If the internet (game) world is seen primarily as 'space', what is posted online, or created on screen, may be treated as data (having been given) and analysed as 'published' text, analogous to film and other publicly available media artefacts. If the game world is seen primarily as place, then what happens on screen might be better viewed ethnographically, with the world seen as a place where people gather and a more 'people-centred' set of ethnographical principles and privacy and permission expectations obtain. McKee and Porter (2009) represent these positions and their implications as a continuum (see Table 14.1).

Tenets relating to ethical considerations, and relationships and behaviours across on and offline worlds therefore include the following:

6. A view of the relationship between 'online' and 'offline' worlds as fluid, and intersecting, with actions, values and behaviours in one having material consequences and influencing and interacting with the other.
7. A view of online worlds as place as much as space.
8. A sensitivity to ethical considerations in data gathering and analysis specific to online games and internet research.

A further tenet of much research from Games Studies, with implications for Literacy-based researchers concerns the researchers' credibility as a player of the game – that is,

9. The researcher must be a player of the game.

While this tenet (that the researcher needs to be familiar with, and participate in, the aspect of digital culture or Web 2.0 participation under discussion), is implicit in much new literacies and digital literacies research, it is not regarded as an essential precondition of analysis. By contrast, it is almost universally explicitly upheld as a core expectation and requirement in Games Studies research. This tenet demands that researchers know the games they discuss intimately and at first hand, just as Shakespearean scholars are expected to be personally familiar with Shakespeare's plays, or students expected to have read books set for study when they write about them in exams. In the case of games, this generally means long-term immersion through play so that the game has been experienced in depth, over a period of time. While not all literacy-based games researchers take this view, it must be recognised and factored into discussion if an alternate research focus, methodology or scenario is in place.

Analysing MMOGs: An Exemplar Study

The discussion in this chapter follows Steinkuehler's analysis of massively multiplayer online games. Steinkuehler utilises approaches and methodologies drawn from functional linguistics, views of literacy as design, Discourse analysis and cognitive ethnography (Steinkuehler 2006, 2007, 2008). This approach entails selecting an utterance, episode or exchange from in-game play and undertaking a close reading to show the ways in which meaning is created through the interaction of multiple elements, at a macro and micro level. The section chosen for analysis is analysed with a view to the immediate focus of that moment, but also with an eye to showing how 'broader forms of life' are enacted within the context of the game, for example, the ways in which affiliations and identities are established, relationships developed and knowledge passed on.

Analysis of Linguistic Data – Traditional Print-based Forms

When the focus of analysis is primarily on linguistic data, grammatical analysis follows functional linguistics frameworks together with 'big-D' discourse analytic approaches – 'the analysis of language as it is used to enact activities, perspectives, and identities' (Steinkuehler 2008, p. 42). Utterances are presented in their original, abbreviated form (as 'Leetspeak'), 'translated' (expanded) into their standard English and then glossed to show their meaning in context, providing in effect a further level of translation where necessary. Thus, for example, 'afk' (original) might be translated into the fuller wording it abbreviates – 'away from keys' – which in the context of the game has the effective meaning of 'wait a minute' (Steinkuehler 2008, p. 42). Syntactic analysis follows, with the utterance parsed according to the functions served, following Halliday (1985) – interpersonal, ideational and textual.

Once grammatical analysis has been completed, discourse analysis follows, which depends amongst other things on the analyst's familiarity with the world of the game, 'situating [the utterance] back in its particular social and material context' (Steinkuehler 2006, p. 49); seeing the utterance as part of an event, shaping what happens in the game and the ways it is played. The final stage is analysis of the utterance in terms of 'big D' Discourse, as 'one instantiation of a big D Discourse operative in the online game' (Steinkuehler 2006, p. 49).

Analysis of Multiple Data Streams – Contemporary Literacy, Literacy as Design

While the analysis of a single utterance or group of utterances as outlined above lends itself to formal grammatical analysis of a highly specialised and literacy form, the analysis of larger chunks of data reflects the interplay of multiple strands as play takes place within a screen environment in which utterances per se are only one subset of a much larger body of data, including diverse semiotic systems and resources. Literacies are seen to 'crucially entail sense making within a rich multimodal semiotic system, situated in a community of practice that renders the system meaningful' (Steinkuehler 2007, p. 300). Sense must be made from a 'seemingly sundry assortment of images, bar graphs, texts, icons and symbols' (p. 300), with game play demonstrating 'fluency and participation in a thoroughly literate space of icons, symbols, gestures, action, pictorial representations and text' (p. 301). Multiple sets of simultaneously occurring data, accompanying and creating game play, are described and analysed using discourse analysis principles, with a view to elucidating the ways in which meaning is made within each set or context; the relationship within and between each, with respect to linguistic and cognitive dimensions; the ways play is advanced, values established, relationships and identities maintained; and the ways in which the player enacts, resists or is inducted into the norms and Discourses of play.

Drawing on different episodes and data sets from her study of the MMOG, *Lineage*, Steinkuehler provides a number of exemplars which demonstrate this methodology (e.g. Steinkuehler 2006, 2007, 2008). While beginning with a reminder of the multiple semiotic elements to which players must attend, and the visual enactment of game play on the screen, these examples particularly focus on (verbal) text-based data streams, located within the broader context of the narrative structures and conventions of the game, the actions entailed and the discourse-mediated values and norms through which players are inculcated into, and demonstrate membership of, the 'big D' discourses of the game. Two examples are given here. The first is the one cited earlier – a single utterance from the game *Lineage*, further elaborated below. The second, also from *Lineage* is an episode in which an experienced player, Myrondonia, apprentices a less experienced female elf, Jellybean, into the Discourses values and practices of the game.

Exemplar 1

The utterance 'afk g2g too ef ot regen no poms' is first expanded into literal translation – 'away from keys got to go to Elven Forest to regenerate no mana potions'. Then this utterance is, in turn, glossed more broadly – 'Just a minute. I have to go to the Elven Forest to regenerate. I'm out of mana potions' (Steinkuehler 2006, p. 42). From there, the utterance is analysed syntactically into interpersonal and ideational functions, so that Galvedor, the speaker, is shown to be acting in the interests of the group to which he belongs, at a time when the group is hunting in a demanding area and needs his presence. Mana potions will be necessary to strengthen his avatar's magic abilities as they come under pressure in the course of attacks he will experience during the hunt. Thus far, knowledge of broad features of the game, and of Lineagese, the form of 'Leetspeak' in the game, together with familiarity with functional grammar analysis of this kind, enables the non-player analyst to make reasonable sense of what is happening. Deeper levels of analysis, however, Steinkuehler argues, are dependent on first hand knowledge of play.

> For those without some understanding of gaming practices, Galvedor's utterance would appear of little consequence. And yet, if we examine the activity in which Galvedor's utterance was situated, we find it most certainly does have consequence. His utterance both reflected and shaped the activity in which it was situated and, as such, can be analysed as one 'move' in a complex coordination not only of language but of (virtual) material objects and people as well.
>
> *(p. 45)*

Small d discourse analysis of the utterance discusses its significance contextually, in relation to 'pledge hunts' and the complex coordination they require. Attention is also paid to the ways in which Galvedor's utterance both reflects and shapes the activity. Big D Discourse analysis identifies ways in which the utterance functions to support community values and goals, strengthening both these goals and Galvador's credibility as an upholder of game values through the actions and explanation for them carried by his words. The goals at issue concern building up the wealth and experience of one's avatar, thus strengthening his value as a member of the hunting party and the group, and the importance of social relationships. Crucially, this brief utterance is also shown to be contributive to the construction and representation of his in-game identity as a member of the *Lineage* community. This low level utterance was chosen to demonstrate how Discourses can be enacted even in routine, everyday exchanges and activities – 'it is through such small, routine accomplishments that big-D discourses are created, maintained, and transformed over time' (pp. 49–50). The analysis

> is one illustration of how attention to the function of language, and not merely its informational content, can be leveraged to better understand the nature of the social and material activity it helps constitute and how that activity is tied to the very community that renders it meaningful in the first place.

Exemplar 2

The second example is a longer exchange, incorporating speech, actions, context and the presence of monsters and other players during the few seconds of in game action described. In this episode, an experienced character, female elf 'Myrondonia' apprentices another female elf, 'Jellybean', a 'newbie' (inexperienced) character played by Steinkuehler, into subtler dimensions of the game. The episode begins after Myrondonia comes to Jellybean's rescue as she is under attack in the Elven forest (Steinkuehler 2004). Following the rescue, Myrondonia shows Jellybean how to hunt and gather 'mithril', required for creating many elven goods. Mithril is dropped by monsters – Zombies and Orcs – who are present in great numbers in one area of the game, the Elven dungeons.

The data consists of a screen shot of Myrondonia and Jellybean in the games landscape, and a detailed transcript of the conversation between them including first person accounts of the actions taken by Steinkuehler/Jellybean in response to Myrondonia's instructions.

Myrondonia tells Jellybean how to navigate to a chosen location through holding the mouse key down, and how to run her mouse over the body of a monster just killed to collect any mithril it might have dropped. She instructs Jellybean to 'try to look for Zombies and to hit them' and the two collect a considerable amount of mithril in this way. Towards the end of the exchange, another character, the elf Irisarker, passes by. Irisarker uses keyboard characters to indicate a smile ('smiley face gesture while passing by'), and Myrondonia uses

FIGURE 14.1 Apprenticeship of JellyBean (source: Steinkuehler 2004, p. 525)

this opportunity to teach Jellybean 'another rule ... if you see someone go one way, go the other ... we are all here for the mithril'.

Analysis of this transcript shows Myrondonia introducing Jellybean to the values of the game through 'joint participation in a meaningful activity [mithril hunting] with a mutually understood and valued goal'. She shows her how to do this, and in doing so draws Jellybean's attention to what needs to happen, where and how, modelling how to find and collect mithril and providing numerous practice opportunities. More than this, however, she also teaches Jellybean to be considerate of others, and to demonstrate what to do should another elf, also hunting mithril, appear. There is plenty of space, plenty of mithril and it is not seemly or collegiate to deny others the opportunity. Jellybean is inducted into the workings of the game with respect to her own survival and advancement, but also into the need to support others and provide opportunities for them too to thrive, thus demonstrating the kinds of values advocated in the ethos of the game: 'Two distinctive but related things are being taught here; one is the *social practice*, the other is *the kind of person/elf* Myrondia wants Jellybean to be' (italics in the original) (Steinkuehler 2006, p. 42). These things are being taught through textual and game play means – explicitly and initially through their chat, scaffolded and enacted by Myrondonia in her own actions within play, and in her choices in rescuing Jellybean and taking her under her wing, embodying compassion and care for others as she plays.

Significance of Video Game and Gaming Analysis

For literacy educators and researchers, the research and method presented here are significant in contributing to understanding young people's literacy practices in online and multimodal contexts and seeing them made visible in action. The method provides increased understanding of the ways in which participation in online spaces and communities has material consequences in shaping players' values, sense of identity and community; and of the operations of 'big D' Discourses, in both on and offline worlds. Analysis of the nature and affordances of the game world, the ways in which presence is established, meanings negotiated and a wide range of cognitive, literate and social skills entailed, provides insights into the possibilities offered by online learning sites and communities such as these for more formal educational purposes.

This method is one amongst many forms of literacy-oriented videogames research. Related approaches analyse the literacy practices observed amongst young players as they play; use talk aloud protocols and recounts as players view recorded segments of their own play; analyse observations and field notes of social and collaborative learning practices around games; use thematic analysis to analyse interviews with players about their experiences of game play; create multimodal analysis of videoed instances of play; adopt visual and literary forms of analysis of games as they are played; and analyse critical, cultural and operational understandings of game play. Methodologies might draw together data of multiple kinds, e.g. screen shots, forum posts, blog entries, interviews, journal notes, drawings, games designs, game 'pitches' and analytic essays on videogames and game play. Related forms of analysis arising from the field of Media Studies (e.g. Burn 2004; Carr, Buckingham, Burn & Schott 2006; Dezuanni 2010) draw on semiotic and media-based frameworks to understand and categorise game play, while also linking game play to production – making games, and to the industrial and commercial contexts from which games arise – that is, through Media Studies' characteristic attention to making as well as viewing; and texts, audiences and institutions.

The length and scope of the methodology outlined here, using ethnographic approaches to collect data in one particular genre of game, from committed and experienced games players, over an extended nineteen-month period, means that in its 'pure' form, this methodology is rarely used or replicated in other literacy settings. However, it offers much to more modest studies and to the analysis of the literacies entailed in games and in-game play. The study models approaches to analysis, and provides insights into ways in which meanings are constructed and games played through the negotiation of complex interrelated linguistic and multimodal signs and symbols and the conventions of the game. It provides a framework for the close analysis of textually mediated action and communication on many fronts simultaneously; a careful mapping of the ways in which the very elements of game play induct players into small and big

D discourses; and link in-world behaviours and experiences to identity, values and community. It renders visible the operation of multiliteracies 'in the wild', highlights the sophisticated knowledge and understanding of multiple semiotic systems required to play, underlines players' agency and reflects the porous nature of supposed boundaries between on and offline worlds.

Aspects of the method, in conjunction with others, can be used in the analysis of smaller studies of game play, or in the analysis of studies that focus on different elements, with school-aged students for example, on the literacy and cooperative learning practices evident as players play. They provide a rationale for the design of curriculum units in English, Media and Literacy classrooms built around videogames, and guidance for the ways in which outcomes might be charted in relation to literacy principles and statutory requirements for English/Literacy as outlined in national reading, writing and technology standards. In conjunction with other approaches to the use and analysis of videogames, the method provides a rich palate of resources with which to analyse cognition, literacies and play.

References

Aarseth, E. (2003). Playing research: Methodological approaches to game analysis. In *Refereed Conference Proceedings, 5th International Digital Arts and Culture Conference* (pp. 1–8), MelbourneDAC, RMIT Melbourne.

Alvermann, D. (ed.) (2010). *Adolescents' online literacies: connecting classrooms: Digital media and popular culture*. New York: Peter Lang.

Apperley, T. (2010). What games studies can teach us about videogames in the English and literacy classroom. *Australian Journal of Language and Literacy, 33*(1), 12–23.

Apperley, T. & Beavis, C. (2011). Literacy into action: Digital games as action and text in the English and literacy classroom. *Pedagogies: An International Journal, 6*(2), 130–143.

Beavis, C. (2012). Multiliteracies in the wild: Learning from computer games. In G. Merchant, J. Gillen, J. Marsh & J. Davies (eds) *Virtual literacies: Interactive spaces for children and young people* (pp. 86–110). New York: Routledge.

Beavis, C. & Apperley, T. (2012). A model for games and literacy. In C. Beavis, J. O'Mara & L. McNeice (eds) *Digital games: Literacy in action* (pp. 12–23). Adelaide, Australia: Wakefield Press/Australian Association for the Teaching of English.

Beavis, C., O'Mara, J. & McNeice, L. (eds) (2012). *Digital games: Literacy in action*. Adelaide, Australia: Wakefield Press.

Bogost, I. (2007). *Persuasive games: The expressive power of videogames*. Cambridge, MA: MIT Press.

Burn, A. (2004). Potter-literacy: From book to game and back again; literature, film, game and cross-media literacy. *Papers: Explorations into Children's Literature, 14*(2), 5–17.

Carr, D., Buckingham, D., Burn, A. & Schott, G. (2006). *Computer games: Text, narrative, play*. Cambridge, UK: Polity.

Consalvo, M. (2007). *Cheating: Gaining advantage in videogames*. Cambridge, MA: MIT Press.

Coiro, J., Knobel, M., Lankshear, C. & Leu, D. (eds) (2008). *Handbook of research on new literacies*. New York: Lawrence Erlbaum Associates.

Dezuanni, M. L. (2010). Digital media literacy: Connecting young people's identities, creative production and learning about video games. In D. Alvermann (ed.) *Adolescents' online literacies: Connecting classrooms, media, and paradigms* (pp. 125–144). New York: Peter Lang Publishers.

Dressman, M., McCarthey, S. & Prior, P. (2012). Literate practices are situated, mediated, multisemiotic, and embodied. *Research in the Teaching of English, 37*(1), 5–8.

Galloway, A. (2006). *Gaming: Essays on algorithmic culture*. Minneapolis, MN: University of Minnesota Press.

Gee, J. (2007). *What videogames have to teach us about learning and literacy* (2nd edn). New York: Palgrave Macmillan.

Gee, J. (2012). *Sociolinguistics and literacies: Ideology in discourses* (4th edn). New York: Routledge.

Halliday, M. A. K. (1985). *Spoken and written language*. Oxford, UK: Oxford University Press.

Kress, G. (2003). *Literacy in the new media age*. London: Routledge.

McKee, H. & Porter, J. (2009). *The ethics of internet research: A rhetorical, case-based process*. New York: Peter Lang.

Merchant, G., Gillen, J., Marsh, J. & Davies, J. (eds) (2012). *Virtual literacies: Interactive spaces for children and young people*. New York: Routledge.

Steinkuehler, C. A. (2004). Learning in massively multiplayer online games. In Y. B. Kafai, W. A. Sandoval, N. Enyedy, A. S. Nixon & F. Herrera (eds) *Proceedings of the Sixth International Conference of the Learning Sciences* (pp. 521–528). Mahwah, NJ: Lawrence Erlbaum Associates.

Steinkuehler, C. (2006). Massively multiplayer online video gaming as participation in a discourse. *Mind, Culture and Activity, 13*(1), 38–52.

Steinkuehler, C. (2007). Massively multiplayer online games as a constellation of literacy practices. *E-Learning, 4*(3), 297–318.

Steinkuehler, C. (2008). Cognition and literacy in multiplayer online games. In J. Coiro, J. M. Knobel, C. Lankshear & D. Leu (eds) *Handbook of research on new literacies* (pp. 611–634). New York: Lawrence Erlbaum Associates.

Stevens, R., Satwicz, T. & McCarthy, L. (2008). In-game, in-room, in-world: Reconnecting videogames to the rest of kids' lives. In K. Salen (ed.) *The ecology of games: Reconnecting youth, games and learning* (pp. 41–66). Cambridge, MA: MIT Press.

15

SOCIAL MEDIA AS AUTHORSHIP

Methods for Studying Literacies and
Communities Online

Amy Stornaiuolo, Jennifer Higgs, and Glynda Hull

Young people today grow up in a profoundly textual world. Encountering digitally mediated texts via computers, television, tablets, cell phones, and gaming
devices, youth have more opportunities than ever before to engage with and
make meaning across many forms and varieties of text. And it appears that
young people are embracing these opportunities in record numbers, with 95%
of young people ages 12–17 in the US using the Internet to search for information, create original content, or exchange messages with others (Lenhart, 2012).
Many of these textual engagements are conducted across social media sites that
connect people and media with one another, with at least 80% of online youth
now participating on these sites (Lenhart et al., 2011). These socially oriented
communicative environments are highly participatory and collaborative, offering amplified authoring opportunities for young people to produce and shape
content online for and with others across a variety of modes.

As more people become authors, writing for purposes of work, learning, citizenship, and leisure, they are writing in the context of other writers, a "mass
daily experience" that is transforming our reading and writing (Brandt, in press,
p. 2). Audiences tend to be interactive, collaborative, and participatory, made
up of other writers who function as engaged interlocutors shaping the writing
process (Ede & Lunsford, 2009). As people write for multiple (often unpredictable, distant, and invisible) audiences, contexts overlap and collapse (boyd,
2011), rendering it necessary as authors to actively and jointly construct contexts
through their interactive textual practices (Haas & Takayoshi, 2011). And they
do so using a variety of rhetorical strategies particularly afforded by the multimodal, global, and participatory potentials of social media (Hull, Stornaiuolo, &
Sterponi, 2013; Stornaiuolo, DiZio, Hellmich, & Hull, 2013) as they compose
in the context of *networked publics*—publics restructured by networked

technologies that offer people the opportunity to connect with others beyond their immediate circle in newly interactive ways (boyd, 2011, p. 39). One of the central challenges facing researchers who investigate these networked literacies is how to study the emergence of "new models of composing" in these contexts (Yancey, 2009; cf. Bezemer & Kress, 2008; Hass & Takayoshi, 2011), particularly the way our practices and understandings of texts and authorship shift, transform, and emerge.

This chapter takes that central methodological challenge as its focus. We first review empirical research on youth's literate, multimodal endeavors with social media, looking particularly at how researchers have addressed key questions of mobility and interconnectivity as they investigated the ways young people read and write online using new tools and engaging with global and interactive audiences. We then briefly describe our own recent efforts to study youth's networked literacy practices, including both insights and challenges from our mixed methods design research project (www.space2cre8.com). We conclude by presenting possible future methodological directions as networked publics shift the methodological landscape for young people and researchers alike. Drawing on boyd's (2011) characterization of networked publics, we examine how the dimensions of persistence, searchability, replicability, and scalability can operate as a generative framework to guide our practices in studying networked literacies. We argue that socially networked environments afford new authoring opportunities for young people to engage in potentially equitable (Warschauer & Matuchniak, 2010), participatory (Jenkins, Clinton, Purushotma, Robison, & Weigel, 2006), and hospitable (Hull et al., 2013) literacy practices in our global, digital world—and that as researchers, we need to develop methodological approaches that can better capture the complexity of these endeavors.

Authoring Practices in Networked Spaces

With the recent "digital turn" in NLS research (Mills, 2010), a number of researchers have begun to study changing semiotic and textual practices associated with digital tool use across various contexts. In this section, we synthesize current empirical research that explicitly examines social media from the standpoint of literacy studies. We are interested in the ways in which scholars aligned with New Literacy Studies (NLS), who understand literacy to be a repertoire of diverse, shifting practices used for communicating deliberately in our multiple social and cultural worlds (Gee, 2000; Lankshear & Knobel, 2006; Street, 1995), have conceptualized and studied literacy practices in social media contexts. To wit, we examine the spectrum of methodologies currently employed to study these new literacies (cf. Coiro, Knobel, Lankshear, & Leu, 2008).[1]

Aiming to gain a fuller understanding of researchers' methodologies across a broad range of socially mediated authoring spaces, we turned to Kaplan and Haenlein's (2010) classification of social media to organize our search. Defining social media as "a group of Internet-based applications that build on the ideological and technological foundations of Web 2.0, and that allow the creation and exchange of User Generated Content" (p. 61), Kaplan and Haenlein identify six categories of social media environments: blogs/microblogs (e.g., Blogger, instant messaging, Twitter, texting); collaborative projects (e.g., wikis); social networking sites (e.g., Facebook, MySpace); content communities (e.g., fanfiction sites, Flickr); virtual social worlds (e.g., Second Life); and virtual game worlds (e.g., World of Warcraft). These categories represent the preponderance of research on online literacy practices.

We searched relevant academic databases (including ERIC, ProQuest, EBSCO, and Google Scholar) using keywords derived from Kaplan and Haenlein's (2010) classification system, such as "blogs AND (literacy OR new literacies) AND data" (including the word "data" to help winnow out non-empirical pieces). Since we were interested in empirical studies on literacy and social media, particularly those addressing social media as potential authoring sites and the methodologies used to examine them as such, we looked for studies that (1) reported observational research; (2) provided details on methodological approaches; and (3) aligned with a New Literacy Studies focus. As of July 2012, the searches of the databases as well as hand searches of reference lists yielded a total of 521 articles, of which 43 were included in our review. We organized the results of our review according to the aforementioned social media categories in order to look for patterns in the methodologies used across them, even though we recognize that many of the studies could fit more than one category.

Our examination of these studies revealed a growing but still nascent body of research attending to social media and literacy practices. Studies on blogging and microblogging have been most common, which may not be surprising given the fact that blogs "look" most like literacy activities and, as bounded texts, may be more straightforward to study than literacy activities in other online environments such as virtual social worlds (e.g., Lee, 2007; West, 2008). Also evident is a pronounced research interest in open and closed social networking sites (SNSs), such as Facebook, Remix World, and Space2Cre8, as spaces for multilingual writing practices and learner–learner interactions (e.g., Reinhardt & Zander, 2011; Hull, Stornaiuolo, & Sahni, 2010; Richards & Gomez, 2010; McLean, 2010; Lam, 2009). The literate practices of content communities are also of increasing interest to NLS scholars (e.g., Black, 2009; Davies, 2007), although this category is less well represented in the current empirical literature, as are the categories of collaborative projects (e.g., Luce-Kapler, 2007), virtual social worlds (e.g., Gillen, 2009; Merchant, 2009), and virtual game worlds (e.g., Steinkuehler, 2007; Sanford & Madill, 2007).

Methodologically, the majority of the reviewed studies featured standard qualitative approaches to capture and analyze the authoring activities represented across the six social media categories. For example, in her case study of a

Caribbean American adolescent's uses of online social networks, McLean (2010) gathered data in the participant's school, home, and physical and online communities, including semi-structured interviews, websites, emails, and researcher field notes. In a similar vein, in their work on the closed Digital Youth Network Remix World site, Richards and Gomez (2010) collected data from the program's in-school and after-school components in the form of thick descriptive field notes, informal surveys on Remix World use, and semi-structured interviews. Mills and Chandra (2011) analyzed preservice teachers' microblogged stories by systematically coding key themes and using concept maps (graphic organizers) to trace characters and plot developments in the stories. In combing through methods sections, we found that certain kinds of qualitative methods predominated: e.g., participant observation in or across bounded virtual or physical sites, field notes, semi-structured interviews, talk-alouds, focus groups, textual content analysis. A smaller number of studies blended qualitative and quantitative approaches (e.g., Lam, 2009).

We appreciate the rich detail such traditional qualitative methods offer, and we hope this kind of work continues, especially given the press of a "big data world." Our review of the most prevalent approaches for studying networked literacies also raises important questions about future methodological directions for NLS scholars. For example, to what extent do new times, new tools, and new practices require us to reconceptualize the role of literacy researchers and reinvent our methods? How might we add new entries to the methodological catalogue, thereby gaining fresh purchase on literacy practices without relying on the assumed "newness" of networked literacies? Davies' (2007) stance as an "auto-ethnographer" on Flickr offers one intriguing answer to these queries, as does Lankshear and Knobel's (2006) call for increased "insider research," or research on new media by those who are also active participants in the studied spaces. Black's (2009) participation as a fanfiction author as well as an interested researcher gestures toward this notion of "insider" investigation that could help scholars explore social media environments from perspectives animated by a willingness to examine familiar environments and/or practices in new ways. Similarly, Gillen's (2009) virtual literacy ethnography, with its diverse interpretive methods and understandings of semiotic practices in virtual worlds, provides a productive methodological model that grapples with the uncertain boundaries of "real life" and virtual environments, as well as the uncertainties surrounding "appropriate" methods for studying these blurred, literacy-rich spaces.

The reviewed studies collectively suggest the potential of various social media as powerful, interactive authoring spaces that can bring together diverse cultures, languages, perspectives, knowledge, and skills (e.g., Greenhow & Robelia, 2009; Dowdall, 2009; Yi, 2008), with implications for literacy learning in and across formal and informal learning contexts (e.g., Leander & Lovvorn, 2006; McLean, 2010; DePew, 2011). For example, the fiction written and read by adolescents in virtual fandoms illustrates an array of literacy practices that often bear a striking resemblance to school-sanctioned composition activities and writing practices valued by professional writers (Black & Steinkuehler, 2009). Our review also demonstrates the need for more studies that explore how users, particularly children and adolescents, employ social media to engage in interactive, multimodal discourse, and how their everyday, technology-mediated literacies might serve as powerful authoring tools in school contexts. As various scholars have noted (e.g., boyd & Ellison, 2007; Greenhow & Robelia, 2009; Hull & Stornaiuolo, 2010; Merchant, 2011), much of the research to date has focused on the presentation of self, identity development, privacy and risk issues, online/offline relationships, and "friending" behaviors. Five years after boyd (2008) highlighted how much youth love SNSs, we still have limited knowledge about young people's literate practices in online authoring spaces, and how those experiences may create discursive spaces for developing as writers across offline and in-school contexts (e.g., Davies & Merchant, 2009; Merchant, 2011). The integration of social media into K-12 schooling in particular looms as a largely unexplored terrain, as college and university students remain the most studied participants of in-school investigations.

Studying Networked Literacies: The Space2Cre8 Project

In order to ground our discussion about the methodological challenges and opportunities of studying youth's networked literacies, we turn now to our own efforts during our three-year mixed methods research study. We examined adolescents' literacy practices on a private social network, Space2Cre8 (S2C8),[2] built in collaboration with a team of programmers, teachers, researchers, and teens in a design research project (Collins, Joseph, & Bielaczyc, 2004). Over four design cycles, guided by interactions with and input from youth participants in Norway, South Africa, India, and the US, we created a social network that could serve as a generative authoring space for youth. Over these iterative, responsive, and theoretically driven design cycles, we created a network that offered participants many ways to share and interact around texts, including multimodal blogging, commenting, video sharing, microblogging, chatting, and profile page design. While the first months of the project were especially challenging as we learned how to imagine, design, and study a social network from the ground up, we found that the design research approach proved fruitful for examining literacy development in the context of social media.

The central benefit of a design research approach for our project was the methodological complexity it afforded, especially the possibility of adjusting and refining our methodologies over several theory-driven cycles in response to participants (Barab & Squire, 2004). Across the multiple design cycles, we worked to understand youth's literacy practices with social networking without making a priori determinations of what such participation looked like, refining our

methodological approaches as we learned, with our participants, what function-
alities worked and which did not. For example, we found that youth wanted to
respond to one another online about their posted artifacts but at times were
reticent to comment (because of a lack of confidence in their writing ability or
language facility, shyness, uncertainty about what to say, etc.). In response to
this concern, we introduced a new icon that participants designed (a happy face
with thumbs up), which allowed participants to mark multimodally their
engagement with texts. Methodologically, this also allowed us to trace youthful
reading patterns in new ways because we could see which texts young people
clicked on, which they labeled via an icon, and which provoked their comments. As we were particularly interested in the ways that the social network
and classroom contexts functioned as complex learning environments that influenced textual engagement, a design research approach offered us not only the
opportunity to examine the ways that social context factored into youth's
textual practices, but also to shape those learning contexts in theoretically
informed ways.

We used a variety of methodological approaches in the project, tweaking
them across the different design cycles to collect a mix of qualitative and quantitative data. Ethnographically, we tried to capture as much rich detail as possible
in the classroom contexts by filming class sessions, writing field notes, collecting
youth-produced artifacts, and conducting a variety of interviews at different
points in time. On the social network, we collected a significant amount of data
via analytics that archived all online activity. In addition to conducting qualitative analysis of all online content, especially multimodal discourse analyses of
participants' online interactions, we analyzed data quantitatively as well, looking
at friendship networks, ascertaining patterns of connectivity and tabulating fre-
quencies of interactions and postings. We worked across the ethnographic and
network data in the analysis, turning to data analysis software (e.g., Atlas.ti) and
creating data matrices using different data visualization tools (e.g., Gephi,
Timeline).

While this mix of qualitative and quantitative data offered the benefit of
seeing patterns over time and across different scales, we faced a number of challenges in studying youth's composing processes in relation to others across
online/offline spaces and across multiple languages and semiotic systems. For
example, we had difficulty tracing intertextual links between participants—how
could we understand the ways that viewing artifacts on the network shaped
youth's composing processes? We often saw references, sampling, and other
remixed elements appearing in youth's compositions, but the trajectories were
difficult to trace, particularly when young people worked collaboratively. Similarly, we tried to track the movement of artifacts through the network, but
observational methodologies coupled with quantitative analysis of viewing and
posting patterns still provided just a partial glimpse of the complex online/
offline movements of texts and the iterative interplay between authors and

audiences across texts and contexts. These queries were made more complex when we attempted to trace collaborative work within and across school sites, especially as youth began to create new genres of radically collaborative texts. We turn now to consider how these challenges, echoed in many of the other studies we examined, can be understood as characteristic of meaning making in the context of networked publics.

Methodological Implications of/for Networked Publics

Clearly, one of the central questions now facing educational researchers who would examine young people's networked literacy practices is how to study the circulation of texts, ideas, and people as social media blurs boundaries between virtual and real, audience and author, public and private, local and global. As authorship becomes more distributed, interactive, and participatory within networked logics, "there is a new intricacy to the choreography of collaborative authoring and feedback" (Gillen, 2009, p. 72). Indeed, social media complicates what it means to compose collaboratively, negotiate audiences, and engage in public life (Baym & boyd, 2012). Networked publics function as a central organizing principle in our cultural and social practices (Varnelis, 2008), with people taking up active roles in producing and circulating knowledge (Ito, 2008). In light of methodological challenges associated with studying shifting relationships among texts, authors, and audiences in the context of networked technologies, we propose that literacy researchers attend more closely to the characteristics of these networked logics to guide their methodological practices.

We have found the work of danah boyd (2011) to be particularly generative in conceptualizing the way networked publics are transforming composing. While boyd finds that networked publics share much in common with other publics—for example, allowing people to interact beyond familiar circles of friends and family and gather for social and cultural purposes—she argues that networked publics are characterized by "fundamental architectural differences" (boyd, 2008, p. 125). As mediated publics in which "spaces and audiences … are bound together through technological networks," networked publics have new affordances for amplifying, chronicling, and circulating information and social activities (p. 125). She (2011) characterizes these affordances along four dimensions that have the potential to destabilize people's assumptions and thus influence their textual practices: persistence, searchability, replicability, and scalability. As these four characteristics of networked publics influence how young people now make meaning with texts, they must also inform researchers' practices, both in how we investigate youth's networked literacies and in how we make meaning in networked contexts. In the following section we draw on boyd's formulation of these four affordances of networked publics to articulate how literacy researchers can expand their methodological horizons in studying networked literacies.

Persistence: What To Do with All That Data?

Persistence refers to the way that online material is recorded and archived, accessible over time and across contexts. Soep (2012) calls this phenomenon the "digital afterlife," arguing that researchers need a robust methodological repertoire for studying the ways in which young people's artifacts persist online well past the processes of production. How can researchers address the persistence of young people's compositions, given the sheer visibility and quantity of their writing as well as their artifacts' unpredictable paths of circulation over time?

One of the central methodological tensions regarding the persistence of data centers on how to adequately account for the deluge of accessible information. How might researchers arrive at their decisions regarding the kinds of data to collect, the contexts of data collection, and the duration of collection? How do they demarcate *data* and the *research field*? As people's literacy practices become increasingly mobile across online and offline spaces (Leander & McKim, 2003), a number of researchers have turned toward ethnographic approaches, especially multi-sited ethnography (Marcus, 1995), as one means of tracing how knowledge, texts, and human and nonhuman "actants" converge and interact over the course of authoring activities (e.g., Leander & Lovvorn, 2006; Soep, 2012). While these kinds of rich ethnographic methods can provide a detailed portrait of youth literacies, we believe that the complexity of meaning making in networked contexts requires researchers to adopt equally complex methods. One way to expand our methodological repertoire, Stornaiuolo and Hall (in press) suggest, is to embrace "methodological heteroglossia" by bringing together a hybrid cross-section of methods from diverse traditions to better capture the multidimensionality of networked learning.

The abundance of data and their relative permanence present ethical challenges to researchers, who bear increased responsibilities to make reasoned, respectful, and justifiable decisions about where to draw methodological boundaries. When information is persistent, researchers are required to articulate methodological choices even more carefully: what they take as an object of study, how they choose to study it, what data are included and not included in their study, and over what period of time. Most importantly, researchers need to consider their own vantage points, or the perspectives, theoretical stances, and historically situated understandings with which they approach the data. In our review of the empirical research literature, we were struck by the paucity of detail regarding researchers' methodological choices and positionality, despite Smagorinsky's (2008) call for researchers to display increased rigor in articulating the methods used in studying writing.

Searchability: How To Make Sense of Everything?

While the archive of material online seems overwhelming, we are greatly assisted in making sense of this wealth of information via the affordance of searchability. Through embedded metadata and search engine algorithms, the capacity to search renders information more manageable and usable. Methodologically, researchers can capitalize on these different search capacities for parsing data meaningfully, using units of analysis that retain sufficient complexity and flexibility. In our design research project, for example, we were able to trace individual artifacts and users through our analytics, but an individual unit of analysis proved inadequate in relation to our questions. We needed more flexible units of analysis that could capture the collaborative composing processes we traced ethnographically, but our system was initially limited in its search capacity, especially in meaningfully tracing youth's interactions and collaborations. We thus need to design and adopt new analytic tools if we are to make sense of data, including algorithms sensitive to multiple parameters and data visualizations that help render patterns viewable in new ways.

While we can improve our own interfaces and search algorithms to make data more useful to us, we would also do well to be attentive to the many ways that networked technologies allow users to categorize and sort data. Tagging, for example, allows users to code material themselves for a variety of purposes, an emergent, participatory literacy practice consistent with other kinds of "hacker literacies" to which researchers should attend (Santo, 2011). These kinds of user-generated search parameters offer insights into the ways in which young people organize their understandings of their worlds and how they see their texts in relationship with others. In as many ways as possible, then, researchers should endeavor to account for users' understandings. Happily, researchers with "insider information" about youth's search efforts may bring a unique expertise and familiarity that will illuminate networked literacy practices.

Replicability: How To Trace Practices?

One of the most vexing challenges in our own work has been around the issue of replicability, or the ease with which people can duplicate and copy material, ultimately making it impossible to identify the original. As more young people remix and recontextualize, it has become increasingly difficult to trace intertextual linkages and creative provenance, particularly as people compose with multiple others. Stornaiuolo and Hall (in press) call these intertextual echoes *resonance* (cf. Hull et al., 2013). While new media tools offer great promise in helping to make this resonance more visible, we have not yet discovered adequately complex methodologies for tracing the movement and relationship between texts as authors repurpose, recontextualize, and revoice texts across different contexts and media. To us, this area offers the greatest challenge—and the most promise—in understanding networked composing now.

Part of the challenge of studying youth's composition practices with easily replicated texts is in negotiating the "digital afterlife" (Soep, 2012). Describing how young people's radio broadcasts have been taken up in mainstream media and responded to by anonymous (and unpredictable) audiences, Soep highlights the importance of attending to the circulatory paths of youth's writing by working with authors to examine the impact of their work. For example, Soep describes how all authors need to be able to access and read analytics that reveal how readers took up their texts, what they clicked on, and so on. While these are important resources for researchers, certainly, Soep calls our attention to the ways in which we might work with young people to develop their online authorship capacities as they advocate for their work and trace its circulations.

Scalability: What Does It Mean To Be Visible?

The last dimension, scalability, refers to the way that material in networked publics spreads and becomes visible to others. One repercussion of scalability is that participants and researchers are visible to one another in new ways. For example, our study participants now have greater access to our published materials and can thus respond to that record of research more easily. And our work can extend to new audiences in ways that were previously unavailable, impacting policy and creating notoriety for researchers in unanticipated ways.

Similarly, our participants' online materials are more visible to researchers, particularly in "public" forums and websites in which participants are not even aware that they are being researched. As young people's work becomes more visible to us—and to unanticipated others—there may be consequences far beyond what young composers might imagine (Hull et al., 2010; Soep, 2012). Further, the ubiquity of online writing—and its social, fleeting, and mundane nature—makes it hard to remember how textually saturated our everyday communications are. Such mundane textualities, often practiced "in spaces and with content that may not be always sanctioned by adults" (Steinkuehler, 2007, p. 315), challenge researchers to gain critical distance and determine how these efforts constitute new models of composing (Yancey, 2009). In light of this increased, reciprocal visibility, researchers and participants engage in relationships that stretch and puncture the more traditional roles of researcher/researched. As we now have access to reams of archived material, made more search-friendly and easily replicable, ethical considerations are heightened and brought into relief. What are our obligations to participants and their online information, as researchers and participants become visible in new ways and operate in new relationships?

Future Directions

Even a decade ago people would have been hard pressed to imagine the ways that authorship would shift for so many people, with new opportunities to write for, with, and to others across great geographical and ideological distances.

These interactive contexts for composing in our everyday lives have transformed how we imagine writing. In this chapter, with a focus on social media as authoring contexts, especially for youth, we have argued that changes are likewise afoot in how we conceptualize the study of these emerging practices. We have turned to boyd's (2011) framework for understanding networked publics in order to highlight how the four dimensions of persistence, searchability, replicability, and scalability are reshaping not just the way youth compose now but our methodological landscape.

These dimensions of networked publics highlight that in an era of proliferating texts and contexts for composing, researchers bear grave greater responsibilities. One responsibility is to become more reflexive in our practices, considering our role in the research as we interact with participants in new ways. Buckingham (2009) helpfully calls for this kind of reflexivity when using creative and visual methods, taking care not to interpret youth's media creations as transparent representations of their "authentic" voice but to understand our role in their creation, interpretation, and circulation in order to redefine and challenge the power dynamics of researcher/researched relationships. Part of this enterprise includes the researcher's examination of his/her positionality in the work, including how we recognize, incorporate, and invite participants' multiple ways of making meaning.

A second responsibility of researchers is to make our work more visible and our methods more transparent, especially to the research field more generally, but also to the participants in our studies. We are obligated as never before to articulate our methodological decisions carefully and thoroughly, a practice, as we noted in our review, that is not yet common. Our continual grappling to understand the literacy practices associated with new technologies must needs be paired with a continual striving to make visible our own procedures and approaches. In this manner we can cull the most effective methods for studying particular social media and devise from these new and potent ways of analyzing and representing data. Last, we encourage researchers to expand their methodological repertoires, learning to exploit the affordances of networked publics. Continually reflexive, methodologically inventive, and ethically alert, all in equal measure—then literacy researchers will be able to trace youth's meaning making across mobile, global, and multimodal contexts.

Notes

1. We focus on peer-reviewed empirical studies rather than non-empirical explanations and descriptions.
2. We gratefully acknowledge the efforts of the entire Space2Cre8 team as well as the support of the Spencer Foundation; the UC Links project of the University of California; the Graduate School of Education at the University of California, Berkeley; and the Steinhardt School of Culture, Education, and Human Development at New York University.

References

Barab, S. A., & Squire, K. (2004). Design-based research: Putting a stake in the ground. *Journal of the Learning Sciences, 13*(1), 1–14.

Baym, N. K., & boyd, d. (2012). Socially mediated publicness: An introduction. *Journal of Broadcasting and Electronic Media, 56*(3), 37–41.

Bezemer, J., & Kress, G. (2008). Writing in multimodal texts: A social semiotic account of designs for learning. *Written Communication, 25*(2), 166–195.

Black, R. W. (2009). Online fan fiction, global identities, and imagination. *Research in the Teaching of English, 43*(4), 397–425.

Black, R. W., & Steinkuehler, C. (2009). Literacy in virtual worlds. In L. Christenbury, R. Bomer, & P. Smagorinsky (Eds.), *Handbook of adolescent literacy research* (pp. 271–286). New York: Guilford Press.

boyd, d. (2008). Why youth social network sites: The role of networked publics in teenage social life. In D. Buckingham (Ed.), *Youth, identity, and digital media* (pp. 119–142). Cambridge, MA: MIT Press.

boyd, d. (2011). Social network sites as networked publics: Affordances, dynamics, and implications. In Z. Papacharissi (Ed.), *Networked self: Identity, community, and culture on social network sites* (pp. 38–57). New York: Routledge.

boyd, d., & Ellison, N. B. (2007). Social network sites: Definition, history, and scholarship. *Journal of Computer-Mediated Communication, 13*(1), 210–230.

Brandt, D. (in press). Deep writing. In R. J. Spiro, M. Deschryver, M. S. Hagerman, P. Morsink, & P. Thompson (Eds.), *Reading at a crossroads: Disjunctures and continuities in conceptions and practices of reading in the 21st century*. New York: Routledge.

Buckingham, D. (2009). "Creative" visual methods in media research: Possibilities, problems and proposals. *Media, Culture and Society, 31*(4), 633–652.

Coiro, J., Knobel, M., Lankshear, C., & Leu, D. (2008). *Handbook of research on new literacies*. New York: Taylor & Francis Group.

Collins, A., Joseph, D., & Bielaczyc, K. (2004). Design research: Theoretical and methodological issues. *Journal of the Learning Sciences, 13*(1), 15–42.

Davies, J. (2007). Display, identity and the everyday: Self-presentation through online image sharing. *Discourse, 28*(4), 549–564.

Davies, J., & Merchant, G. (2009). *Web 2.0 for schools: Learning and social participation*. New York: Peter Lang.

DePew, K. E. (2011). Social media at academia's periphery: Studying multilingual developmental writers' Facebook composing strategies. *Reading Matrix, 11*(1), 54–75.

Dowdall, C. (2009). Impressions, improvisations and compositions: Reframing children's text production in social network sites. *Literacy, 43*(2), 91–99.

Ede, L., & Lunsford, A. (2009). Among the audience: On audience in an age of new literacies. In E. Weisler & B. Felhler (Eds.), *Engaging audience: Writing in an age of new literacies* (pp. 42–72). Urbana, IL: NCTE.

Gee, J. P. (2000). The New Literacy Studies: From "socially situated" to the work of the social. In D. Barton, M. Hamilton, & R. Ivanic (Eds.), *Situated literacies: Reading and writing in context* (pp. 180–196). London: Routledge.

Gillen, J. (2009). Literacy practices in Schome Park: A virtual literacy ethnography. *Journal of Research in Reading, 32*(1), 57–74.

Greenhow, C., & Robelia, B. (2009). Old communication, new literacies: Social network sites as social learning resources. *Journal of Computer-Mediated Communication, 14*(4), 1130–1161.

Haas, C., & Takayoshi, P. (2011). Young people's everyday literacies: The language features of instant messaging. *Research in the Teaching of English, 45*(4), 378–404.

Hull, G. A., & Stornaiuolo, A. (2010). Literate arts in a global world: Reframing social networking as cosmopolitan practice. *Journal of Adolescent and Adult Literacy, 54*(2), 85–97.

Hull, G. A., Stornaiuolo, A., & Sahni, U. (2010). Cultural citizenship and cosmopolitan practice: Global youth communicate online. *English Education, 42*(4), 331–367.

Hull, G. A., Stornaiuolo, A., & Sterponi, L. (2013). Imagined readers and hospitable texts: Global youth connect online. In D. Alvermann, N. Unrau, & R. Ruddell (Eds.), *Theoretical models and processes of reading* (6th ed., pp. 1208–1240). Newark, DE: International Reading Association.

Ito, M. (2008). Introduction. In K. Vernelis (Ed.), *Networked publics* (pp. 1–14). Cambridge, MA: MIT Press.

Jenkins, H., Clinton, K., Purushotma, R., Robison, A. J., & Weigel, M. (2006). *Confronting the challenge of participatory culture*. Retrieved from the John T. and Catherine T. MacArthur Foundation: http://digitallearning.macfound.org/atf/cf/%7B7E45C7E0-A3E0–4B89-AC9C-E807E1B0AE4E%7D/JENKINS_WHITE_PAPER.PDF http://digitallearning.macfound.org/atf/cf/%7B7E45C7E0-A3E0–4B89-AC9C-E807E1B0AE4E%7D/JENKINS_WHITE_PAPER.PDF.

Kaplan, A. M., & Haenlein, M. (2010). Users of the world, unite! The challenges and opportunities of social media. *Business Horizons, 53*(1), 59–68.

Lam, W. S. E. (2009). Multiliteracies on instant messaging in negotiating local, translocal, and transnational affiliations: A case of an adolescent immigrant. *Reading Research Quarterly, 44*(4), 377–397.

Lankshear, C., & Knobel, M. (2006). *New literacies: Everyday practices and classroom learning*. Buckingham, UK: Open University Press.

Leander, K., & McKim, K. K. (2003). Tracing the everyday "sitings" of adolescents on the Internet: A strategic adaptation of ethnography across online and offline spaces. *Education, Communication and Information, 3*(2), 211–240.

Leander, K. M., & Lovvorn, J. F. (2006). Literacy networks: Following the circulation of texts, bodies, and objects in the schooling and online gaming of one youth. *Cognition and Instruction, 24*(3), 291–340.

Lee, C. K.-M. (2007). Affordances and text-making practices in online instant messaging. *Written Communication, 24*(3), 223–249.

Lenhart, A. (2012). *Teens & online video*. Retrieved from Pew Research Center's Internet and American Life Project: http://pewinternet.org/Reports/2012/Teens-and-online-video.aspx.

Lenhart, A., Madden, M., Smith, A., Purcell, K., Zickuhr, K., & Rainie, L. (2011). *Teens, kindness and cruelty on social network sites*. Retrieved from Pew Research Center's Internet and American Life Project: http://pewinternet.org/Reports/2011/Teens-and-social-media.aspx.

Luce-Kapler, R. (2007). Radical change and wikis: Teaching new literacies. *Journal of Adolescent and Adult Literacy, 51*(3), 214–223.

Marcus, G. E. (1995). Ethnography in/of the world system: The emergence of multi-sited ethnography. *Annual Review of Anthropology, 24*, 95–117.

McLean, C. A. (2010). A space called home: An immigrant adolescent's digital literacy practices. *Journal of Adolescent and Adult Literacy, 54*(1), 13–22.

Merchant, G. (2009). Literacy in virtual worlds. *Journal of Research in Reading, 32*(1), 38–56.

Merchant, G. (2011). Unravelling the social network: Theory and research. *Learning, Media and Technology, 37*(1), 4–19.

Mills, K. A. (2010). A review of the "digital turn" in the new literacy studies. *Review of Educational Research, 80*(2), 246–271.

Mills, K. A., & Chandra, V. (2011). Microblogging as a literacy practice for educational communities. *Journal of Adolescent and Adult Literacy, 55*(1), 35–45.

Reinhardt, J., & Zander, V. (2011). Social networking in an intensive English program classroom: A language socialization perspective. *CALICO Journal, 28*(2), 326–344.

Richards, K. A., & Gomez, K. (2010). Participant understandings of the affordances of Remix World. *International Journal of Learning and Media, 2*(2–3), 101–121.

Sanford, K., & Madill, L. (2007). Understanding the power of new literacies through video game play and design. *Canadian Journal of Education, 30*(2), 432–455.

Santo, R. (2011). Hacker literacies: Synthesizing critical and participatory media. *International Journal of Learning and Media, 3*(3), 1–5.

Smagorinsky, P. (2008). The method section as conceptual epicenter in constructing social science research reports. *Written Communication, 25*(3), 389–411.

Soep, E. (2012). The digital afterlife of youth-made media: Implications for media literacy education. *Comunicar, 19*(38), 93–100.

Steinkuehler, C. (2007). Massively multiplayer online gaming as a constellation of literacy practices. *E-Learning and Digital Media, 4*(3), 297–318.

Stornaiuolo, A., DiZio, J. K., Hellmich, E. A., & Hull, G. A. (2013). Expanding community: Youth, social networking, and schools. *Comunicar, 40*(20), 79–87.

Stornaiuolo, A., & Hall, M. (in press). Toward methodological heteroglossia: Qualitative research in a networked world. In G. B. Gudmundsdottir & K. B. Vasbø (Eds.), *Methodological challenges when exploring digital learning spaces in education.* Rotterdam: Sense Publishers.

Street, B. (1995). *Social literacies.* Cambridge, UK: Cambridge University Press.

Varnelis, K. (2008). *Networked publics.* Cambridge, MA: MIT Press.

Warschauer, M., & Matuchniak, T. (2010). New technology and digital worlds: Analyzing evidence of equity in access, use, and outcomes. *Review of Research in Education, 34*(1), 179–225.

West, K. C. (2008). Weblogs and literary response: Socially situated identities and hybrid social languages in English class blogs. *Journal of Adolescent and Adult Literacy, 51*(7), 588–598.

Yancey, K. B. (2009). 2008 NCTE presidential address: The impulse to compose and the age of composition. *Research in the Teaching of English, 43*(3), 316–338.

Yi, Y. (2008). Relay writing in an adolescent online community. *Journal of Adolescent and Adult Literacy, 51*(8), 670–680.

16

ANALYZING DIGITAL TEXTS AS LITERACY ARTIFACTS

Vivian Maria Vasquez

Increasing access to digital technologies in many parts of the world has changed the conditions of possibility for literacy events resulting in the development of new diverse literacy practices (Janks & Vasquez, 2011). Nowadays readers of all ages can download books, music, and images, and Web 2.0 has given young people a global audience for anything they choose to upload. As such there are new spaces in which they can produce and re-produce identities and enter global online communities. The current generation of students are out-of-school creatives, driving how expressive technologies are used and circulated and, as a result, how schools will respond, adopt, and adapt new literacies practices (Vasquez, Harste, & Albers, 2010). Gee (2003) maintains that children today are learning more about literacy outside school than they are in school. For students, YouTube, cell phones with still, video, and audio capabilities, and other digital devices are not new; they are the everyday tools used to communicate in and navigate their worlds (Albers, Vasquez, & Harste, 2008). As such,

> the possibilities presented by the new communication landscape, new modes of meaning making, the ongoing transformation of digital texts, the interactivity and immediacy of access – for some – to the information highway, continue to provide challenges to language and literacy teachers and researchers at all levels of education.
>
> *(Janks & Vasquez, 2011, p. 1)*

In this chapter I take up one of these challenges and examine what it means to analyze digital texts produced for, with, and by children. In particular I will focus on analyzing podcasts, for the stories they tell about children as text creators, producers, and consumers. In doing so I will explore possible effects of their choices for themselves and on their audience.

Critical Literacies from an Artifactual Literacies Perspective

One method of analyzing podcasts lies at the intersection of Critical Literacies and Artifactual Literacies. Critical literacy has been a topic of debate for some time. Much of this is due to the growing belief that, as a theoretical and pedagogical framework for teaching and learning, critical literacy should look, feel, and sound different and accomplish different sorts of life work depending on the context in which it is being used (Comber and Simpson, 2001; Luke, 2007; Vasquez, 2004, 2001). In previous publications I have referred to this framing as a way of being, where I have argued that critical literacy should not be an add-on but a frame through which to participate in the world (1994). What this means is that the issues and topics that capture learners' interests as they participate in the world around them can, and should be, used as text to build a curriculum that has significance in their lives. Key tenets that comprise this perspective are as follows (Vasquez & Felderman, 2013):

- Critical literacy involves having a critical perspective or stance (Vasquez, 2004, 1994).
- Students' cultural knowledge and multimodal literacy practices should be utilized (Comber & Simpson, 2001; Vasquez, 1998).
- Texts work to create particular subject positions that make it easier or harder for us to say and do certain things; therefore we need to interrogate the perspective(s) presented through texts (Meacham, 2003).
- We read from (a) particular subject position(s), and so our readings of texts are never neutral and we need to interrogate the position(s) from which we read (speak, act, do . . .) (Foucault, 1988).
- What we claim to be true or real is always mediated through Discourse (Gee, 1999).
- Critical literacy involves understanding the sociopolitical systems in which we live and should consider the relationship between language and power (Janks, 1993).
- Critical literacy practices can contribute to change and the development of political awareness (Freire & Macedo, 1987; Freebody & Luke, 1990).
- Text design and production can provide opportunities for critique and transformation (Janks, 1993; Larson and Marsh, 2005; Vasquez, 2005).

From an artifactual literacies perspective, texts are themselves material objects, shaped by a series of choices (Pahl & Rowsell, 2010). The choices are modal, meaning choices are made as to the particular way or manner in which something exists or is experienced or expressed. According to Pahl and Rowsell modal choice can reveal the habitus – everyday lives and practices – of the text producer. They further note that artifactual literacy represents a methodology for approaching literacy research that draws from a social–cultural, ethnographic perspective of multimodal meaning-making and from semiotics, design, and the materiality of texts.

A digital text draws on different modes such as visual, aural, or written. As such it offers different affordances than a strictly print-based text. For instance a text that is combined with music and visuals helps a reader to better feel and experience the text by awakening the senses in ways that are not possible with strictly print-based text.

Pahl and Rowsell (2010) argue that "artifacts give power to meaning makers" (p. 56). They continue by saying "artifacts can leverage power for learners, particularly learners who feel at the margins of formal schooling" (p. 56). In terms of the podcasts, analyzing the episodes from these perspectives creates a space for considering how this leveraging of power takes place, in particular for students who see themselves outside the curriculum. Critical literacies, on the other hand, create spaces for disrupting the social practices and Discourses that create and/or maintain social inequities and inequitable power relations.

When applying this method to their studies teachers might ask questions such as the following.

- How might artifacts be used as tools for creating spaces to disrupt inequitable social practices and inequitable Discursive practices?
- What literacies are produced when learners use artifacts, within a critical literacy curriculum, to leverage power? What difference might this make? To whom would this make a difference and in what ways?

What is a Podcast?

A podcast is an on-demand Internet audio broadcast distinguished by its capability to be downloaded automatically using software that can read RSS (Really Simple Syndication) feeds. According to Albers, oral language texts, including podcasts, must be viewed in light of the messages conveyed, visible, and/or hidden (Albers, 2007).

Sheridan and Rowsell (2010) note, "it has never been easier to produce digital media" (p. 85). As such, more and more spaces have been created in school settings where teachers and students together have explored opportunities for using digital technologies in their settings (Evans, 2005; Marsh, 2005; Vasquez & Felderman, 2013; Wohlwend, 2011). Janks (1993, 2010) and Vasquez (2004, 2010) argue that the more complex and multimodal texts become, the more important it is to understand the politics of semiosis and the textual instantiations of power. How do we come to such understandings? We can begin with close examination and analysis of these complex multimodal texts.

Analyzing Podcasts: A Study of Digital Texts

In this study, podcasts were written, recorded, and co-produced with a group of second-grade children from the ages of six to eight. The classroom teacher was Carol Felderman. The world in which Carol's students were born was, of course, technologically very different from the world in which she and I were born. Most of these children came to school with knowledge of and experience with new technological stuff and new ethos or mindsets (Lankshear & Knobel, 2009) about the role that technology can play in their lives. It is therefore no surprise that after she shared with them audio of children that I had included in my podcast, the Critical Literacy In Practice Podcast (www.clippodcast.com), they became very interested in becoming podcasters themselves.

In this section of the chapter, I describe some of the podcasting work done by the children that takes into account the stuff of everyday life, everyday social issues and events, and their existing literacy practices. I will do this to set a context for particular data that I will use as an example of some of what I do as I analyze digital texts.

The second-grade classroom is located in a school with over 800 students. According to the school website, the students represent over 40 countries of origin and over 20 different languages spoken at home although the most dominant of these is Spanish. The neighborhood is located about 25 minutes outside Washington, DC, in a neighborhood that is experiencing increased gang activity and where most of the children are on free or reduced-cost lunch. On average there were 20 students in the class. A total of 50% of the children were English learners; 65% were on free or subsidized meals. There was one student identified with learning disabilities and another eight in referral process for identification as having learning disabilities. This was a complex mix of children with varied needs.

After a number of discussions regarding what their podcast should be about, the children decided on doing a show that focused on ways they could help make a difference in the world and contribute to change in some way. In general, they wanted to share, on the podcast, those issues they had been taking up that focus on injustice. They did this to make accessible to potential listeners how they have attempted to make change in different spaces and places. After some deliberation, the children decided to call their show *100%Kids* to indicate that they would generate the topics to be discussed and that the voices a listener would hear would be primarily the children's voices. Some of the topics they addressed in their show included animal rights, global/environmental issues, identity, and positioning where they took up issues of language use and power and engaged in deconstructing injustice. In addition, the students attempted to do some re-design or re-constructive work within their own school and beyond. For instance, one of the actions the children took was to re-instate a school field trip that had been removed from the school curriculum.

For years the second-grade classes had gone to the Baltimore Aquarium. For many of the children this school trip was the only chance they had to be able to visit the aquarium. Some of them had looked forward to the trip since their Kindergarten year. During the podcasting year the school principal decided the trip was too costly. It was therefore canceled without warning. The children were both saddened and outraged. After much discussion they decided to ask for a meeting with the school principal. The children presented their case focusing on the learning that could come from such a trip. Unsuccessful at convincing the principal to reinstate the school trip the children proposed that if they could raise the funds themselves that they ought to be allowed to go to the aquarium. The principal agreed setting into motion several fund-raising events that were held before, during, and after school. In the end the children were able to raise enough funds for all the second graders to go on the trip. They then took to the airwaves to podcast about the work that they did encouraging other children to never give up because change is possible.

Creating Episodes for the Podcast

Together with Carol, the children spent Monday to Thursday organizing, researching, writing, and rehearsing scripts for their show. The scripts were focused on different show segments the children had decided would be entertaining and informative for their listeners. The segments sometimes varied depending on the topic being addressed. Common to each episode was a welcome or introduction, a dedication, news items, and an acknowledgment or thank you section. Other segments included songs, stories, jokes, and other interest items. To listen to the children's show, go to www.bazmakaz. com/100kids/.

On Fridays, I went to their classroom to record the audio using a digital recorder. Together we discussed what sorts of transitional sounds or bumpers we might use between the various segments along with how long these transitions should last. We also talked about any additional sound effects and confirmed the order of the different segments. We used the sounds and music from the Garageband library, which is the audio editing software built into my computer (MacBook Pro). This music is copyright free and part of the public domain. The children also created an image to be included with the audio when it was posted on the podcast homepage located at www.bazmakaz. com/100kids/.

After recording the various segments, I used an instruction sheet outlining the order of the segments and the music/sound bumpers to insert. I spent time over the weekend editing the audio into a show episode to be posted along with the art piece on the podcast website. Monday morning became our release day when the new episode went live for all to hear. Every Monday morning Carol and the children gathered together on the carpet and listened to their show. As they listened they would critique their performances and take notes on what to maintain and what to change or add to enhance the show.

Carol and I immediately recognized the powerful learning that was taking place as the children took on the role of podcaster. The numerous anecdotal narratives, journal entries, recordings, photographs, and children's writings and drawings provided evidence of this. The more episodes the children created the more Carol understood the cross-curricular connections being made as well as the impact the experience had on shifting relationships between the children and on constructing identities. Seeing this made it easier for Carol to create more and more spaces for the children to do their podcasting work for sustained periods of time throughout the week. (For more on this work refer to Vasquez and Felderman, 2013.)

The effects on individual children also became more apparent. In the following section, I focus on a case study of an eight-year-old girl named Maria. All the children's names are pseudonyms. Some of the names are ones that the children gave themselves. They referred to these as their radio names.

About Maria

Maria was born in the USA in 1999 to a mother and father from Mexico. Her mom worked as a cleaning lady and her dad took jobs whenever he could. She had three siblings: Manuela 18, Andres 13, and Beto 12. Together they lived in a basement apartment in a neighborhood known for increased gang activity, in Falls Church, Virginia. Also living with them was Manuela's newborn baby.

Carol first met Maria's family when Maria was a baby and her oldest brother Andres was in Carol's class. Carol recalls her first encounters with Maria's mother.

> What struck me about the family was that the mother did not speak much English, but knew what to ask for to best help her son with his home-work. She asked for texts that I did not know about as a first year teacher. Her wanting to work with her son so he could do well was outstanding in my mind. She was the only parent in the class who just wanted to be educated on how to work with her child. She also asked for books to take home to read with her son, not only so she could assist him, but she knew this would help her learn English. This parent stood out as a learner and someone who truly craved the best for her children. I also cannot forget that she arrived on time for all conferences, meetings (unlike many of the other parents) and dropped Andres off and picked him up with a sweet little girl in a stroller. Andres was a very proud older brother and let me hold his little sister when his mom came in – these were my first days with Maria.

(Reflection August 20, 2007)

By the time Maria became Carol's student she had been identified with a number of learning difficulties from her speech development to her hearing. She joined Carol's class with an individualized education plan for developing social skills, speech, and language. Carol reflected "The first days of school were reassuring with Maria because we already 'knew' each other. I watched her with the children from the year before and how they interacted. Maria had plenty of struggles to manage throughout the year" (Reflection September 11, 2007). Carol and the other children had difficulty understanding Maria's speech. It is not surprising, therefore, that Maria was very withdrawn when I first met her. She seemed to deliberately shy away whenever she knew I would be in the room. In fact she was rarely ever in the classroom when I was there. She preferred to be doing other work elsewhere in the school than doing work with me. She barely spoke and did not have much to do with the other children. She especially stayed away from the work on podcasting.

I spent one to two mornings a week in the classroom during the fall 2006 and spring 2007. As we worked on the first three episodes, Maria sat or stood along the periphery of the classroom. From show #1 to show #3, however, she began to move in closer and closer to where her classmates gathered to listen to their newly released episodes on Monday morning. Then, one day, without warning, three weeks into podcasting, as we were putting together show #4, Maria told Carol that she wanted to podcast. Prior to beginning podcasting, we had sent home permission forms to the children's families explaining what we were doing, so Maria's parents had previously given permission for her participation. Also prior to recording we had talked to the children about safety issues with regards to the Internet and the use of radio names.

It is two pieces of data, in the form of Maria's contributions to the show (show #4 and show #8), that I will look at more closely. In particular, I will look more closely at what happened from the release of show #4 to the production of show #8. The following chart summarizes the data produced, the analytical tools used to unpack the data, along with the reason for analyzing each category of data.

The Telling of New Stories

As Maria watched what her classmates were doing and as she listened in on some of their conversation, she became more and more interested in what they were doing, how they were doing it, and the joy they were exuding from hearing their voices "on the radio." As she listened there was a look of surprise on her face. She looked back and forth between the computer where the audio was playing and her classmates. We interpreted from her actions that she was surprised to think that the voices coming through the broadcast were those of her classmates. Our interpretation was confirmed when we heard her ask a couple of the children, "that's you?" They had different names and some had

TABLE 16.1 Data analysis chart

Data type	Analytical tool employed	Analyzed for...	Example
Classroom observations in relation to show #4 and #8	Narrative analysis	Illuminating the journey of Maria to Queen Patterns and anomalies Complexity of learning	Maria getting beyond feeling silenced in the classroom to using new modalities as an entry point into joining the classroom conversation
Transcripts of language use in audio recordings	Discourse analysis	Positioning and shifts in positioning Identity work How language is used to produce particular effects	Maria's movement from being on the outside of the classroom community to being "Queen," on the inside of the classroom community
Audio recordings	Multimodal analysis	Modal choice and ideological situatedness Transformation in participation and the social effects that are produced	In her role as Queen, Maria was able to project a new identity that had transformative social effects

taken on different personas, and this seemed to make listening to the podcast even more interesting. If they could be someone else then maybe she could be someone else too. Eventually she took on a new persona as Queen. When Carol and I asked her about this name, Maria told us this was a nickname her mom called her. She said being called Queen made her feel good, safe, and made her feel wanted. In some ways this was the opposite of how she felt as Maria: shy, hesitant, scared, marginalized. It is no wonder that as Queen, Maria was able to tell new stories.

Queen's debut performance consisted of one line with nine words; "We hope you like our painting of the world." This would be part of the art section of the podcast where there was a brief discussion regarding the piece of art used in the show notes. She decided on what to say after some conversation with Carol, about her possible contribution. Prior to the first recording session, for show #4, I talked with Queen about the equipment I was using and reassured her that we could record as many times as she wanted. The first recording session lasted about 15 minutes and was done in the hallway away from any of the other children. Recording was challenging for Queen as she struggled through saying each of the nine words. She repeated word after word over and over again. Carol confirmed that in the past Maria would likely have given up or not participated at all. Queen hung in there. I had explained to her that we could cut out the pieces she was not happy with and leave in the pieces she liked. Knowing these editing tools were available, according to Gee (2003), lowered the consequences of failure and kept her in the game. It increased the opportunity for her to succeed and created a space for her to take on this new challenge.

It took six or seven takes and approximately 25 minutes of editing to produce Queen's 2.5 seconds of audio. The ear-to-ear smile on her face as she heard herself on air for the first time was a demonstration of how she felt about her contribution.

Treating her recording as an artifact that reflected what Queen was capable of doing resulted in her being positioned very differently by her classmates. No longer did they position her as being incapable of participating with them. For instance in her identity as Queen, Maria was able to position herself as part of a group of classmates who by the end of the year had become her friends. No program of study or mandated curriculum could have helped her with this! In a way the podcasts as artifacts helped "establish connections between [the children]" (Pahl & Rowsell, 2010, p. 64). Queen's segments became artifacts through which her classmates were able to construct different stories about her and therefore build different relationships with her. Bartlett (2005) notes, artifacts themselves are not innocent but instead are situated in relations of power (p. 5). There were definite shifts in power that resulted once the children heard each other on the podcast.

In subsequent episodes, such as show #8, Queen participated in singing songs, which she helped create with her classmates. She also can be heard contributing to unscripted dialogue with phrases like "you go girl" or "that's right girl." These sorts of contributions from this eight-year-old girl were not the kinds of contributions that Carol might have imagined earlier in the year.

From Maria to Queen

Pahl and Rowsell (2010) note, "some stories themselves are artifacts" (p. 11). Maria's transition as Queen began as she witnessed her classmates shifting identities while taking on different roles and personas on the show. The recorded episodes that had been uploaded online became artifacts that created "new opportunities for storytelling … for students to tell their stories and become heard" (p. 50). For Maria witnessing these artifactual stories became "a moment of transformation for [her], creating a shift in [her] way of seeing the world" (p. 50). It was while observing these recorded episodes in the making that Maria took on the persona of Queen and experienced a "shift in consciousness" (p. 50). The transformational power of artifacts (Csikszentmihalyi & Rochberg-Halton, 1981; Pahl & Rowsell, 2010) is therefore an important element in my theoretical toolkit for this study.

Sedimented Identities

Artifacts produced by people can be seen as a process by which identities are sedimented into texts (Rowsell & Pahl, 2007). Unlike her initial venture into podcasting during show #4, in show #8, a different Queen emerged. She physically and emotionally moved from the periphery of the classroom to the center with her classmates. Gee (2003, 2004) talks about new technology, like podcasting, as opening up possibilities for new forms of interacting that are quite motivating and compelling. From a critical literacy perspective, for Maria, the act of renaming herself into a different existence as Queen was transformative. This once shy and hesitant child, for whom the curriculum was difficult to access, began taking on new roles in the classroom. The podcast itself became a critical artifact through which she and some of her classmates storied new or different versions of their lives.

This fits Nixon and Gutierrez's (2008) notion of identity play whereby children can extend the ways in which they are able to express themselves and tell their stories. As they play with language for publication in the online space, they develop a point of view from which they communicate their ideas. In doing so they develop new identities as meaning makers (Nixon & Gutierrez, 2008). Critical literacy helps us to understand the ways in which these new identities come with different relations of power and access to literacy events in the classroom and beyond.

In this story of podcasting, Maria started off from the position of being an outsider. Although she was very much a participant in her home life, the same could not be said of her life at school where she was disconnected from many of the experiences with which her classmates participated. Her digital stories as Queen, "bear the traces of a movement from being outside an experience to being inside" (Pahl & Rowsell, 2010, p. 94). For Queen, the experience of podcasting was therefore transformative as it was for other children in the class.

Since artifactual literacies and critical literacies cut across disciplines and curricular areas, this work would have utility in other literacy settings regardless of the age group of participants or their areas of study.

References

Albers, M., Vasquez, V., & Harste, J. (2008). A classroom with a view: Teachers, multi-modality and new literacies. *Talking Points, 19*(2), 3–13.

Albers, P. (2007). Visual discourse analysis: An introduction to the analysis of school-generated visual texts. In D. W. Rowe, R. T. Jimenez, D. L. Compton, D. K. Dickinson, Y. Kim, K. M. Leander, & V. J. Risko (Eds.), *56th Yearbook of the National Reading Conference* (pp. 81–95). Oak Creek, WI: NRC.

Bartlett, L. (2005). Identity work and cultural artefacts in literacy learning and use: A sociocultural analysis. *Language and Education, 19*(1), 1–9.

Comber, B., & Simpson, A. (Eds.). (2001). *Negotiating critical literacies in classrooms.* Mahwah, NJ: Lawrence Erlbaum Associates.

Csikszentmihalyi, M., & Rochberg-Halton, E. (1981). *The meaning of things.* London: Cambridge University Press.

Evans, J. (Ed.). (2005). *Literacy moves on.* London: David Fulton Publishers.

Foucault, M. (1988). Technologies of the self. In L. H. Martin, H. Gutman & P. H. Hutton (Eds.), *Technologies of the self* (pp. 16–49). Amherst: The University of Massachusetts Press.

Freebody, P., & Luke, A. (1990). Literacies programs: Debates and demands in cultural context: Prospect. *Australian Journal of TESOL, 5*(7), 7–16.

Freire, P., & Macedo, D. (1987). *Literacy: Reading the word and the world.* South Hadley, MA: Bergin & Garvey.

Gee, J. P. (1999). *An introduction to discourse analysis theory and method* (2nd ed.). New York: Routledge.

Gee, J. P. (2003). *What video games have to teach us about learning and literacy.* New York: Palgrave/Macmillan.

Gee, J. P. (2004). *Situated language and learning: A critique of traditional schooling.* London: Routledge.

Janks, H. (1993). *Language, identity, and power.* Johannesburg, South Africa: Witwatersrand University Press.

Janks, H. (2010). *Literacy and power.* New York: Routledge.

Janks, H., & Vasquez, V. (2011). Critical literacy revisited: Writing as critique. *English Teaching: Practice and Critique, 10*(1), 1–6. Retrieved from http://edlinked.soe.waikato.ac.nz/research/journal/view.php?id=54&p=1.

Lankshear, C., & Knobel, M. (2009). New ways of knowing: Learning at the margins. In K. Hall & S. Jones (Eds.), *Pedagogy and practice: Cultural bridging and identities* (pp. 161–176). London: Open University Press.

Larson, J., & Marsh, J. (2005). *Making literacy real.* New York: Routledge.

Luke, A. (2007). The body literate: Discourse and inscription in early literacy. In T. Van Dijk (Ed.), *Discourse studies* (vol. IV, pp. 1–22). London: Sage Publications.

Marsh, J. (Ed.). (2005). *Popular culture, new media and digital literacy in early childhood.* New York: Routledge.

Meacham, S. J. (2003). *Literacy and street credibility: Plantations, prisons, and African American literacy from Frederick Douglass to Fifty Cent.* Presentation at the Economic and Social Research Council Seminar Series Conference, Sheffield, UK, March.

Nixon, A. S., & Gutierrez, K. D. (2008). Digital literacies for young English learners: Productive pathways toward equity and robust learning. In C. Genishi & A. L. Goodwin (Eds.), *Diversities in early childhood: Rethinking and doing* (pp. 121–136). New York: Routledge.

Pahl, K., & Rowsell, J. (2010). *Artifactual literacies: Every object tells a story.* New York: Teachers College Press.

Rowsell, J., & Pahl, K. (2007). Sedimented identities in texts: Instances of practice. *Reading Research Quarterly, 42*(3), 388–404.

Sheridan, M. P., & Rowsell, J. (2010). *Design literacies: Learning and innovation in the digital age.* London: Routledge.

Vasquez, V. (1994). A step in the dance of critical literacy. *UKRA Reading, 28*(1), 39–43.

Vasquez, V. (1998). Building equitable communities: Taking social action in a kindergarten classroom. *Talking Points, 9*(2), 3–7.

Vasquez, V. (2001). Constructing a critical curriculum with young children. In B. Comber & A. Simpson (Eds.), *Negotiating critical literacies in classrooms* (pp. 61–73). Mahwah, NJ: Lawrence Erlbaum Associates.

Vasquez, V. (2004). *Negotiating critical literacies with young children.* New York: Routledge.

Vasquez, V. (2005). Creating spaces for critical literacy with young children: Using everyday issues and everyday text. In J. Evans (Ed.), *Literacy moves on* (pp. 78–97). Abingdon, UK: David Fulton Publishers.

Vasquez, V. (2010). *Getting beyond I like the book: Creating spaces for critical literacy in K-6 settings.* Newark, DE: International Reading Association.

Vasquez, V., Harste, J., & Albers, P. (2010). From the personal to the worldwide web: Moving teachers into positions of critical interrogation. In B. Baker (Ed.), *The new literacies multiple perspectives on research and practice* (pp. 265–284). New York: Guilford Press.

Vasquez, V., & Felderman, C. (2013). *Technology and critical literacy in early childhood.* New York: Routledge.

Wohlwend, K. (2011). *Playing their way into literacies.* New York: Teachers College Press.

LIST OF CONTRIBUTORS

Peggy Albers is a Professor of Language Education in the Middle and Secondary Education and Instructional Technology Department in the College of Education at Georgia State University, Atlanta, GA, USA. Her research focuses on the analysis of student-generated visual texts created in language arts classrooms. Peggy developed visual discourse analysis as a method and theory to understand the relationship between how students convey meaning visually and the discourses that underpin these meanings.

Catherine Beavis is a Professor of Education at Griffith University in Queensland, Australia. She teaches and researches in English and Literacy Education, young people, and digital culture, with a particular focus on videogames as new narrative and communicative forms, and the implications of young people's engagement with digital culture and videogames for education.

David Bloome is EHE Distinguished Professor of Teaching and Learning in the School of Teaching and Learning of the Ohio State University College of Education and Human Ecology in Columbus, OH, USA. His research focuses on how people use spoken and written language for learning in classroom and non-classroom settings, and how people use language to create and maintain social relationships, to construct knowledge, and to create communities, social institutions, and shared histories and futures.

Stephanie Power Carter is an Associate Professor in Literacy, Culture, and Language education at Indiana University Bloomington, IN, USA. Her scholarship in the field of education focuses primarily on discourse analysis, issues of language and diversity, and Black education. She has co-authored two books: *Discourse Analysis and the Study of Classroom Language and Literacy*

Events: A Microethnographic Perspective and *On Discourse Analysis in Classrooms: Approaches to Language and Literacy Research*, and published work in various journals and book chapters.

Catherine Compton-Lilly is an Associate Professor in Curriculum and Instruction at the University of Wisconsin Madison, USA. She engages in longitudinal research projects that last over long periods of time. In her most recent study, she followed a group of eight inner-city students from grade 1 through grade 11. Her interests include examining how time operates as a contextual factor in children's lives as they progress through school and construct their identities as students and readers. Among the books she has edited or authored are: *Reading Families: The Literate Lives of Urban Children* (Teachers College Press, 2003), *Rereading Families* (Teachers College Press, 2007), and *Reading Time: The Literate Lives of Urban Secondary Students and their Families* (Teachers College Press, 2012).

Amy Seely Flint is an Associate Professor at Georgia State University in Atlanta, GA, USA. Her research interests include early literacy development, critical literacy, and teacher professional development. She was a lead researcher in a large-scale study involving eight universities examining exemplary teacher preparation programs, and is now serving as a professional development liaison in elementary schools in the metro-Atlanta area.

Jennifer Higgs is a doctoral student in the University of California Berkeley's Graduate School of Education in Berkeley, CA, USA, with an emphasis in new media studies. Her research, which focuses on the intersection of new media and English language arts instruction, is informed and inspired by her experiences as a middle and high school English teacher.

Teri Holbrook is an Assistant Professor of literacy and language arts in the Department of Early Childhood Education at Georgia State University in Atlanta, GA, USA. Broadly, her research—including text creation, analysis, and use—looks at how arts-infused, multimodal composition alters notions of literacy education, academic and literary writing, and qualitative inquiry.

Glynda Hull is Professor of Education in the Graduate School of Education at the University of California Berkeley, USA. Her recent research has focused on university-community collaboratives, multi-modal composing, and social networks as sites of cosmopolitan practice. Recent books include *School's Out! Bridging Out-of-School Literacies with Classroom Practice* (co-edited with Katherine Schultz, 2002); *Changing Work, Changing Workers: Critical Perspectives on Language, Literacy, and Skills* (1997); *The New Work Order: Behind the Language of the New Capitalism* (with J. Gee and C. Lankshear, 1996) (all Teachers College Press).

Rita L. Irwin is a Professor of Art Education, and Associate Dean of Teacher Education, at the University of British Columbia, Vancouver, Canada. She is also the current President of the International Society for Education through Art. Rita publishes widely, exhibits her artworks, and has secured a range of research grants to support her work. Her most recent co-edited books include *Curriculum in a New Key: The Collected Works of Ted T. Aoki* (co-edited with William F. Pinar), *Revisions: Readings in Canadian Art Teacher Education* (co-edited with Kit Grauer and Mike Emme), and *Being with A/r/tography* (co-edited with Stephanie Springgay, Carl Leggo and Peter Gouzouasis).

Jodi Kaufmann is an Associate Professor, Department of Educational Policy Studies at Georgia State University, Atlanta, GA, USA. As qualitative research methodologist, her work currently focuses on autoethnography, the construction of meaning, and experimenting with poststructural theories and qualitative inquiry.

Carl Leggo is a poet and Professor in the Department of Language and Literacy Education at the University of British Columbia. His books include: *Growing Up Perpendicular on the Side of a Hill; View from My Mother's House; Come-By-Chance; Teaching to Wonder: Responding to Poetry in the Secondary Classroom; Lifewriting as Literary Métissage and an Ethos for Our Times* (co-authored with Erika Hasebe-Ludt and Cynthia Chambers); *Being with A/r/tography* (co-edited with Stephanie Springgay, Rita L. Irwin, and Peter Gouzouasis); *Creative Expression, Creative Education* (co-edited with Robert Kelly); and *Poetic Inquiry: Vibrant Voices in the Social Sciences* (co-edited with Monica Prendergast and Pauline Sameshima).

Jackie Marsh is a Professor of Literacy at the University of Sheffield, England. Jackie is interested in the role and nature of popular culture, media, and new technologies in young children's early literacy development, both in and outside school. She has conducted research projects that have explored children's access to new technologies and their emergent digital literacy skills, knowledge, and understanding. She has also examined the way in which parents/carers and other family members support this engagement with media and technologies.

Carmen Medina is an Associate Professor in the Literacy, Culture, and Language Education at Indiana University in Bloomington, IN, USA. Her research interests are literacy as social and critical practices, critical performance/drama pedagogies, biliteracy education, and Latino/a children's literature. She also is examining Puerto Rican children's engagement and interpretive practices at the intersection of global/local landscapes and networks.

Lorri Neilsen Glenn is a Professor of Education at Mount Saint Vincent University in Halifax, Nova Scotia, Canada, where she teaches qualitative research and writing. Lorri is the author and editor of 11 books of non-fiction, scholarly work, poetry, and memoir. She was Halifax Poet Laureate for 2005–2009, has served as writer in residence and scholar in residence internationally. Her academic and literary awards include CEE's Richard Meade Research Award in English/Language Arts, Mount Saint Vincent University's Research Excellence Award, as well as numerous Canadian awards for poetry and creative non-fiction.

Sue Nichols is a Senior Lecturer in the Division of Education, Arts, and Social Sciences at the University of South Australia in Adelaide, South Australia. Among Sue's research interests are Media and consumer culture participation of new arrival families, children's personal consumption choices, and parental networks. Her upcoming book is entitled *Resourcing Early Learners: New Networks, New Players* (2012) (with J. Rowsell, S. Rainbird, and H. Nixon).

Sigrid Norris is an Associate Professor of Communication Studies and Director of the Multimodal Research Centre at Auckland University of Technology in New Zealand. She is the author of *Analyzing Multimodal Interaction: A Methodological Framework* (Routledge, 2004) and *Identity in (Inter)action: Introducing Multimodal (Inter)action Analysis* (de Gruyter, 2011); she is the co-editor of *Discourse in Action: Introducing Mediated Discourse Analysis* (Routledge, 2005), editor of *Multimodality in Practice: Investigating Theory-in-practice-through-methodology* (Routledge, 2011), and founding and ongoing editor of the journal *Multimodal Communication* (published by the Multimodal Research Centre since 2011). Sigrid's main research interests are multimodal theory, methodology, and multimodal identity production.

Kate Pahl is a Reader in Literacies in Education at the University of Sheffield, England. She conducts ethnographic fieldwork in homes and communities and has directed a number of research projects that engage with young people's everyday literacies. She is the co-author of *Artifactual Literacies* (with Jennifer Rowsell).

Mia Perry is an Assistant Professor of theatre and education at the University of Regina, Saskatchewan, Canada. Working in the intersections of performance, philosophy, and pedagogy, Mia's background spans England, Ireland, Russia, and Canada. In these various contexts, Mia's work and scholarship has revolved around the application and the analysis of contemporary performance and cultural practices in community and educational contexts.

Rebecca Rogers is an Associate Professor of Literacy and Discourse Studies at the University of Missouri-St. Louis, USA. Her scholarship focuses on the socio-political contexts of literacy and language education and situates critical discourse studies within an ethnographic tradition. She has published many articles and books, the most recent is the second edition of *An Introduction to Critical Discourse Analysis in Education* (Routledge, 2011). She was recently a Fulbright Scholar in Critical Discourse Studies at the Universidad de San Martín in Buenos Aires, Argentina.

Jennifer Rowsell is an Associate Professor and the Canada Research Chair in Multiliteracies in the Department of Teacher Education at Brock University in St. Catherines, Ontario, Canada. She researches and writes in the areas of multimodality, ecological and spatial methodologies, and New Literacy Studies. She is the co-author of *Artifactual Literacies* (with Kate Pahl).

Amy Stornaiuolo is an Assistant Professor in the Graduate School of Education at the University of Pennsylvania, Philadelphia, PA, USA. She studies young people's multimodal composing practices across contexts, teachers' uses of digital technologies, and the cosmopolitan implications of social networking in educational spaces.

Vivian Maria Vasquez is a Professor of Education at American University, Washington, DC. Her research interests are in critical literacy, early literacy, and information communication technology. Her publications include eight books and numerous book chapters and articles in refereed journals including her newest book, *Negotiating Critical Literacies with Teachers* (with Stacie Tate and Jerome C. Harste).

Karen Wohlwend is an Assistant Professor in Literacy, Culture, and Language Education at Indiana University in Bloomington, IN, USA. She studies play as an embodied literacy that young children use for producing multimedia and as a social practice for participating in early childhood settings and digital spaces. She is the author of *Playing their Way into Literacies* (2011). Karen's research in the area of play has been recognized through the International Reading Association's 2008 Outstanding Dissertation Award and the 2007 American Educational Research Association's 2007 Language and Social Processes Emerging Scholar Award.

INDEX

Page numbers in *italics* denote tables, those in **bold** denote figures.